AUTHORITY AND DEMOCRACY

STUDIES IN MORAL, POLITICAL,
AND LEGAL PHILOSOPHY

General Editor: Marshall Cohen

A list of titles in the series
appears at the back of the book

AUTHORITY AND DEMOCRACY

A General Theory of Government and Management

Christopher McMahon

PRINCETON UNIVERSITY PRESS
PRINCETON, NEW JERSEY

Library of Congress Cataloging-in-Publication Data

McMahon, Christopher, 1945–
Authority and democracy : a general theory of government and
management / by Christopher McMahon.
p. cm. — (Studies in moral, political, and legal philosophy)
Includes bibliographical references (p.) and index.
ISBN 0-691-03662-4
ISBN 0-691-01629-1 (pbk.)
1. Authority. 2. Democracy. 3. Management—Employee participation.
I. Title. II. Series.
HM271.M39 1994
350—dc20 94-1366 CIP

This book has been composed in Palatino

Princeton University Press books are printed on acid-free paper
and meet the guidelines for permanence and durability of the
Committee on Production Guidelines for Book Longevity of the
Council on Library Resources

Second printing, and first paperback printing, 1997

Printed in the United States of America
by Princeton Academic Press

3 5 7 9 10 8 6 4 2

For Ruth McMahon and Janine Scancarelli

CONTENTS

CONTENTS

CONTENTS

PREFACE

Radical political theory gives the concept of power pride of place. It views society as an arena of clashing interests, in which contending groups seek to marshall power to dominate others as interest dictates. More sophisticated theories of this sort view the power at the disposal of dominant groups as encompassing not only the ability to promise rewards or threaten punishments but also generally accepted ideas, including moral ideas. By assimilating morality to power, however, these theories limit what they can sincerely say about the good society, as Marx's sketchy descriptions of communism attest. Indeed, the radical ideal sometimes seems to be a utopian fantasy, a world in which no one has power over anyone else or all have the power to get everything they want.

If we ask what distinguishes moderate political theory from radical political theory, one plausible answer is that moderates give a central role to the concept of legitimate authority. Accepting authority involves deferring to the assertions or directives of various individuals or groups, including, in the case of democratic authority, groups of which one is a member and whose authoritative communications one helps to generate. In embracing the idea that such deference can be legitimate, moderates show that they think that not all subordination is domination. Sometimes there are good reasons for it from the standpoint of those in subordinate positions. They can live better with deference of certain kinds than without it. This means that for moderates, the good society is not one in which nobody has power over anybody else, but rather (to oversimplify a bit) one in which power does not exceed legitimate authority.

The authority of individuals or groups is not the only form of authority that moderates acknowledge. They also accord authority to morality. They regard our basic moral ideas, if not the specific moral conventions accepted at a given time and place, as legitimately constraining what we may do.[1] One of the most interesting

[1] For discussion of the authority of morality see Butler (1983), esp. sermon 2, and Scheffler (1992), chap. 5.

questions for moderate political theory concerns how clashes between the authority of particular individuals or groups and the authority of morality are to be resolved. What should one do when a particular authority that one regards as legitimate directs something that seems morally wrong, or when one judges that there are good moral reasons for resisting a particular authority?

The topic of the moral limits of legitimate authority has received much attention in the case of governments, but governmental authority is not the only sort of authority exercised by particular individuals or groups that moderates regard as legitimate. They are also prepared to accord this status to managerial authority, the authority of the managers of nongovernmental organizations.

Unlike governmental authority, there has been little discussion of what makes managerial authority legitimate. One of the reasons for this, I believe, is that it has been thought that since nongovernmental organizations are voluntary associations, consent theories of legitimate authority are straightforwardly applicable to them. Their members can be regarded as having promised to obey those who occupy managerial offices within the organization. One of my goals in this book is to show that this way of understanding legitimate managerial authority is tenable only if one supposes, contrary to fact, that there are seldom good moral reasons for questioning what managers direct. When the possibility of conflict between morality and managerial authority is fully appreciated, we are forced to reconsider what makes this form of authority legitimate. As we shall see, the answer has implications for the sorts of institutional structures in which managerial authority can appropriately find expression.

This book has two parts. The first provides an account of authority in general and, specifically, in government. It distinguishes three kinds of authority—the authority of experts, authority grounded in a promise to obey, and authority that facilitates mutually beneficial cooperation within a group—and examines the considerations that justify them. It also develops an account of democracy as reflexive authority, the collective exercise of authority by those subject to it. The second part applies the results of the first to the phenomenon of managerial authority.

The title of the book may suggest a contrast between authority and democracy as two different ways of directing the actions of groups, but this is not my intention. I believe that in large groups, at least, democracy is best viewed as a way of exercising authority. The account of democracy as reflexive authority that I present is of interest for two reasons. First, although the best recent work on authority is primarily concerned with the authority of governments or the state, it is surprisingly silent on the topic of democracy. It says virtually nothing about whether, and if so why, the democratic exercise of authority is preferable to its nondemocratic exercise. One of the objectives of the first part of this book is to remedy this defect. Second, interesting light is shed on democracy when it is viewed as a way of exercising authority. My account of democracy as reflexive authority can be distinguished both from views that justify democracy by reference to the idea that people have a right to participate in decisions that affect them and from theories of "deliberative democracy" that understand democracy in terms of a deliberative process that aims at a consensus.

I have characterized the first part of the book as a discussion of authority in general and of authority in government. It is a discussion of authority in general because many of the issues addressed may be applied to all the settings in which authority is found. And it is a discussion of authority in government because it covers essentially the same ground as recent accounts of the authority of governments or the state. Some topics that would have to be treated in a full-scale discussion of the authority of governments, for example, the nature of law and its authority, are omitted. Given the discussion of democracy it contains, however, the first part actually provides a more complete treatment of the authority of governments than other recent accounts. The authority of governments might also be called political authority, although for reasons that will become clear as we proceed, I believe that in important respects managerial authority deserves the label "political" as well.

The principal goal of the second part of this book is to determine whether nongovernmental organizations should be democratically managed by their employees. The central case deals with large business corporations, but the account is meant to be general, encompassing such institutions as hospitals and schools as well. I argue that managerial authority is best regarded not as the authority of a principal over an agent but rather as authority that facilitates mutually beneficial cooperation among employees with divergent aims. And the results of the first part are invoked to establish that if managerial authority is understood in this way, there is a presumption that it should be democratically exercised by the employees. The case for managerial democracy is presumptive only, however. The book concludes by considering whether certain countervailing considerations—in particular the desirability of securing investment by nonemployees and the need to utilize technical expertise effectively—are capable of rebutting the presumption in favor of democracy. I argue that while these considerations have some force, it will seldom be sufficient to justify institutional structures that give employees no role at all in formulating ultimate managerial policy.

My intellectual debts are acknowledged in the footnotes. My work was supported by a sabbatical quarter from the University of California, Santa Barbara, and by a fellowship from the National Endowment for the Humanities. I also thank the College of William and Mary and its philosophy department for extending me library privileges during the 1991–1992 academic year, and Lesley Beneke for editorial assistance.

AUTHORITY AND DEMOCRACY

CHAPTER ONE

INTRODUCTION

This book is an essay in political philosophy. It depicts government and management as two components of an integrated system of social authority that is essentially political in nature. A variety of issues relating to authority and democracy are discussed, but the principal goal is to determine when the democratic exercise of authority, both in government and in nongovernmental organizations, is appropriate.

In the first part of the book I consider what kinds of authority there are, which of them can be exercised democratically, and what supports their democratic exercise. This discussion of authority in general is, at the same time, a discussion of the governmental case, since it is conducted in the same conceptual space as the best recent discussions of political authority.

The second part of the book is concerned with managerial authority and managerial democracy. Most writers who advocate the democratic management of nongovernmental organizations by their employees base their case in some way on the value of participation. Thus, Marxists, who regard human flourishing as self-realization through labor, typically hold that self-realization is more complete when workers participate in the decisions that determine how their work will be organized. This approach, however, confronts the problem that many people do not care about participating on a regular basis in the decision making that guides their work.[1] Rather, they see their work as a way of financing self-realizing activities that take place in other contexts.

Arguments for democracy in the political sphere, that is, arguments for democratic government, usually do not depend on the value of participation. Instead, they claim that only democratic governments can hold legitimate political authority. In the second part of this book, I take a similar approach to the problem of managerial

[1] For related discussion, see Arneson (unpublished), esp. sect. 7, and Arneson (1987).

3

democracy. I address the question of whether democracy is required if managerial authority is to be appropriately exercised. This involves examining different ways that managerial authority might be justified and considering their implications for managerial democracy.

That authority is exercised by governments and that some consideration must be given to how it might be justified are not controversial claims. This is familiar ground in political philosophy. Much less familiar is the idea that there is a problem about how the authority of managers might be justified. Thus I devote the remainder of this introductory chapter to the managerial case, presenting some of the themes of the discussion of managerial authority in Part II. Part I, the discussion of authority and democracy in general and in government, begins with the account of the concept of authority in Chapter Two.

Management and Government

One of the principal problems of political philosophy is the justification of government, that is, of political authority. A justification of political authority would provide an answer to the question: Why obey the law? Of course, one reason is that if one does not, one may be punished. But this reason comes into being only after government is in place, and thus cannot justify the existence of government. A justification of political authority must provide a reason for obeying the law that operates even when there is no threat of punishment for violation. If such a reason can be found, it may be possible to regard the punitive power of at least some governments as a social mechanism for forcing people to do what they have, independently of this power, sufficient reason to do.

Since the collapse of the idea that governments get their authority from God, one of the most important strategies for justifying political authority has been to suggest that if government did not exist, it would be necessary to invent it. Writers taking this approach argue that, without government, social life would be marked by chaos or inconveniences of certain kinds and that everyone would regard the elimination of these conditions by a government as worth the monetary and other costs entailed. To use the image historically associated with this approach, the people in a territory that lacked a government would find it in their interests to enter into a social contract to constitute themselves as a political society and establish a government. Further elaboration of the idea that we can see why political authority is justified by reflecting on what life would be like without it enables us to distinguish between better and worse forms of government. The better forms are those that better promote (in a particular social context) the ends that justify establishing a government.

My goal in the second part of this book is to investigate the parallel problem of the justification of managerial authority. A justification of managerial authority would provide an answer to the question: Why obey one's employer? The answer seems obvious to most people: because he, she, or it is paying one to obey. And they might add that, unlike nation-states, corporations are voluntary organizations, so if one does not want to implement a particular managerial directive, one can (and should) quit.[2]

I do not believe that this answer is satisfactory. The account of managerial authority that I provide explains why, proposes what I regard as a better answer, and traces its implications for current economic institutions. The argument is complex, but the basic idea is easily stated. While it would doubtless be morally impermissible to continue to accept pay from an employer while disobeying managerial directives for purely selfish reasons, the situation is more complicated when one's reasons for disobeying are moral. Suppose, for example, that some civilian employees of the German State Railroad during World War II had been ordered by their superiors to facilitate the conveying of detainees to concentration camps, but they discovered that without any risk to themselves, they could allow some of the detainees to escape en route. Moreover, they knew that if they were to quit, they would be replaced by people who would comply fully with the directives of the railroad's managers. I suspect that virtually everyone today would agree that the appropriate course of action for employees in this position would be to retain their jobs and continue to accept their pay—in part to meet their needs and in part because to decline it would arouse suspicion—while disobeying their bosses.

I argue that this case, while extreme, is by no means anomalous. Employers in modern societies routinely make decisions that are appropriately assessed on moral grounds, and where the employer is a large organization, the consequences, good or bad, of its decisions are typically much greater than those of the decisions of isolated individuals. But not all of the employees of a particular employer will find the employer's policies morally acceptable. Thus, for some employees at any given time, and for virtually all at some point

---

[2] A common theme in discussions of authority is that the exercise of authority in voluntary organizations is unproblematic. Thus, attention has focused on the authority of the state.

in their working lives, to comply with managerial directives will be to contribute to a moral or political agenda that they do not share. As the above example shows, this problem arises whether the employer is a publicly or a privately owned enterprise. To be sure, only the largest organizations will make decisions that have moral implications at the national or international level. Yet, even the actions of small firms can have moral implications at the local level. While the fact that one is being paid is a good moral reason for complying with a managerial directive, then, it may conflict with other morally relevant considerations that count against compliance. And sometimes these considerations will be strong enough to justify continuing to accept pay while disobeying managerial directives.

Of course, the policing of the work force by employers usually makes keeping one's job while disobeying managerial directives impossible. This police power derives from the fact that the law gives employers the virtually absolute right to exclude from their property anyone they choose. Like the threats that governmental officials can make, however, the threat of being excluded from one's workplace does not provide the sort of reason for obedience that can justify the authority of managers. A justification of managerial authority must provide a reason for complying with managerial directives that is prior to and independent of the employer's legal powers. If such a reason can be found, we can consider whether the legal powers that employers possess can be defended as a social mechanism for forcing employees to do what they have, independently of these powers, sufficient justification for doing. Our objective, then, is to find a reason for complying with managerial directives that is independent of the threats managers can make to recalcitrant employees, and that operates not just sometimes, for some employees, but routinely for all. If the fact that one is being paid is not this reason, what does justify managerial authority?

My answer is similar to that provided by the contractarian tradition in political philosophy. If every employee who disagreed on moral grounds with the policies of his or her employer disobeyed managerial directives, the result would be economic chaos. Like political authority, then, managerial authority can be justified as eliminating a certain kind of chaos. This answer gives employees sufficient reason to comply with most managerial directives that they find morally questionable, while leaving room for disobedience in such extreme cases as that of the German railway workers.

If we accept this answer, however, we must reexamine the powers that the law accords to managers. If the task performed by managers is the same as that performed by governmental officials—that is, to eliminate certain obstacles that would otherwise confront groups of people trying to live what they regard as morally acceptable lives—management and government are appropriately viewed as two aspects of a larger system of authority with a single rationale. And the legal powers given to managers, including the legal property rights they exercise, will have to be adjusted to reflect this understanding of their role.

The Public and the Private

The foregoing points can also be made by saying that on the view that I present, the idea that government and management fall on different sides of the public-private divide—that is, that managers work in the "private sector"—becomes dubious. The claim that management is private reflects a view of the public-private distinction according to which actions are public if they employ publicly owned resources and private if they employ privately owned resources. But if, as I have suggested, legal property rights cannot be taken as morally basic, we need another way of making the distinction.

One way of drawing the line that might place management and government on the same side would be to regard the defining feature of public authority as the application of coercive power. The state, our paradigm of a public entity, is often defined, following Max Weber, as an organization that possesses a monopoly on the legitimate use of coercion in a certain territory.[3] The essence of permissible private activities, by contrast, is that they are not coercive. But some writers, especially in the socialist tradition, have claimed that management, like government, involves the application of coercive powers. Their argument asserts that humans must have access to productive resources in order to live—or to live well—and this enables those who have the legal right to control access to such resources, in the form of employment, to force those who do not own them to do what they want. If this is correct, management is relevantly similar to government.

This way of making the public-private distinction is, however, open to the same objection as the first we considered. To justify authority, we need a reason for subordinates to comply with authoritative directives that is independent of and prior to any legal powers, coercive or otherwise, that a given authority may possess. And it would be desirable to have a definition of public authority

[3] See Weber (1947), pp. 154–57.

that is tied to how authority is justified rather than to the power that a particular society's laws or conventions confer on those exercising authority in certain contexts. The "contractarian" justification of authority provides one such definition. Following it, we can define the public sphere of human life as the sphere of those social mechanisms that make it possible for people with conflicting aims, especially moral aims, to live together. I argue that the managers of nongovernmental organizations play this sort of public role. The private sphere then becomes the sphere of association among people with coincident aims.

A contractarian justification of authority has implications for issues such as the accountability of managers. In large, contemporary organizations, governmental and nongovernmental, decision makers are accountable to those who choose them. Thus, in contemporary democracies, few if any decisions are made directly by citizens. Government is "by the people" to the extent that the people choose the top-level, political decision makers. Similarly, decision makers in the nongovernmental organizations are accountable to those who choose them. The question is, Who does this?

Most important nongovernmental organizations in contemporary capitalist societies have a certain legal form, that of the corporation. Legally, a corporation is a locus of legal rights and duties that are independent of the legal rights and duties of the natural persons associated with it. It can enter into contracts, and sue and be sued, in its own name.[4] But a corporation can act only through the people associated with it, and the law divides them into various groups: shareholders, a board of directors, senior executive officers, and other employees. The shareholders of a corporation have the legal right to determine, by voting, who the directors will be and to make decisions bearing on what philosophers would regard as corporate identity and survival—decisions concerning merger, sale, and dissolution, for example. Boards of directors have the right and duty to make decisions regarding basic business policy, such as what dividends to declare. They also hire the senior executive officers of the corporation. The senior executives manage the day-to-day opera-

---

[4] I often use the terms "organization," "corporation" and "firm" interchangeably, but strictly speaking, they have different meanings. "Organization" is a sociological term referring to a group with an internal decision-making apparatus. "Corporation" is a legal term having the meaning just specified in the text. "Firm" is an economic term referring to an entity that buys in order to sell—either what has been bought or something made out of what has been bought. An organization need not be a corporation or a firm, a corporation need not be an organization (it could consist of only one person) or a firm, and a firm need not be an organization or a corporation. Still, in the typical case, a nongovernmental organization is both a corporation and a firm.

tions of the corporation, including the hiring and firing of the rest of the employees. The senior executive officers and other employees are agents of the corporation, but the board is not the agent of the shareholders. The shareholders do not have the same rights with respect to the board that principals typically have with respect to agents.[5]

The decision making that takes place in most corporations usually does not conform to this legal model, however. Membership on boards of directors is typically controlled not by the shareholders but by the board itself. Although shareholders must vote each year to determine board members, it is very difficult and expensive for any shareholder who wants to replace the slate of directors proposed for election by the current management to contact all of the other shareholders, or enough to secure a majority of voting shares for an alternative slate. The annual election usually endorses the choices of those presently running the corporation. Similarly, the actions of boards of directors are typically controlled by the senior executives. Boards meet infrequently and do not have as much knowledge of the issues confronting the corporation as the senior executives. Thus, the control of most corporations—or at least those that are not "closely held" by a small group of shareholders—is actually in the hands of the senior executive officers. Because senior executives are usually members of the board, however, we may continue to speak of the board of directors as the locus of ultimate managerial authority, bearing in mind that a subgroup within the board often controls the rest.

When we apply the test of accountability proposed above—that decision makers are accountable to those who choose them—to the top managers of corporations, then, we find that these decision makers are accountable only to themselves as a group. In the normal course of events, decisions regarding membership in what is in fact the ultimate decision-making unit, the board of directors, are made by those who are already members, either through decisions to hire or fire those upper-level mangers who are also members of the board or by proposing for endorsement by the shareholders a certain slate of candidates. In general, we can say that membership in the group of top-level economic decision makers in our society is determined like membership in a club: Those who are already members decide who will join or be removed. One of the tasks of this book will be to determine whether this way of selecting top-level, economic deci-

---

[5] See Eisenberg (1976), pp. 1–6. The legal relations described are, of course, those that obtain in the United States.

sion makers is compatible with their role as wielders of a certain kind of public authority.

Managerial Democracy

The idea that managers are public officials, or that corporations play a quasi-governmental role or have some of the properties of a state, is not new, but it is usually formulated differently from the way that I formulate it here. In my view, if productive organizations are like states, their citizens are the employees. The usual way of making the point that corporate activities have a public aspect, however, is to note that these activities affect the lives many different "publics"— most importantly, shareholders, employees, consumers, suppliers, and neighbors of corporate facilities—and thus cannot be regarded as the private concern of those who own or operate corporations.[6] To be sure, some have argued that corporate managers should consider only the interests of the shareholders,[7] but many commentators have taken it for granted that corporate decision making should give weight to the interests of other groups as well.

It may seem that giving weight to the interests of other publics or constituencies or "stakeholders" is possible only to the extent that firms operate in noncompetitive industries; in competitive industries, the requirement of survival drastically limits options. Less stringent oligopolistic competition is the norm in many industries, however, and even where firms to do not have a financial cushion that allows them to promote actively goals that conflict with profit seeking, hard thinking can often reveal ways of making economic survival compatible with the satisfaction of various moral demands. It should also be noted that there will be times when it would be better, morally, for a firm to go out of existence than to do what is necessary to survive.

The suggestion that managerial decision making must balance the claims of various constituencies provides a provisional way of interpreting my earlier assertion that to comply with a managerial directive is often to contribute to a moral or political agenda that one does not share. An employee may disagree with the weighting of the claims of the various affected groups that underlies a particular managerial policy or decision. A more sophisticated account of the moral dimension of management is provided in Chapter Six.

[6] For a good exposition of this view, produced at the high point of post–World War II complacency about the American economy, see Mason (1959), especially the essays by Mason, Chayes, Rostow, Brewster, Kaysen, and Latham.

[7] See M. Friedman (1979).

Given that the interests of various constituencies must be taken into account, there are three main mechanisms by which this can be accomplished. A society can rely on the top management of a corporation to give the various interests affected by their decisions the morally appropriate weight. Or, it can devise mechanisms by which representatives of the affected groups—or those other than the shareholders, for whom such a mechanism already (in theory, it least) exists—can participate in corporate decision making. Or, it can legally regulate the operations of corporations to secure corporate actions that give appropriate weight to the various competing interests.

Democratic principles seem to give some support to one or the other of the latter two suggestions, but in fact both are problematic. Participation by representatives of the various affected groups—through membership on boards of directors—is usually advocated as a way of empowering various relatively powerless people. But the most important shareholders, customers, suppliers, or neighbors of a corporation are often other corporations, and providing for the participation by corporations—that is, their managers—in each other's decision making would certainly not be a way of making a self-selected managerial elite more responsive to the concerns of ordinary people.[8] The third suggestion also faces a problem. Since virtually all important managerial decisions have a moral dimension, to place all morally laden decisions in the hands of regulatory agencies would be to place general management in their hands, with the result that the benefits of economic decentralization associated with a system of independent corporations would be lost.

There is a deeper philosophical issue that counts against "stakeholder" participation in corporate governance. The suggestion that representatives of such groups should participate is associated with a widely held, but I believe fundamentally mistaken, conception of democracy. This is the view that democracy requires that, or is more fully realized to the extent that, people have a say in what affects them. A little reflection shows that this is not a principle that we accept in the political sphere. Virtually everyone in the world is affected by the foreign policy decisions of the U.S. government, but we do not suppose that they therefore have a right to participate in making these decisions or in choosing those who make them. They have a right that their morally legitimate claims be taken into account by those who formulate the foreign policy of the United States, and this may imply a duty on the part of policy makers to give

---

[8] I take this point from Eisenberg (1976), p. 21.

11

them a hearing, but they do not have a right to be among those who make the decisions by which this policy is formulated. Only the citizens of the United States have this right.

Citizens have the right to formulate foreign policy, or to choose who will formulate it, because the laws and policies of their country organize their collective actions—organize what they collectively do and allow. This yields the following general principle: The people who have a right, under democratic principles, to participate in a decision are not those who are affected by it but those whose actions are guided by it. That is, if the possession of authority is a matter of having a right to direct the actions of some group, democracy is *reflexive authority*—the generation of authoritative directives by those who will be subject to them. The say in determining a group's decision that democracy confers is a say in determining what one will do or allow as a member of a group. This point can also be made by regarding democracy as group autonomy. When an autonomous individual makes the decisions that will guide his actions, all those potentially affected have a right that their legitimate claims be taken into account, but the final decision is his alone. Similarly, when an autonomous group of individuals performs a collective action, those potentially affected have a right that their legitimate claims be taken into account, but the final decision is for the members of the group alone.[9]

This point does not count against the third of our proposals for insuring that corporations take into account the interests of all affected parties. The legislation enacted by a government determines what the individuals in a given territory will, as a political society, do or allow. Thus, those affected by corporate actions can participate in determining these actions by participating in the generation of regulatory legislation—that is, if they are citizens of a political unit that encompasses the corporate activities that affect them. In so acting, they are not, in the first instance, participating in the control of what affects them but rather in the control of what they do or allow as a political society. If regulation by the larger society is not total, however, so that nongovernmental organizations function to a certain

[9] If democracy were a matter of having a right to a say in what affects one, it would replace moral deliberation as the vehicle by which the interests of affected others found expression in the decision making of agents. Instead of deciding what the applicable moral reasons required, one would simply solicit the votes of all affected parties. Or at least this would be so for parties capable of participating in a democratic process; morality would remain the vehicle by which the interests of those affected were conveyed to decision makers when the affected parties were incompetent, or members of future generations, or animals. We shall consider these issues in more detail in Chapter Five.

extent as independent loci of decision and action, democratic principles do not support participation in organizational decision making by affected parties viewed simply as such. In this case, the decisions in question do not guide their actions.[10]

It seems, then, that the least attractive of the possibilities for securing attention to the interests of the various groups affected by organizational actions, namely, counting on managers to act responsibly, cannot be dispensed with entirely. But our survey of democratic possibilities overlooked one option. If micromanagement of corporations by agencies of democratically elected governments is undesirable and participation by representatives of various affected groups constitutes a misunderstanding of the requirements of democracy, then we must indeed rely on those who manage corporations to assess responsibly the claims of the various groups affected by corporate actions. We need not, however, understand this set of managers as simply the board of directors and the senior executives. We can design corporations so that they are managed democratically by their employees, or, more realistically, so that managers are accountable to and chosen by the employees.

If democracy is to be introduced into corporate affairs, this is the form it should take: the democratic management of corporations by their employees. Democracy is reflexive authority, that is, the exercise of authority by those who are subject to it, and those who are subject to managerial authority are the employees. Of course, it would be morally incumbent on employees, as the ultimate corporate decision makers, to consider the effect of corporate actions on other groups. The democratization of management does not alter the fact that these other groups have a right that their legitimate claims be taken into account.

There is no reason to suppose that an arrangement in which the decisions left open by regulation are made democratically by a firm's employees would be worse from the standpoint of consideration of the claims of the different affected groups than one in which these decisions are made by a self-appointed elite. The members of such elites may have greater expertise than most employees in a variety of technical matters relevant to the management of a firm, which has a bearing on the appropriateness of managerial democracy. But it is highly implausible that professional managers have greater *moral* expertise than ordinary employees. Therefore, the quality of the

---

[10] The encompassing political society could order participation in managerial decision making by representatives of affected groups if it thought that *its* aims would be best achieved by such measures.

13

consideration given to the interests of various affected groups cannot be a reason to favor management by a self-appointed elite over management by the employees or their representatives.

One of the most striking facts about corporate governance is that it is not, at present, democratic. A variety of explanations might be offered for this, some reflecting the conviction that legitimate social purposes are served by the absence of democracy in nongovernmental organizations, others reflecting the conviction that the absence of democracy in such organizations is a manifestation of a conspiracy by a ruling class to maintain its privileges. I consider arguments for curbing managerial democracy in Chapter Nine. For present purposes, the important point is that *if* corporate management is to be democratized, the group to whom corporate decision makers should be accountable—the group that should get to choose these decision makers—is the employees. They are the people whose actions are guided by managerial directives.

The picture that emerges from the considerations in this section is that of a federal system in which profit-seeking firms and other nongovernmental organizations such as hospitals and schools form, along with state and local governments, subordinate loci of political decision making. Like the idea that corporations have a public character, the idea of "corporate federalism" is not new.[11] But again, my way of formulating it is different. As previously formulated, the main point of the analogy is that if corporate managements are to be viewed as analogous to governments, they should be regarded as analogous to state or provincial rather than national governments. They should be regarded as possessing the sort of public authority that is itself subordinate to a higher authority that can regulate its exercise. With this I am in complete agreement.[12] The above considerations, however, enable us to make the analogy more specific and judge the employees of a corporation, rather than the shareholders or the other "stakeholders" as its citizens. It is they who, like the citizens of a state or municipality, have their actions organized by the relevant form of authority, and it is they who should constitute the voting population if corporate "states" are to be democratically managed.

The integrated framework of public authority mentioned earlier is, then, to be understood as a federal system. A federal system is

---

[11] See Brewster (1959), pp. 72–84.

[12] In my view, even multinational corporations should be regarded as subordinate loci of decision making in a federal system. The divisions of such firms that operate in other countries are subordinate nongovernmental organizations in those countries, participating with the local governments in a single system of public authority there.

not just a nested hierarchy of governments that perform the public function of making cooperation among people with conflicting conceptions of the moral good possible within a given territory. It also contains organizational "governments" that make possible cooperation among people with conflicting views about what constitutes morally acceptable conduct in their working lives.

Two Rejected Theses

The disenfranchisement of all corporate constituencies but the employees—their exclusion from participation in managerial decision making except through the medium of regulation by the political societies of which they are citizens—might be accepted with respect to consumers, suppliers, and neighbors but not with respect to shareholders. Shareholders own the productive resources that the employees put to use, and this seems to give them a legitimate say in the management of firms.

As we have seen, shareholders often have little actual say in the management of corporations, and it can be argued that respect for their interests does not require that they have a say. Where developed capital markets exist, shareholders have the option of selling any shares they may hold in a firm whose performance they find unsatisfactory. To invoke a well-known distinction, they do not need voice because they can exit.[13] From the moral point of view, however, shareholders are the owners of a corporation, and the fact that it is their property that is being put to use by the employees seems to entitle them to a say in management if they want one. Moreover, one could argue that the moral basis of the authority of managers is the property rights of the shareholders—reworded, managers have the authority to manage because they exercise the property rights of the shareholders. One of the standardly acknowledged incidents of ownership, the right to manage, is the right to determine who will use a particular item and how they will use it; and managers can be regarded as exercising this right for the owners.[14] But if the authority of managers is grounded in the fact

[13] See Hirschman (1970). As presented by Hirschman, voice is more a matter of complaining to decision makers than exercising a constitutional right to participate in decision making.

[14] For an account of the incidents of ownership see Honoré (1961). For our purposes, the most important are the right to use, the right to possess (to exclude others), the right to manage (the power to permit use and contract for use), the right to the income derived from productive use, and the right to the capital (the right to alienate, modify, or destroy).

15

that they exercise a property right of the owner-shareholders, it would seem that the shareholders should be free to exercise this right themselves if they so choose.

The thesis that property rights confer a right to direct the actions of employees is an instance of a broader thesis that I call the thesis of the moral unity of management. According to this thesis, the same basic moral consideration underwrites, and confers legitimacy on, both of the two main aspects of the management of a productive organization: the management of property (or capital) and the management of personnel (or labor). In the version we are now examining, property rights in productive resources are held to justify personnel management as well as property management. This view should not be understood as peculiar to defenders of capitalism. Defenders of socialism often seem to accept it as well, supposing that if management must be public to be legitimate, all that is necessary to achieve managerial legitimacy is the institution of public ownership of productive property.

Feudal conceptions of property may have satisfied the thesis of the moral unity of management. As property in land was understood at that time, it carried with it with it a right to direct, in certain respects, the actions of those living on the land.[15] But property rights as they are now understood force us to reject the thesis of the moral unity of management. The "right to manage" that forms a part of our concept of ownership cannot be regarded as a right to direct the activities of others.

This can be seen as follows. What is in some respects the central incident of ownership, the right to possess, is the right to exclusive physical control of something.[16] The emphasis here is on "exclusive." Central to ownership is the right to exclude others from contact with an item. Ownership thus gives the owner of an item the right to control the uses to which others put it in the sense that he may veto any use of it proposed by someone else. But it does not give him the right to tell anyone to put that property to the use that he wants. It is not a right to command labor. My ownership of my car, for example, gives me the right to tell someone who is driving it to refrain from certain courses of action—to exclude them—but it does not give me the right to direct her to do anything with it. If she

---

[15] As Parsons puts it: "under feudalism it was impossible to simply 'own' land in the modern sense. The holder of a fief was, in the German terms, not merely a *Grundbesitzer* but necessarily also a *Grundherr*. That is to say, what we treat as property rights, and political jurisdiction (in certain respects) were inseparable" (1947, p. 43).

[16] See Honoré (1961), pp. 113–15. Honoré calls the right to possess "the foundation on which the whole superstructure of ownership rests" (p. 115).

refuses to do what I want, I can order her out of the car. And I can leave her with only one option (if she wants to stay in the car) by vetoing all others. But my property rights do not constitute a moral reason for her to take that option. If she is disinclined to, she can simply leave. Similarly, property rights in productive resources cannot provide a moral basis for managerial authority, understood as the authority to tell employees what to do, as opposed to what to refrain from doing.[17]

The moral disunity of management has been overlooked because property in productive resources confers power. Humans must have access to productive resources, at least in the form of employment, in order to live well, and this gives an owner of such resources the ability to force nonowners to do what he tells them to by threatening them with unemployment if they do not. In the terms of the example above, nonowners do not want to be ordered out of the car. But the de facto *power* to direct the actions of employees that arises from the combination of the moral right of owners to exclude nonowners with the contingent fact that humans need access to productive resources in order to live well is not a *right* to direct their actions and thus does not in itself constitute legitimate authority.

Management, then, understood as the direction of the actions of employees, takes place within a practical space—a set of alternatives—determined by what the owners of the productive resources involved will allow. But something other than property rights is required to establish a license to tell employees to bring about one of these alternatives. From the standpoint of the individual or group holding the right to determine how the employees will act, owners holding a right to veto certain uses of the productive property employed are simply another constituency whose legitimate claims must be taken into account in determining what the organization—that is, the employees—will do.

Of course, nothing in this account of the moral basis of management precludes the same individual or group from holding both the right to manage the property and the right to manage the personnel. Nonemployee owners could hold a right to direct the actions of

---

[17] It may be useful to make this point another way. A right to direct actions could be either categorical or hypothetical. A categorical right to direct would be independent of the wants or desires of the person directed. A hypothetical right to direct, by contrast, would be a right that was conditional on the other person's wanting to do something. Property does not confer a categorical right to direct but does seem to confer a hypothetical right. If someone wants to drive my car, I have a right to tell her how to do it. But this right is essentially a right to prohibit uses. What I am doing when I rightfully tell her how to drive my car is rightfully leaving her with only one option by which she can satisfy her wants by driving my car.

employees as well, at least if managerial democracy was not required, and employees could own the resources with which they work. The point is simply that a given individual or group needs *two moral licenses* to run a productive enterprise.

Support for the contention that property management and personnel management are normatively distinct can be found in the law. The law does not regard managers as having a right to direct the actions of employees by virtue of the fact they exercise the legal property rights of the owners. Rather, the authority of managers over employees is grounded in the law of agency; employees are agents of their employers. A relation of agency is created when one party, the agent, consents to act on behalf of and under the direction of another party, the principal, and the principal consents to having the agent's actions count as the principal's for legal purposes—primarily purposes of assessing liability. The principal may be either a natural person or an organization.[18]

The law, then, does not regard the two parts of management as having a unified normative basis. As I have already indicated, however, from the standpoint of an inquiry into the legitimacy of authority, legal relations are not fundamental. They are social conventions of a certain kind the acceptability of which depends on their having an adequate moral justification.[19] Thus, we cannot simply take the legal view of the normative basis of personnel management at face value.

This brings us to the second of the theses that I reject, the mirror thesis. According to the mirror thesis, the legal picture of the relations between individuals in a productive organization mirrors the underlying moral relations. Sometimes the legal considerations that govern a particular action—the legal rights and duties that the people acting in that area have—mirror exactly, or at any rate very closely, the underlying moral considerations. Thus, murder is against the law and is also morally impermissible. But sometimes laws are justified not as mirroring an underlying moral reality but simply because the system of conventional rights and duties that

---

[18] Legal acceptance of the normative disunity of management is revealed by Honoré's account of the right to manage as a property right. It is, in part, a power to contract with nonowners for certain uses by them of an item. But the power to contract is not itself a contractual right. The contract must be struck.

[19] For the purposes of this book, I adopt a positivist account of law according to which laws need not reflect moral requirements to count as valid. The law is simply a system of conventional rules distinguished from other such systems by its structure, the most notable feature of which is a rule of recognition by means of which those conventional rules that are to count as laws are identified. See Hart (1961), esp. Chaps. 5 and 6.

they create gives rise to social behavior that advances morally important goals. The legal requirement to drive on the right-hand side of the road (in the United States) corresponds to no moral requirement; it simply facilitates orderly transportation.

Legally, an agency relation is created by the consent of both parties, and the moral analogue of the employee's legal consent to act under the principal's direction is a promise to this effect. If the mirror thesis is true, then, employees should obey their employers because they have promised to, typically in return for pay. While the law may regard consent as sufficient to underwrite routine obedience, however, I argue that promissory obligation does not have enough moral power to do so, at least in large organizations.

The law of agency does not require an agent to perform an illegal action if so directed by a principal. That is, the legal duties of an agent are nullified when they clash with a legal prohibition. Since most of the things employers want employees to do are not illegal, this restriction does not seriously limit the legal powers of managers—who are usually lieutenants exercising the rights of the employer as principal. When we move to the moral sphere, however, things are different. An employee might easily regard as morally impermissible a perfectly legal action by a corporate employer. As we have seen, corporate actions affect many different groups of people, and there is often disagreement about the morally correct balancing of these interests even when the alternatives at issue are all legally permissible. Thus if managerial authority is to be robust for a given employee—if he is to have a good moral reason to comply with managerial directives in a wide variety of possible situations—what justifies managerial authority must be capable of underwriting his compliance with managerial directives even when this would mean contributing to an effort that he regards as morally suboptimal. I argue that promissory obligation is not a strong enough moral consideration to give managerial authority this sort of robustness. While there may, then, be no legal barrier to regarding employees as agents of their employers, there is a moral barrier. We must find some other way of thinking about the relation of employees to their employers. Contractarian theories of political authority can, I believe, provide what we need.

Political Philosophy or Business Ethics?

In contemporary philosophical discussion, moral questions concerning how people should behave in economic contexts are often treated under the heading of "business ethics." Earlier I characterized this book as an essay in political philosophy. In one sense, this is merely a terminological issue, but there are several reasons why I think that even the parts of the book that discuss management are better understood as political philosophy than as business ethics.

First, two different questions can be raised about institutions that contain offices from which authority is exercised. There is the question of why a society should create institutions that contain such offices, and there is the question of what those who hold these offices (or aspire to them) should do. This latter question may be further subdivided into the question of what policies the occupants of offices should implement and the question of how the occupants of offices should treat those with whom they come into contact in the course of discharging their duties. In the governmental case, questions of the last sort might be called questions of political ethics. Business ethics has mostly concerned itself with questions of policy and official ethics as they arise in corporate contexts.[20] One of the main objectives in this book, however, is to show that there also needs to be discussion of the first sort of question, regarding the justification for creating offices from which authority is exercised, with respect to all large nongovernmental organizations. Because the inquiry that is required to answer this question is essentially the same as that required to answer the question of what justifies government, my discussion, even in the managerial case, should be classified as political philosophy.

Second, although the role of manager is found in all economic systems, and in government as well as industry, the term "business" suggests economic activity in a market, and in particular a capitalist system. Thus, business ethics becomes the study of ethical behavior in a capitalist system. For some people, however, this begs what they regard as the most important moral question that arises in connection with economic activity, the question of whether private ownership of the means of production, or private ownership by nonemployees, is morally permissible. For these people, business ethics seems comparable to an "ethics of slavery" that articulates such propositions as: slaves should never be sold in a way that breaks up primary family units. Of course this is true, but it is also beside the point. Morally, people cannot be owned by other people at all.

The argument of this book bears on the question of whether pro-

---

[20] An anonymous reader pointed out the need for clarification here. I discuss why business seems problematic from the moral point of view in McMahon (1981, 1982).

ductive resources should be publicly owned, but it approaches it by an unfamiliar route. The usual route is through an investigation of distributive justice. The question is taken to be whether private ownership of the means of production, the means of creating the material prerequisites of human life, is in accordance with our best understanding of the requirements of distributive justice. But private ownership of productive resources is compatible with a just distribution of the *products* produced with these resources if appropriate tax and welfare policies are in place.[21] The decisive question is whether control of productive *activity* by private owners is morally permissible.

Given the moral disunity of management, however, this is not a question that a theory of distributive justice, understood as a theory of just ownership, can answer alone. Property in productive resources implies only a right to veto uses of one's property of which one does not approve. As we have seen, given the circumstances of human life, an individual exercising this right has the power to control productive activity. But to have the right to control it, she needs an additional moral license, one that gives employees a sufficient reason to do what she tells them to. Moreover, this remains the case even if the best theory of distributive justice supports public ownership of productive resources. Public ownership implies only that the society as a whole, or its agents, has the right to veto any use of its productive resources and the power that this entails. It does not imply that the society as whole has a right to direct workers (its members) to do certain things.[22] I suggest, then, that the best way to approach the question of whether socialism is required is to determine what justifies managerial authority and then consider whether productive property must be in public hands if the de facto powers that ownership confers are to be exercised in a way that is compatible with managerial legitimacy.

There is a third reason why the discussions of management that this book contains are appropriately regarded as political philoso-

[21] It might be argued that the enactment of the tax and other legislation required to effect a just distribution of the social product is, as a matter of political fact, unlikely when ownership is in private hands. But any political movement strong enough to overthrow capitalism in the United States would, well before it attained that degree of power, be strong enough to pass the laws necessary to assure a just distribution of what is produced with privately owned productive resources.

[22] It may be useful to say a bit more about the case of productive property. A group of individuals sharing a certain interest could use their just earnings to buy or build a factory. But unless they had a right to direct the actions of employees, their purpose in doing this would have to be limited. Their purpose in building it would have to be, say, that they liked the figure it cut against the sky, or in buying it that they liked to hear the hum of the machinery (when they operated it themselves).

phy. As I understand political philosophy, it is the branch of moral philosophy that is concerned with how people who disagree about moral or nonmoral matters but live together in the same society should manage their common affairs. Each substantive moral theory—utilitarianism, say—will have implications for this question, and thus each will contain a political theory as a part. But if there is moral disagreement, the problems of political philosophy will reemerge as problems about how people holding political theories grounded in different substantive moral conceptions should manage their common affairs. The emphasis that I place on the concept of authority is meant to address these higher-order problems. It may be that we can provide an account of legitimate authority that does not require us to commit ourselves to a particular substantive moral conception, or that draws only on very general values shared by a variety of conceptions.

It should be noted that these points have application even when someone's substantive moral theory is described as a theory of justice. Such a theory will undoubtedly have implications for the exercise of authority, deeming some ways of exercising it just and some unjust. But the moral conceptions of some of the members of a society may not be conceptions of justice at all, and those whose substantive moral conceptions are conceptions of justice may understand justice in different ways. Thus, it will be desirable to have an account of legitimate political authority that is independent, at least initially, of considerations of justice, and that explains how those holding different substantive conceptions of justice can acknowledge the same authority.[23]

If disagreement among people holding different substantive moral conceptions is the mark of the political sphere, however, nongovernmental organizations are as political as states. Managers routinely put into effect policies that take sides on the moral issues that divide the larger society, and since employees are members of the larger society, it can be expected that they will be divided about these issues as well. Inquiries into what justifies compliance with managerial directives despite these disagreements, then, are inquiries into a political matter—a matter regarding how the common affairs of people who hold conflicting substantive moral views should be managed.

[23] John Rawls's writings can be regarded as moving in this direction. His *A Theory of Justice* (1971), seems simply to work out the political implications of a certain substantive conception of the requirements of justice. But in his more recent work, he argues that his theoretical apparatus is the appropriate basis on which to organize a society in which people hold a variety of competing substantive moral conceptions. See Rawls (1980, 1985, 1987, 1988).

PART I

AUTHORITY IN GENERAL
AND IN GOVERNMENT

AUTHORITY

Authority is one of the central concepts of political philosophy. It is usually defined as a mode of influence distinct from both coercion and persuasion by argument.[1] A subordinate in an authority relation complies with authoritative directives without being coerced and also without necessarily being convinced that what they direct is the best course of action in the circumstances. Authority so understood is indispensable for the management of the affairs of large groups. It is impossible to coerce or convince everyone.

Power and Authority

The concept of authority may be introduced by sketching its relation to the concept of power. For present purposes, power can be defined as the ability to get what one wants.[2] To be more precise, one has power to the extent that there are sequences of actions available to one (where availability includes knowledge of their existence) the performance of which will produce a state of affairs that one wants.[3] Both individuals and groups can have power in this sense. For an account of authority, the most important kind of power is the power to make the lives of other people the way one wants them to be and especially the power to make them do certain things. Not all such power is important, however. I have characterized authority in terms of the idea of compliance with a directive, and we can introduce a corresponding species of power, the ability to get others to act or refrain by issuing directives, that is, by telling them what to do. To take an example that Alvin Goldman uses to make a different point, a skywriter has the ability to make people look up, but he does not

---

[1] See, for example, Arendt (1958) and Peters (1958). For the case of managerial authority, see Simon (1976), pp. 123–53.

[2] At the most general level, as Tom Wartenberg has pointed out to me, power is the ability to produce an effect.

[3] Here I am following Goldman (1972).

tell them to do anything.[4] Let us call the ability to get people to do things by telling them to do these things *directive power*.[5]

Leaving aside cases in which one secures compliance with a directive by a causal mechanism that bypasses the will, such as hypnosis, there are three ways that one can come to possess directive power: (1) a person may want, without any manipulation of the situation on one's part, to comply with one's directive; (2) one may be able to create such a want in him; or (3) one may be able to attach consequences to compliance or noncompliance (rewards and punishments) that make it rational for him to comply with one's directive, given the wants he already has. A potential source of confusion should be noted here. Somebody's wanting to comply with one's directives is his wanting to do what one tells him to do. But this can be construed either as his wanting independently to do the thing one happens to tell him to do or as his wanting to do whatever (within some range) one tells him to do. It is the latter construal that is relevant to the possession of directive power.

Corresponding to the idea of the power to direct the actions of others we can introduce the idea of a right to do this—a right to tell others, within certain limits that will vary from case to case, what to do. This is authority. The right to direct involved in authority need not be a personal right of the individual holding authority. It can be a right to direct in the weaker sense that compliance with the authority's directives is the right course of action for those who have the status of subjects.[6]

If the right to direct is understood descriptively or sociologically, as a claim that is as a matter of fact acknowledged by all the relevant agents—both those whose performance is required if the claim is to be sustained and those whose noninterference is required—we may speak of de facto authority. De facto authority is a form of directive power distinguished from other forms by the fact that those whose compliance is obtained accept that the individual or group issuing the directive has a right to do so, and they comply for this reason. That is, they want to do what they are directed to do, without any manipulation of the situation by the person issuing the directive,

---

[4] Goldman (1972), pp. 261–62. Goldman uses the example to support his contention that the ability to make people do certain things is not sufficient for having power over them, which he takes to be tied rather to the ability to affect their welfare. For a discussion of the distinction between "power over" and "power to" see Wartenberg (1990), chap 1.

[5] My concept of directive power is roughly equivalent to Weber's concept of "imperative control." He defines this as "the probability that a command with a given specific content will be obeyed by a given group of persons" (1947, p. 152).

[6] Cf. Peters (1958), pp. 217–18.

because they believe that it is right to comply with this person's directives. By contrast, if the notion of a right is taken normatively rather than descriptively, we may speak of de jure or legitimate authority. A legitimate authority is one that actually has the right to direct, in certain specified respects, the actions of certain other individuals.

I shall assume that only an individual or group that has some form of directive power can be a legitimate authority. In part this is because, as Joseph Raz has emphasized and as we shall see in detail later, the ability to effect coordination is one of the properties that confers legitimacy on an authority. I shall not, however, assume that a legitimate authority must be a de facto authority. An individual or group that has a right to direct can be a legitimate authority even if most of those whose compliance it seeks mistakenly suppose that it lacks this right, provided that it has some other kind of power, for example, coercive power, sufficient to insure that most comply with its directives.

Subordination and Authority

To have authority is to have a right to direct the actions of some other people. But what distinguishes this right from other considerations that give one the moral ability to call on others to act in certain ways? Using a concept introduced by Raz, we can say that although all such considerations present others with reasons for action, when one has authority, one's *directives* are taken as—or are, in the case of legitimate authority—*preemptive* reasons for some other people to do what is directed.[7] Let us consider further what this means.

Sometimes I may have a right to direct another to behave in a particular way because I have an independently existing right that he behave in that way. An example would be my right to direct someone with hostile intentions to take his hands off me. I have this right because I have an antecedently existing right not to be touched without my consent. Let us call a right to direct of this sort a derived right to direct. The right to direct characteristic of authority is not derived in this way from an independent right (or other consideration that makes it the case that the person to whom the directive is addressed ought in any case to perform the action he is directed to perform). It is a right to direct another to perform certain actions even if no independent considerations require their performance.

---

[7] See Raz (1985) and (1986), chaps. 2–4. Chapter 3 of the book is a somewhat expanded version of the article.

To say that the right to direct involved in authority is not derived from an independent consideration that makes performance of the directed act the right thing to do is not, of course, to say that authority cannot be justified. Other considerations can establish the existence of a right to direct.

It might be supposed that what distinguishes a derived from a nonderived right to direct is the degree of latitude associated with the latter. When one's right to direct is derived, one may direct someone to perform only the particular act that the individual in question ought in any case to perform. When it is nonderived, however, one may direct the performance of whatever action one chooses, within some specified range. But while latitude for choice is often associated with a nonderived right to direct, it cannot be taken as a defining feature. The range of choice that a particular nonderived right to direct provides may be so limited that it is coextensive with the range of choice possessed by someone who has a derived right to direct, namely, the choice between calling for the performance of a particular act or refraining from calling for it.

The true mark of a nonderived right to direct is the simple fact that it is not derived. It is a right that someone perform an action simply because one has told her to perform it, rather than because it is something that, for some independent reason, she ought to do. Following H.L.A. Hart, it has become customary to refer to this feature of authority as content-independence.[8] An authoritative directive provides the subject to whom it is directed with a content-independent reason to perform the action in question, where this means a reason that does not depend on the content of the directive, that is, it does not depend on the fact that the directed action is of a kind that the subject already has some reason to perform.

From the standpoint of the subject in an authority relation, the phenomenon of content-independence can (with a little oversimplification) be understood as follows. When we speak of such a relation, we have in mind a set of actions that could be performed by the subject, and we suppose that she has some ranking of the alternatives in this set determined by her assessment of the applicable content-dependent reasons. Her acceptance of authority consists, in part, in her willingness to regard the fact that one of the actions in this set is directed by the person whose authority she acknowledges as a sufficient reason to perform it even though it is not the action that she, consulting content-dependent reasons, ranks first.

Although the distinction between content-dependent reasons

[8] Hart (1982). For further discussion of content-independence, see Green (1988), pp. 29–56.

and content-independent reasons is well-established in the literature, I employ a different but related distinction to mark the non-derived character of an authority's right to direct. This is the distinction between what the recipient of a directive would regard herself as having sufficient *directive-independent* reason to do—that is, what she would regard herself as having sufficient reason to do if the directive in question had not been issued—and what she regards herself as having sufficient *directive-dependent* reason to do—that is, what she regards herself as having sufficient reason to do given that the directive has been issued. Directive-dependent reasons comprise all the reasons that support acting on the directive, but that would not have applied to the situation had it not been issued.[9]

In a de facto authority relation, the subject does not act on her judgment about what there is sufficient directive-independent reason to do, but rather performs the action she is directed to perform. And in a de jure authority relation, the subject ought to act in this way. But this is only a necessary condition for an authority relation since there are ways of performing an action because one is directed to that do not involve the acceptance of authority. An example would be a case in which someone, usually but not necessarily the person issuing the directive, has indicated that he will reward the agent for complying, and this reward is perceived by the agent as sufficient to tip the balance of reasons in favor of doing so— sufficient to make complying the course supported by the balance of reasons when it would not otherwise have been. What, then, distinguishes the ways of acting for sufficient directive-dependent reason that are characteristic of the acceptance of authority from those that are not?[10]

For our purposes, the most important difference between accepting authority and acting for directive-dependent reasons that take the form of rewards is that authority involves subordination. Someone who does what A says solely because he expects a reward for doing so is not in a relation of subordination to A. But someone who complies with an authoritative directive is in a relation of subordination to the person issuing it.

[9] The distinction between directive-independent and directive-dependent reasons is not equivalent to the distinction between content-dependent and content-independent reasons because the applicable directive-independent reasons may include promissory obligations (especially to someone other than the person issuing the directive) and these are content-independent reasons. The reason they provide depends not on the nature of the promised act, but the fact that one has promised to perform it.

[10] Since in all of these cases the agent has no reason to do anything until a directive is issued, the label "directive-dependent" is appropriate.

To be in a relation of subordination to somebody is to have one's behavior controlled by that person. Not all ways of controlling someone's behavior involve subordination, however. Control by hypnosis does not, for example. The difference is that the behavior of a hypnotic subject is controlled in a way that bypasses his will, while the behavior of someone in a relation of subordination is controlled in a way that engages his will. To be more precise, to be subordinate to someone is to have her will, in a certain sense, replace one's own as the determinant of one's actions. This may be understood as follows. In a subordination relation, the subordinate's judgment of what the applicable directive-independent reasons require is displaced from its normal, action-inducing relation to his will by a directive.[11] Something that can be regarded as the judgment's being knocked away from the will by the directive occurs. Of course, this talk of displacement needs to be made more precise.

To say that authority involves subordination does not, however, give us a sufficient condition for an authority relation since there are two species of subordination. One way the displacement of judgment by a directive can take place is through coercion. I consider in the next section how this is to be understood. For the time being it is enough to note that subordination effected by coercion, or by mechanisms relevantly similar to it, is not (de facto) authority. An armed robber subordinates his victim, in the sense in which I am using the term, but to comply with the directive of an armed robber is not to accept him as having authority in the situation.

De facto authority involves subordination effected without the use of coercion or mechanisms relevantly similar to it. This means that the displacement involved is voluntary. The subordinate allows his will to be shaped by the directive of another rather than his own judgment of what the situation requires—or perhaps we should rather say, the subordinate makes it the case that his will is shaped by someone else's directive. How, then, can we speak of displacement? Why does the element of voluntariness not mean that the judgment is no longer displaced—knocked away—from its normal relation to the will? How is voluntarily allowing displacement different from voluntarily complying with a directive because a reward has been offered?

---

[11] For convenience, I speak of an individual in a relation of subordination as a subordinate. Strictly speaking, however, the term "subordinate" designates the occupant of a role that involves subordination. As I understand subordination, B can be said to be A's subordinate though B does not occupy such a role.

The answer lies in the nature of the reasons that justify giving the directive precedence over one's directive-independent judgment. Here we finally come to the preemptiveness of authoritative directives that is distinctive of Raz's account of authority. In addition to ordinary reasons for performing certain acts, there are reasons to take, or more typically not to take, certain ordinary reasons into account in reaching a conclusion about what to do.[12] When the reasons are reasons not to take certain ordinary reasons into account, Raz terms them exclusionary reasons. Exclusionary reasons do not nullify the ordinary reasons to which they apply, in the sense of making it the case that they are no longer reasons. Rather, they are reasons for not giving these ordinary reasons any weight when deciding what to do, and thus reasons for not acting on these reasons in a particular situation.

One simple example, discussed by Raz, is decision. When one makes a decision, one closes off further consideration of the ordinary reasons pro or con of a certain course of action and resolves to act on the judgment that the applicable ordinary reasons support at the time the decision is made. Insofar as deciding is rational, it must be because there are good reasons not to entertain, for the purposes of determining a course of action, any additional considerations that may emerge at a later date—perhaps because the expected gain from doing so, in the sense of the expectation of acting more successfully when the time comes, is not great enough to outweigh the costs of further deliberation. These reasons for not entertaining any further considerations are exclusionary reasons, reasons to judge and act on the basis of a proper subset of the reasons that are potentially relevant.

Decisions, however, are not merely judgments that no further deliberation is appropriate. They are also judgments that the ordinary reasons available when they are made support a certain course of action. By relating these ordinary reasons for action to a particular action, decisions count as reasons for action as well. They convey the force of ordinary reasons for action. Decisions do more than exclude certain ordinary reasons for action from consideration, then; they also replace these reasons. To be more precise, they put the rational force of the ordinary reasons on which they are based in place of the total set of reasons, including the excluded reasons, that would otherwise bear on what was to be done. Raz terms considerations that have this status preemptive reasons for action. Decisions

[12] Here I am following Raz (1978).

are, then, preemptive reasons for action; they are reasons to act on a proper subset of the available reasons.[13]

Similarly, in an authority relation, the directives of the authority are preemptive reasons for action. Accepting authority involves excluding from consideration, for practical purposes at any rate, certain reasons—namely, the directive-independent reasons that support one's own judgment about what the situation requires—and thus declining to act on these reasons. But unlike the preemption characteristic of decision, the preemption characteristic of authority involves the replacement of the excluded reasons not with an earlier judgment of one's own but with somebody else's directive, which thus acquires the status of a preemptive reason for action.

We are now in a position to say why the acceptance of authority involves subordination. The subject's judgment of what the applicable directive-independent reasons require is displaced from her will because the reasons supporting it are excluded and replaced, that is, preempted, by the authority's directive. If the replaced reasons are all those the subject regards as applicable to the situation, the result is full subordination, doing just what the authority says. It is worth noting, however, that there could be what might be called partial subordination if the replaced reasons were not all those the subject regarded as relevant. In such a case, the subject would have to somehow combine the authoritative directive with the nonreplaced reasons to reach a judgment about what to do. The main point, however, is that in either case, de facto authority involves the subordinate's believing that there is sufficient reason not just for excluding certain reasons but also for replacing her judgment of what they require with a directive issued by another. And legitimate authority involves there actually being sufficient reason for both these operations. To justify authority is to establish its legitimacy—that is, to establish that there is sufficient reason for the subordinate to allow the authority's directives to preempt her judgment of what the applicable (directive-independent) reasons require.[14]

To avoid confusion, two points should be made clear. First, as Raz and others have emphasized, while to accept authority is to exercise one's will in accordance with someone else's directive rather than one's own judgment (of what the applicable directive-independent reasons require), it does not involve a surrender of judgment in the

[13] There is a potential for confusion here since exclusionary reasons are sometimes referred to as "peremptory." But "peremptory" means "closing off debate" while "preemptive" means "replacing." Preemptive reasons are more than peremptory; they not only exclude, but also replace, other reasons.

[14] The justification of authority is the topic of Chapter Four.

further sense of declining to exercise one's one judgmental capacities. One remains free, as someone subject to authority, to consider what the applicable directive-independent reasons require as long as one does not act on the resulting judgment. Indeed, we can go further. Not only does one remain free to do this, but doing so may be a necessary part of the procedure by which one determines whether authority is legitimate. Whether there is reason to accept preemption may depend in part on what there would be reason to do in the absence of preemption.

Second, as Raz has also emphasized, preemption is to be distinguished from the outweighing of one reason by another.[15] Preemptive reasons are not to be understood as simply added to and balanced against the reasons that one already acknowledges. Rather, preemptive reasons exclude and take the place of other reasons. The difference between this and outweighing can be brought out by reverting to our discussion of exclusionary reasons. Such reasons may tip the balance of considerations supporting a certain action, but they do this not by taking a place alongside other considerations on the scale of reason, but by removing certain other considerations from the scale. Of course, preemptive reasons are not merely exclusionary; they are considerations pro or con of action in their own right. But because they are in part exclusionary, they take a place on the scale of reason by knocking other considerations off.

Now we can see more precisely what distinguishes complying with the directive of an authority from complying with the directive of someone who has offered a reward for compliance. In the latter case, the directive does not displace the agent's judgment of what the applicable directive-independent reasons require. Instead, the reason that justifies compliance (the reward) merely takes a place alongside the directive-independent reasons for and against compliance and works by tipping the balance of all these reasons taken together toward compliance. This point can be generalized. When the reasons that justify complying with a directive do this by simply outweighing the contrary directive-independent reasons that the recipient of the directive regards as applicable to the situation, the relation between the person issuing the directive and the recipient is not an authority relation.

Autonomy and Authority

Let us return to the question of how the displacement of judgment characteristic of the forms of subordination that do not involve au-

[15] For discussions of this and the preceding point, see Raz (1986), pp. 38–42.

thority is to be understood. My account of these forms of subordination makes use of the fact that they violate the autonomy of the subordinate. It is sometimes claimed that authority, too, is incompatible with autonomy. If the distinction between forms of subordination that involve authority and those that do not is made in the way that I suggest, however, this latter claim must be rejected.

As we have seen, the acceptance of authority can involve acting against one's judgment of what the directive-independent reasons applicable to a situation require. It can involve performing an action that there would be no reason to perform had one not been directed to perform it. But while there may be a strong presumptive objection to acting contrary to one's directive-independent judgment of what a situation requires, it is a mistake to characterize doing this as abandoning one's autonomy. One does not typically abandon one's autonomy if one complies with a directive because one has been offered a reward for doing so, and one judges that the incentive offered is sufficient to justify acting against one's directive-independent judgment of what the situation requires. And although the reasons that support complying with an authoritative directive cannot be regarded as merely outweighing the considerations that they replace, acting on them can also be compatible with autonomy.[16]

This point becomes clear if autonomy is understood in the way proposed by Gerald Dworkin.[17] At the most general level, autonomy is self-determination, but in Dworkin's view it must be carefully distinguished from other notions that are closely tied to self-determination. One of these is liberty. Liberty is a matter of the absence of de facto obstacles to goal attainment, understood as the satisfaction of what Dworkin and others have called first-order desires, desires for states of the world the characterization of which does not involve reference to other desires that one may have. An example would be the desire to eat an apple. The obstacles to goal attainment the absence of which constitutes liberty are barriers in the case of negative liberty and diminished opportunities in the case

[16] Wolff says, "The autonomous man, in so far as he is autonomous, is not subject to the will of another. He may do what another tells him, but not because he is told to do it" (1970, p. 14). The first of these sentences states that autonomy is incompatible with subordination, the second that it is incompatible with acting on (certain) directive-dependent reasons. As we shall see, both claims are dubious. In McMahon (1987), I argue that authority is compatible with autonomy, understood as acting on directive-independent reasons. I would now characterize the argument of that article simply as an attempt to show that under certain conditions, the available directive-independent reasons alone can justify complying with an authority's directives.

[17] See G. Dworkin (1988).

of positive liberty. Another notion closely tied to self-determination is voluntariness. Negative liberty does not suffice for the voluntary performance of an action. Someone who gets me to do something by deceiving me does not block my performance of any action, but nevertheless brings it about that I do not perform the action in question voluntarily.

Although being an autonomous person usually involves having negative and positive liberty and acting voluntarily, liberty and voluntariness are neither necessary nor sufficient for autonomy. They are not sufficient because an addict who freely and voluntarily acts on his first-order desire for drugs is not normally autonomous. They are not necessary because one can autonomously put oneself in a position where one is not at liberty or where one does not act voluntarily. Dworkin uses the example of Odysseus and the sirens. Odysseus autonomously arranged to have his liberty restricted so that he could hear the song of the sirens without endangering himself or his crew. Similarly, one might autonomously arrange to have one's doctor lie to one in the event that one was diagnosed to have terminal cancer.

Dworkin accounts for these facts about autonomy by linking autonomy to second-order desires, desires to be the sort of person who is motivated or not motivated by certain first-order desires. The desire not to crave cigarettes, for example, is a second-order desire. According to Dworkin, one is autonomous or self-determining when one is (1) able to reflect critically, from the standpoint of one's second-order desires, on one's first order desires; and (2) able to endorse from this standpoint the first-order desires that move one to act—which involves being able, to a certain extent, to harness the motivation associated with one's second-order desires to modify one's first-order desires, should this be necessary to bring them into conformity with one's second-order desires. It should be noted, however, that the core of this account of autonomy is the possibility of adopting a critical stance toward the desires that move one, and we may have the conceptual resources to do this without invoking second-order desires.

Given this, one can autonomously accept authority if one can endorse, from one's critical standpoint, the motivation that manifests itself in one's acceptance of a directive as a preemptive reason for action.[18] Let us consider this in more detail. De facto authority is

[18] There is a sense in which exclusionary reasons are second-order, since they apply to other reasons. Indeed Raz sometimes uses this terminology to describe them. But both exclusionary reasons and the reasons they exclude are first-order considerations in Dworkin's sense, since we can raise the question of whether be can endorse, from our critical standpoint, being motivated by them.

subordination undertaken because the subject accepts the directives he receives as preemptive reasons for action. A subject in such a relation might despise himself for being moved to accept the directives of the authority as reasons of this sort, in which case his participation in the relation would not be compatible with his autonomy. But if his being moved to accept the directives as preemptive reasons is something that he can endorse from his critical standpoint, his participating in the authority relation will be compatible with his autonomy. Plausible examples are not hard to find. Thus Dworkin suggests that the acceptance of authority associated with entering a monastery could be endorsed from a monk's critical standpoint.[19]

Dworkin's account of autonomy can be used to shed light on the form of subordination that does not involve the acceptance of authority. I have described subordination as the displacement, by the superior's directive, of the subordinate's judgment of what the applicable directive-independent reasons require from its normal, action-inducing relation to his will. We have seen how this works in the case of an authority relation. The displacement reflects the subordinate's grasp of specifically displacing reasons: preemptive reasons.

Somewhat different considerations justify our speaking of displacement in the case of coercion. Here, too, the subordinate acts contrary to his judgment of what the applicable directive-independent reasons require. But in one respect, the situation is similar to the offering of a reward. In the latter case, one acts as one does because someone has attached to compliance incentives that are sufficient, combined with any directive-independent reasons that may support compliance, to outweigh the directive-independent reasons that argue against compliance. Similarly, when one gives one's wallet to a robber who says, "Your money or your life," one complies because one judges avoidance of the threatened harm to be a weightier consideration, when combined with any others that may justify compliance, than those that support resisting. This means that just as in a case in which a reward is offered, in coercion there is no preemption. What then, justifies speaking of subordination in such a case?

We are justified in doing this because one does not usually act

[19] This view seems to imply that a slave could be autonomous. (This was pointed out to me by Alan Fuchs and Dworkin appears to agree. See Dworkin [1988], p. 29.) But Dworkin makes it clear that any such case would have to be regarded as deviant. While liberty and voluntariness are not logically necessary for autonomy, large-scale restrictions of either usually make it impossible for humans to develop the second-order capacities required for autonomy (p. 18).

autonomously when one is coerced; the directive-dependent reasons which move one to act are not reasons that one can endorse acting on from one's critical standpoint—or perhaps better, one cannot endorse being presented with them in this way. Rather, one endorses acting on the directive-independent reasons that argue against compliance but that are outweighed by the coercer's threat. This means, however, that there is a sense in which one is not acting on one's own judgment, for the judgment that shapes one's will is not based on reasons that one endorses. When another person has violated one's autonomy in getting one to comply with his directive, then—has put one in the position of being motivated by considerations the operation of which one cannot endorse—we are justified in speaking of the displacement of one's judgment by the directive and thus of subordination.[20]

It is a consequence of this account of subordination outside authority relations that whenever someone violates one's autonomy by getting one to act on a directive for reasons that one cannot endorse, one is placed in a position of subordination. This means that one can be subordinated, as I am using this term, not only by being coerced, by also by having one's autonomy violated in other ways. An example would be a case in which another obtains one's compliance with his directives by inducing weakness of will, that is, by offering incentives which induce one to act against one's all-things-considered judgment of what is required in the situation.

Let us summarize our discussion to this point. There are three ways of acting on someone's directives for directive-dependent reasons, reasons that are activated only when a directive is issued. One may do this because (1) a reward is offered for compliance, (2) punishment is threatened for noncompliance, or (3) one wants to do what the person in question tells one to do—in the sense of wanting to comply with her directives, as opposed to already wanting to perform the act that one happens to be told to perform. Cases of type (1) usually do not involve subordination while cases of type (2) usually do. And when cases of type (3) involve wanting to do what someone says because one regards her directives as preemptive reasons for action, subordination is also present.[21] Unlike the subor-

---

[20] This means that coerced compliance with directives will not involve subordination if the agent endorses being motivated by the threat. Arranging for someone credibly to threaten to hit one if one tries to start drinking again might be an example. Compare Dworkin's Odysseus case.

[21] If someone just wants to do what another tells him to do because it would make her feel good—say he is humoring an imperious friend—we would not, I think, speak of a relation of subordination. Here the agent's desire to do whatever he is told simply outweighs any contrary desires he may have.

dination involved in most cases of type (2), however, this latter form of subordination is usually compatible with autonomy.

The last point has the consequence that where subordination is being effected by means that are incompatible with autonomy, eliminating the subordination relation is not the only step that respect for autonomy can support. One can also convert the relation into the sort of subordination relation that is compatible with autonomy by convincing the subject that she can endorse, from her critical standpoint, regarding the superior's directives as preemptive reasons for action. Normally this will be accomplished by providing arguments that the directives in question really are good preemptive reasons, that is, arguments that the superior is a legitimate authority. It should be emphasized, however, that the reconciliation of authority with autonomy does not entail its justification. A de facto authority relation need not be legitimate, and it can be compatible with autonomy even if it is not legitimate. All that is necessary is that the subject endorse, from her critical standpoint, accepting the directives in question as preemptive reasons for action.

The Priority of Right to Directive Power

As we have seen, there are several different forms of directive power. I now propose a normative thesis regarding them, which I call the thesis of the priority of right to directive power. This thesis states that the exercise of directive power in a particular case—the exercise of an ability, whatever its source, to get someone to do something by telling him to do it—is permissible only if one has a right to direct the action that one directs in that case.

The force of this thesis can be brought out by considering the various instances of it. One sort of directive power is de facto authority, and here the thesis implies that one may exercise one's powers as a de facto authority only if (1) one is (in the case at hand) a legitimate authority, and thus has a nonderived right to direct the action in question, or (2) one has a right to direct it derived from the fact that it is an action that the agent ought, for independent reasons, to perform. Another sort of directive power is the power to coerce: to get people to do what one says by threatening them with bad consequences if they do not. Here, again, the thesis implies that one may exercise this power only if one is a legitimate authority and thus has a nonderived right to direct the particular action in question, or one has a right to direct it derived from the fact that the agent ought for independent reasons to perform it. It should be borne in mind that the fact that someone ought, for independent reasons, to do something does not always give another person a derived right to direct it. I am concerned only with the cases where the conditions requisite for the existence of a derived right to direct are met. I do not consider here what these conditions are.

The final sort of directive power that we have considered is the power to get people to do what one tells them to do by attaching a reward for compliance. It might seem that here there is no need for power to conform to right since the people over whom this sort of power is exercised are not subordinated by its exercise. But leaving aside the fact that subordination can be effected by offering rewards if weakness of will is induced, in all cases of this sort, there is a sense in which the exercise of directive power is controlled by right. One must have at least a liberty right to secure compliance with one's directives by offering rewards, which normally means that what one directs others to do must be morally permissible.

The thesis of the priority of right to directive power should not be problematic. In general, morality dictates that one may exercise whatever powers one has only in morally permissible ways. That is, what one may do takes precedence over what one can do. For example, one may use bargaining power only to secure results that accord with the requirements of distributive justice. Here, however, we are concerned with cases in which the power at issue is directive power, the power to get people to perform certain actions by telling them to perform them. Thus, it will be useful to have before us a thesis that specifies the general point by stating explicitly that directive power may only be brought to bear where the individual employing it has a right to direct the action whose performance he secures.

It should be emphasized that the thesis states only the priority of right to directive power, not the priority of legitimate authority. As we have seen, one need not be a legitimate authority to be justified in bringing directive power to bear. It is sometimes enough that the other person ought, for independent reasons, to do what one directs, or, in the case of rewards, that he have no duty not to.[22] The thesis of the priority of right to directive power can, then, be more fully stated as the disjunctive thesis of the priority of right or authority to directive power. In most of the situations that we shall be discussing, however, only the second disjunct will be engaged. These situations will be marked by disagreement about substantive questions of right, and when such disagreement exists, a justification for exercising directive power that appeals to the independent

---

[22] Thus, legitimate authority cannot be defined as justified power. See Raz (1986), pp. 23–28.

rightness of what is directed has little prospect of winning general acceptance. But it is desirable that power be exercised on a basis that those subject to it can, in principle at least, be brought to accept. For the most part, then, I consider only whether a given source of directives can be regarded as a legitimate authority, and if so on what basis. I also sometimes speak simply of the thesis of the priority of authority to directive power.

The thesis of the priority of right or authority to directive power has implications for Max Weber's definition of the state as an entity that claims a monopoly on the legitimate use of coercion in a given territory.[23] In theory, the state's right to coerce could be basic, that is, a right to use coercion to get its subjects do whatever it happens to want them to do. But to my knowledge, no political theorist has regarded the state's right to coerce as having this character. What makes coercion legitimate is not that the state has a basic right to coerce, but that it has a (limited) right to direct the actions of the inhabitants of a territory. Coercion is then justified as a way of making the subjects do what, given the state's right to direct, they have sufficient reason to do. This allows us to dispense with the notion of coercion in the definition of the state. What is characteristic of a state is not that it claims a right to coerce but that it claims a supreme right to direct: It claims to be an undirected issuer of directives. If a state's right to direct were accepted by all within its territory—if all accepted its legitimacy—and this were common knowledge (so that the assurance problem was solved), it would not need to exercise coercive power at all. Indeed, if the state's right to direct can be regarded as taking the nonderived form characteristic of authority, we can go farther and define the state simply as an entity that claims to have supreme authority in a given territory.

Similar points apply to managerial authority. In the managerial sphere, the thesis of the priority of right to directive power is related to the thesis of the moral disunity of management discussed in Chapter One. The latter thesis states that an individual or group needs two moral licenses to run a productive enterprise, one justifying its control of the productive property associated with the enterprise, and the other giving it a right to direct the actions of the personnel. As we saw in Chapter One, however, the license to direct the actions of employees is prior to the license to control the property since the power to get people to comply with directives that property rights confer must be exercised in a way that accords with

23 Weber (1947), pp. 154–57.

whatever right to direct the managers may have. This is an instance of the thesis of the priority of authority to directive power.

The Varieties of Authority

Preemption is common to all forms of authority, but there are also important differences among them. One important distinction is that between the subordinating kind of authority that we have been considering so far and the authority of expertise, which I call *E-authority*. We use the term "authority" to describe not only people whom we obey because we regard their directives as good preemptive reasons for action, but also people who are experts on certain matters of fact. Thus, someone might be said to be an authority on the species of beetles or the causes of earthquakes.[24] The distinction between de facto and de jure or legitimate authority applies to E-authority as well as to subordinating authority. A de facto E-authority is someone who is generally thought, in a given community, to know more about some subject than the rest of the members of the community, and whose pronouncements (in the area of her presumed expertise) are believed for this reason. A legitimate E-authority is someone who is both thought to be an expert and who really does know more. As is generally the case with authority, a de facto E-authority need not be a legitimate E-authority.

The acceptance of someone as an E-authority usually manifests itself in belief formation; one believes that something is the case because someone whom one acknowledges as an expert in that area says that it is the case. This involves a distinction like that between directive-independent and directive-dependent judgments about what to do. One believes that P is the case because an authority has asserted that it is so even though one would not have believed it were one assessing the evidence for oneself. As we have seen, when accepting authority takes the form of doing what someone says, the distinction between directive-independent and directive-dependent judgments does not by itself give us the authority relation. There must be subordination, the control of someone's action in a way that involves the displacement, by a directive, of his judgment of what the applicable directive-independent reasons support

[24] Another expression sometimes used to characterize this form of authority is "an-authority," from the fact that someone who has it is *an* authority on a particular subject. This is contrasts with "in-authority," the sort of authority someone has when she is in authority in a particular situation. This usage appears to have originated with Peters (1958).

41

from its normal, action-inducing relation to his will. But subordination in this sense does not seem to play a role in E-authority because belief-formation is not under the control of the will.

The difference between E-authority and subordinating authority may be understood as follows. In the forms of authority that involve subordination, a directive displaces a judgment from the will-affecting position. In E-authority, the will need not be involved at all. Instead, we are operating entirely within the sphere of belief. Belief is normally a result of one's assessment of the evidence supporting various claims. One's assessment of the evidence finds expression as belief. When one acknowledges someone as an E-authority, however, her assertions determine one's beliefs. To be more precise, her assertions exclude and replace the reasons that would otherwise have determined one's beliefs on the matter concerned; they are treated as preemptive reasons for believing what she asserts.

The association of E-authority with the determination of belief is, however, potentially misleading. The reasoning involved (and replaced) in E-authority can be practical as well as theoretical reasoning. That is, if there are moral and evaluative facts—facts about what people ought to do or what ought to be the case—some people could have E-authority in practical matters. They might, for example, be experts on what morality requires in a certain class of cases, experts in identifying and assessing the implications of moral reasons of a certain kind. Acceptance of such authority might initially take the form of a belief that one ought to behave in a certain way that then determines the will in combination with a desire to do what one (believes that one) ought to do. Alternatively, if practical reason is capable of directly informing motivation, the judgment might shape the will immediately. Even in the latter case, however, we can speak of the judgment as expressing a belief about what one ought to do.

When one accepts the authority of a practical expert, then, displacement occurs in the sphere of belief. The expert's assertion replaces one's own assessment of the applicable reasons for action as the determinant of one's belief about what one ought to do (or judgment about what one ought to do). One changes one's mind about what one ought to do as a result of the assertion. This is different from the way that subordinating authority has practical consequences. There, displacement takes the form of the preemption by the authority's directive of one's final directive-independent belief about what one ought to do (however formed) from its normal, action-inducing relation to the will. Thus, one might form a belief about what one ought to do as a result of the assertion of some practical authority, yet act differently because one regards oneself as

42

having good reason to place oneself in a position of subordination to someone else.[25]

I have contrasted E-authority with subordinating authority, but there is also an important distinction to be made within the latter sphere. This may be introduced by considering two concepts James Coleman employs in his recent account of authority.[26] For Coleman, the right to direct involved in an authority relation (and indeed any right) is understood descriptively, as a claim that is in fact accepted by those who must accept it if it is to be sustained—both those who must perform and those who could intervene to block performance. Because our investigation is a normative inquiry, however—an inquiry into the way things ought to be—I give Coleman's concepts a normative construal. A right, then, is a claim that certain people ought to accept.

Coleman divides the cases in which one person has a right to direct the actions of another into two kinds. In both, people are understood to enter into, or remain in, authority relations only because they believe that doing so is in their interest. This condition may be satisfied in either of two ways. In what Coleman calls "conjoint authority," the subject believes that his acceptance of authority is directly conducive to his interests. That is, he believes that complying with the authority's directives is in itself in his interest, and thus he does not need to be induced to comply with rewards or threats. In the second form of subordinating authority, which Coleman calls "disjoint authority," the subject does not believe that complying with the authority's directives is in itself in his interests. Indeed, he may believe that it is contrary to his interests. But he complies nevertheless because he expects to receive an extrinsic reward for compliance, and regards this reward as outweighing the damage to his interests that compliance per se involves.

Let us understand the idea that the acceptance of authority is in itself in one's interests as the idea that one better complies with (what are from one's point of view) the applicable directive-independent reasons by obeying the authority's directives. How can the acceptance of authority be in one's interests in this sense? One possibility is that the authority is better at determining what the applicable reasons require, and her directives reflect this superior competence. This is the situation that obtains when E-authority is based on superior competence in practical reasoning. To be sure, we

---

[25] Practical E-authority could also play a role in leading one to accept subordinating authority if a moral expert asserted that the applicable (directive-*dependent*) reasons were sufficient to support such a course.

[26] James Coleman (1990), chap. 4.

are now supposing that the authoritative communication takes the form of a directive rather than an assertion. But the acceptance of this directive does not involve subordination; rather, it involves changing one's mind about what it would be right to do in the circumstances.

It can also, however, be in one's interest to accept the authority of someone who is not superior in deliberative ability, that is, where one does not expect to acquire from her a more accurate belief about what the applicable directive-independent reasons require. This is the case when the authority's directives facilitate cooperation within a group of which one is a member. As is well-known, it sometimes happens that when each of the members of a group acts as she believes reason requires, each does worse, by her own lights, than she would if all cooperated to achieve some single objective. Each may regard the achievement of this objective as suboptimal but still superior from her own point of view to the state of affairs that would result if each went her own way.[27] One of the main roles for subordinating authority is to direct the members of groups to act cooperatively in such situations. Let us call this cooperation-facilitating kind of authority *C-authority*. Classical contract theories of government characterize governments as playing this cooperation-facilitating role. Such theories can, then, be regarded as presenting political authority as C-authority.

We should be clear about one important difference between E-authority and C-authority. When an individual is accepted as an E-authority on some matter by the members of a group, her pronouncements eliminate disagreements within the group about these matters. A C-authority, by contrast, facilitates cooperation among individuals with contrary aims without eliminating disagreement, at least in the sense of securing the adoption by all of the same substantive goals. Rather, it makes it possible for each member of the group to promote his or her goals more effectively.

As I have characterized conjoint authority, the idea that one better promotes one's interests by accepting authority is understood as the idea that one better satisfies the applicable directive-independent reasons. So characterized, there is a close connection between conjoint authority and Joseph Raz's normal justification thesis. In a form appropriate for practical cases, this states that

> the normal way to establish that a person has authority over another person involves showing that the alleged subject is

---

[27] Among the more prominent situations of this sort are multiperson prisoner's-dilemmas.

likely better to comply with the reasons that apply to him (other than the alleged authoritative directives) if he accepts the directives of the alleged authority as authoritatively binding and tries to follow them, rather than by trying to follow the reasons that apply to him directly.[28]

In our terms, "reasons that apply to one, other than the alleged authoritative directives" are directive-independent reasons. The idea is that one can better satisfy the applicable directive-independent reasons by complying with someone's directive. In the case of C-authority, the directive-dependent reason that justifies compliance is thus in some way derived from the applicable directive-independent reasons, but the subject is incapable of acting on it without authoritative guidance.

Raz's normal justification thesis enables us to distinguish authority from domination. A relation of subordination may involve domination if it serves only the interests of the person in the superior position. This is so even if the relation is a de facto authority relation believed by the subordinate—and indeed by the superior—to be in the subordinate's interests. If it actually serves only the interests of the superior, it may involve domination. If it serves the interests of the person in the subordinate position, however—in the sense of enabling him to better comply with the reasons that apply to him—it is not a relation of domination.

Let us turn now to disjoint authority. Coleman defines this as authority that is accepted because a reward is offered, but this definition will not do for our purposes. The acceptance of nonexpert authority involves subordination, and as we have seen, in the standard case, doing something because a reward is offered does not involve subordination. There is no displacement of the subject's judgment of what the applicable directive-independent reasons require. The reward simply tips the balance of applicable reasons in favor of compliance. Coleman may feel that we may still speak of authority when rewards are offered because one's ability to direct the actions of others is underwritten by a right, namely the property right that one exercises in offering the reward. But as we saw in Chapter One, the power to direct that derives from exercising property rights must be distinguished from the right to direct characteristic of authority.

How, then, can there be a form of legitimate authority in which compliance with authoritative directives is not in itself in the interests of the subject? To establish the possibility of such authority, we

[28] Raz (1986), p. 53.

45

need a consideration that is capable of justifying the preemption of the applicable directive-independent reasons by a directive without displaying compliance with this directive as better satisfying the preempted reasons. Raz and others have argued that preemption is a feature not just of authority but of obligation in general. I consider this claim in more detail in Chapter Four. For the time being, however, let us suppose that it is true. Then we can say that what we need to make sense of disjoint authority is a source of obligations that can obligate one to comply with a directive—that is, to do whatever someone says (within a certain range)—without displaying doing so as better complying with the applicable directive-independent reasons. A source of obligations that has this character is promising. One can promise to comply with someone's directives. If promises create obligations and obligations are preemptive reasons for action, the result will be a preemptive reason to comply with a directive, which will establish the directive itself as a preemptive reason for action. I call the form of subordinating authority established by a promise to obey someone *P-authority*. I suggest, then, that Coleman's disjoint authority can be understood as P-authority.

It will be useful to make this point in terms of the concept of consent. Viewed as a general source of reasons for action, consent is a mechanism for changing the normative situation of another. Promising is one of the most important species of consent. When one promises, one changes the normative situation of another by creating an obligation to her to perform a certain action. Not all consent involves undertaking an obligation, but consent to obey someone's directives does, in particular a promissory obligation.[29] We must take care, however, when we say that P-authority is authority justified by a species of consent. The claim that an authority relation is justified by the consent of those over whom it is exercised can be understood in two different ways. Both involve a claim to the effect that consent is tied to legitimacy, but only one involves P-authority.

Any form of de facto authority can be regarded as grounded in the consent of the subjects in the sense that they accept that they have some sufficient reason to comply with authoritative directives. But here consent is not being understood normatively, as a mechanism for altering moral relations, but rather descriptively, as voluntary acquiescence for what seems to the agent to be a good reason. This reason need not have anything to do with promising. It might, for example, be that compliance is traditional in the society in question,

---

[29] For this and the preceding points in this paragraph, see Raz (1986), pp. 80–88.

or that those exercising authority have been elected by what is deemed a fair procedure. The claim that government must be by the consent of the governed in this sense may be formulated as a necessary condition for legitimacy or as a necessary and sufficient condition. In the latter case, it is the claim that all and only de facto authorities are legitimate authorities.

The claim that legitimate authority must be by the consent of the governed can also, however, be understood in the narrower sense that views consent as a particular source of reasons for action of which promising is the most important species (for the purposes of justifying authority). Here, the claim is that the only good reason for complying with a government's directives—the only condition under which it can be legitimate—is that one has promised it, or the other members of the group whose actions it directs, to comply.

In this section I have introduced two overlapping distinctions that encompass three species of authority. There is one species of authority that governs belief-formation (E-authority) and two that involve subordination (C-authority and P-authority). And, there are two species of authority in which, ideally, the subject better complies with the applicable directive-independent reasons for action, or assertion-independent reasons for believing, by entering into the authority relation (C-authority and E-authority), and one in which this is not so (P-authority).

Agency and Authorization

Our discussion of authority has understood having authority, at least when it is subordinating, as having a right to direct the actions of someone else. But there is another use of the word "authority" that we should consider. This is the use in which someone who is authorized to perform a certain action is said to have the authority to perform it.

One important place where this form of authority is found is agency relations. A relation of agency exists when one person, the agent, consents to act under the direction of, and on behalf of, another person, the principal, and the principal consents to have the actions of the agent count as hers for moral or legal purposes.[30] The duties of an agent include performance (to do for the principal what he has undertaken to do, if legally and physically possible), obe-

[30] For an account of the law of agency, see Frascona (1964). The principal's consent, while normative, is of a form that does not involve the undertaking of an obligation, at least to the agent. Rather, it authorizes the actions of the agent, in the sense that I explore below.

47

dience (to accept the reasonable directions of the principal within the scope of the agency relation), and loyalty (not to act contrary to the interests of the principal, for example, by selling certain goods as she directs, but at an unusually low price to a dummy corporation he has set up).[31]

The law makes a number of distinctions involving agency. First, an agent is distinguished from a trustee. A trustee has a fiduciary duty to act in the interests of the beneficiary of the trust, but no duty to act as the beneficiary directs.[32] Second, an agent is distinguished from an independent contractor. An independent contractor is a person who contracts to produce a definite result but is not subject to the other party's control and is not regarded as acting on behalf of (that is, in place of) the other party.[33] And third, a nonservant agent is distinguished from a servant.[34] A nonservant agent undertakes to act on behalf of the principal in achieving a particular objective directed by the principal. A servant, by contrast, is an agent who contracts to allow the principal to control his physical conduct, that is, contracts to do what he is told without necessarily knowing what purposes it will serve. This sort of agency is particularly important in the managerial case. Employees often have the legal status of servants.

Relations of agency can be quite complex. This can be brought out by applying to the authority of a principal some distinctions that Coleman makes in his discussion of authority.[35] First, he distinguishes between the person in whom authority is vested—to whom the right to direct associated with authority is in the first instance granted—and the person who exercises authority, the one who exercises this right. This distinction makes possible a further distinction between simple and complex authority relations. In a simple authority relation, authority is exercised by the person in whom it is vested; in a complex relation it is delegated by the person in whom it is vested to a lieutenant, who exercises it on the right-holder's behalf. This distinction presupposes that authorities have not only a right to direct the actions of others but also a right to transfer this right. These rights are separable; one could hold the first without holding the second.

Coleman also distinguishes between authority relations and authority structures, which are social objects constructed out of author-

31 See Frascona (1964), pp. 90–99.
32 Frascona (1964), pp. 6–7.
33 Frascona (1964), p. 5.
34 Frascona (1964), p. 13.
35 James Coleman (1990), pp. 162–72.

ity relations. Complex authority relations play a large part in the authority structures with which we are familiar; they are structures that involve the delegation of authority. This delegation could be directly to an individual who then exercises the rights of the principal or other authority as his own personal rights. But as Coleman notes, modern authority structures typically take the form of bureaucracies, or systems of offices. In such structures, the delegation of authority is in the first instance to offices and only derivatively to the persons occupying those offices. Even in these cases, however, the basis of the authority relation can be an agent's consent to obey a principal. Weber says that the authority of an employer over an employee in a bureaucracy originates in a contract.[36]

Since the agent has a duty of obedience, the principal in an agency relation has authority in the sense that we have been discussing up to now: she has a right to direct someone's actions. Legally, an agency relation is created by the consent of both parties, and the moral analogue of the agent's consent is a promise. Thus from the moral point of view, the principal in an agency relation has what I have called P-authority. To be sure, P-authority can encompass more than the authority of a principal. One could promise to obey another without any reciprocal consent on her part to have one's actions count as hers for moral purposes. That is, one could promise to do what she said while assuming oneself any moral or legal debts incurred as a result. One could also promise to do what someone said without promising not to undermine her aims by acting contrary to them in ways the possibility of which she failed to foresee. Still, the authority of a principal in an agency relation is one clear case of P-authority.

It is important to note, however, that an agency relation involves authority in a second sense as well. The agent is said to have authority to act for the principal, in the sense of being *authorized* by the principal to act on her behalf. This sense of authority does not in itself involve a right to direct. In general, to authorize someone to do something is to enable him to exercise one's right to do it. There are two ways a right might be transferred to another. One involves the

---

[36] Weber (1947), pp. 325–26. For Weber, an important feature of bureaucracies is that authority is finally located in an impersonal order of rules, and only derivatively in the occupants of the offices that these rules create. He may regard the pure case as that in which even the person ultimately responsible for all directives occupies an office to which authority is delegated, which means that there is a sense in which the principal in the agency relations associated with bureaucracy must be understood as the organization itself. Legally, employees can contract with organizations, but as we shall see, there is room for doubt whether an organization can hold a promissory right.

alienation of the right, so that it passes from the first party to the second. An example would be selling a car, which involves the transfer in this sense of a property right. But one can also arrange to have someone exercise a right that one has while retaining possession of the right. This is granting him authority to act.[37] Granting someone authority in this sense is a feature of agency, but is not limited to this case. Typically, one will authorize actions in the expectation that they will benefit oneself, but the person to whom one grants this authority need not have a obligation to act in one's interests or to accept one's directions. Thus, in granting oil companies leases to drill in an area it controls, a government authorizes them to do so, but the companies do not function as agents of the government.

Richard De George emphasizes the importance of this form of authority in the economic sphere.[38] But we must distinguish the authority that corporations have to use the resources of a country from managerial authority understood as the authority of managers over employees.[39] If we regard property rights as entirely legal creations—that is, we deny the possibility of natural property rights that people can acquire independently of any legal provisions and that place moral constraints on the laws governing property that a government may enact—then there is a sense, even in a capitalist system based on private ownership of productive resources, in which all property is ultimately owned by the state. The state can modify property relations at will by changing the laws governing them. This means that all social entities that work with productive resources can be regarded as having been authorized to do so by the ultimate political authority.

In granting corporations the authority to use productive resources in certain ways, however, the ultimate political authority does not grant them managerial authority in our sense. As has been noted several times, the conditions of human life are such that property in productive resources gives those who hold it directive power. But the thesis of the priority of right or authority to directive power implies that the exercise of this power must be in accordance with a derived or authoritative right to direct the actions of those over whom power is exercised, which in turn limits what corporations

---

[37] See Hobbes: "So that by Authority is alwayes understood a Right of doing any act: and done by *Authority*, done by Commission, or Licence from him whose right it is" (1968, chap. 16.)

[38] De George (1985), pp. 165–85.

[39] De George regards the authority of managers over employees as grounded in promissory obligations.

may do with the property that they have been authorized to use. By extension, this limits the powers that a government can grant them in authorizing the use of productive resources. To authorize organizations to use the resources of the society in which they operate is not, then, to confer on them legitimate managerial authority, in the sense of a right to direct the actions of their employees.

CHAPTER THREE

MORAL PRINCIPLES AND SOCIAL FACTS

In Chapter Two, authority was conceived, for the most part, as a relation between two natural persons. The sorts of authority that are the principal concern of this book, the authority of governments and of the managers of nongovernmental organizations, do not seem to conform to this paradigm. The entity in which authority is vested—that in the first instance holds the right to direct—appears to be an organization. This raises two main questions: Can an organization hold a right to direct the actions of an individual?[1] And, does the fact that organizations are part of the context of action alter the directive-independent considerations that bear on what individuals should do?

The Ontological Status of Organizations

The Structure of the Problem

Issuing directives is an action of a certain sort. Thus, the first question we must address in considering whether an organization can have a right to direct the behavior of individuals is whether organizations can perform actions.

One of the problems in the philosophy of the social sciences is whether realism about social entities—the view that social entities are something over and above the individual human beings that comprise them—is tenable. A variety of positions have been taken. Ontological individualism holds that social objects distinct from the individuals that comprise them do not exist. This view is often joined with claims to the effect that statements about social entities, events, and states of affairs can be reduced to statements about relations among individuals that do not employ social terms, or that all social phenomena can be explained adequately by explaining the

---

[1] Organizations as well as individuals can be subordinates in an authority relation, but I only discuss the case where individuals are subordinates.

52

behavior of the individuals involved in them.[2] Among writers who reject individualism and admit the existence of real, in the sense of irreducible, social phenomena, a further distinction can be made between those who are prepared to speak of some of these phenomena as goal-directed systems and those who are not. And among those who are willing to ascribe goals to some social entities, there is room for further disagreement about how similar to natural persons they are. They may be regarded as having goals only in the way that plants or lower animals do, or they may be regarded as possessing in their own right the higher psychological attributes that would justify regarding them as rational agents or persons.[3]

All parties in this debate agree that we routinely ascribe actions to groups, especially if they are organized in the sense of possessing some internal decision-making procedure. But we also routinely speak of the sun as rising and setting, so these linguistic facts cannot be taken as decisive. We need to consider whether some of these positions are more philosophically respectable than others.

Questions of realism regarding putative entities of a certain sort can be posed as questions about the referential status of (uses of) terms. Certain terms in our language are, by virtue of their grammatical form, capable of being used to talk about things, typically by being used as the grammatical subjects or objects of declarative sentences. Not everything that we can talk about really exists, however. We can talk about ghosts, for example, but most people think that ghosts do not exist. The question of realism is the question of whether a term—or better, a set of terms comprising a theory—that is used to talk about things should be understood as genuinely referring, in that use, to extralinguistic items.

Contemporary philosophical discussion approaches this question as follows. With respect to any term capable of being used to talk

---

[2] Methodological individualism, on one interpretation, claims that the best explanations for social phenomena are explanations that refer only to nonsocial properties of individuals, such as what they want and what they believe about their environment. It is sometimes objected to methodological individualism that we cannot explain social phenomena without ascribing to individuals beliefs and desires that have an irreducibly social content, a content that can only be expressed with social concepts—for example, a desire that a certain party win the election. Even if this is so, however, it does not follow that our explanations commit us to the existence of anything beyond individuals and their properties. It may be that we can only explain certain kinds of religious behavior by ascribing irreducible beliefs and desires about gods, but we do not thereby commit ourselves to the existence of these gods. For an account of methodological individualism see Lukes (1973), chap. 17.

[3] Recent discussions of the ontological and moral status of organizations include Quinton (1976), Copp (1979, 1984), Donaldson (1982), French (1984), Werhane (1985), Dan-Cohen (1986), May (1987), and Keeley (1988).

about things, we can ask what purposes of ours are served—or could be served—by using it in this way. One possibility is that explanatory purposes are served. We can provide better explanations for certain phenomena if our explanations use the terms in question. But explanatory purposes are served by talking about things of a certain kind only if the things of this kind really exist. So we may infer from the fact that the best explanation of some phenomenon talks about certain things that these things really exist. To put it more precisely, we are justified in regarding a particular use of a term as referring to a kind of thing that really exists if the assumption that there are items of this kind figures in the best explanation of some phenomenon that we observe.[4] The test of whether things of a kind that we can talk about really exist, then, is whether talking about them increases the explanatory coherence of our experience.

Such theoretical purposes, however, are not the only purposes that might be served by using terms to talk about things. Sometimes talking about things of a certain sort serves practical purposes, in the sense that assuming that there are things of the sort talked about (or making believe that there are such things) and acting accordingly enables us to achieve our practical ends more efficiently or effectively. When talk about things of a certain kind is best regarded as serving practical, as opposed to explanatory purposes, the items ostensibly referred are appropriately regarded not as really existing but as fictions.[5] Thus, the debate between scientific realists and instrumentalists in the philosophy of science concerns whether talk about things like subatomic particles is best regarded as serving explanatory or practical purposes. And in the social sphere, to say that the personhood of corporations is a legal fiction is to say that the purposes served by speaking of corporate persons are practical rather than explanatory, namely, the purposes of commercial law in facilitating economic activity.[6] To take talk about things that is best

---

[4] See Harman (1965). Inference to the best explanation is a form of nondeductive inference. The basic idea is that if the truth of some proposition P is part of the best explanation, given certain background conditions, of other things that we take to be the case, we have some reason to regard P as true. Here I am following Brink (1989), p. 169.

[5] Things that there is no good reason to talk about, such as ghosts, are also fictions. The point in the text is simply that we cannot regard everything that we have good reason to talk about as really existing. It matters whether the reasons are theoretical or practical.

[6] Legal personhood may just be a matter of the ascription of rights, rather than personal attributes such as memory and intention, to entities of a certain sort. See French (1984), chap. 3. As several writers have pointed out, a locus of activity carried out solely by machines guided by a computer could have the status of a legal person. See Werhane (1985), chap. 1, and Dan-Cohen (1986), chap. 3. The question of whether

regarded as serving only practical purposes as genuinely referential is to make the mistake of reification.

We can apply these points to the question of the ontological status of organizations. That organizations exist is not controversial. What is controversial is whether organizations understood as entities distinct from the individuals that they contain exist. The kind of thing picked out by a social term such as "organization" might be nothing but a kind of relation between individuals that can be specified without countenancing social entities at all—for example, a relation specifiable in terms of what the parties want, what they believe about their environment (including the likely behavior of other individuals), and the actions that result. Realism can take the form of reductionism. In order to decide between the competing hypotheses canvassed above, then, we must determine whether regarding talk of organizations as referring to something over and above individuals in certain relations specifiable in nonsocial terms better serves explanatory purposes than regarding this talk as referring only to individuals in relations.

Arguments of two sorts may enable us to dispense with the task of determining which explanations are best. The first claims that admitting talk about social entities, events, or states of affairs that is not reducible to talk about individuals couched in nonsocial terms is metaphysically extravagant because it commits us to the existence of social organisms or group minds, and such entities are bizarre. One reply to this objection is that we can admit irreducible social phenomena without regarding them as having biological or psychological properties in their own right. One might regard the social kind "riot" as irreducible to nonsocial kinds, for example, without regarding a riot as a kind of organism. But it is not necessary to make this reply because social organisms and group minds could be as metaphysically respectable as biological organisms and individual minds. Metaphysical respectability can be achieved by employing the strategy favored by realists in many fields today, namely, that of regarding the relatively more problematic kinds of phenomena as supervening on relatively less problematic kinds.[7]

The basic idea behind realist approaches that emphasize supervenience is to view the "higher-order" theories and conceptual schemes that seem to bring with them unacceptable metaphysical

the practical purposes of the legal system would be best served by ascribing the fictional status of person to such a locus of activity is different from the theoretical question of whether the behavior of some computers might be best explained by regarding them as persons.

[7] For an account of the relation of supervenience see Kim (1978).

commitments as really just different ways of carving up the same stuff described by lower-order theories. To take a biological example, to speak of something as an organism, or as alive, is not to regard it as matter combined with a "soul" that animates this matter. It is merely to ascribe a certain kind of property to a material thing, albeit a property that cannot be equated with any property, no matter how complex, that can be ascribed to it by a lower-order theory such as chemistry.[8] To be sure, everything that is alive is alive only because it is in some chemical state. But biological talk has uses that chemical talk does not—the language game of biology is different from that of chemistry—and thus there is no reason to suppose that the way biological kinds carve up the world can be exactly matched by chemical kinds. Life is realized by different chemical processes in different actual organisms and could be realized by an even greater variety of processes in possible organisms.[9] That is, the set of chemical processes that could count as realizing life is open-ended. All we can say in general about the relation of biology to chemistry is that anything that is alive has a set of chemical properties such that anything else that has those properties will be alive too. This is what is meant by saying that biological facts supervene on chemical facts.

This approach has also been employed in the philosophy of mind, where it is claimed that mental properties supervene on neurophysiological properties, and it seems to be equally applicable to social theory. Here, antirealists (about distinct social phenomena) claim that the kinds of social phenomena that we talk about can be equated with kinds of relations between individuals that are fully specifiable using psychological terms. But realists who accept the existence of distinct social objects can avoid metaphysical embarrassment by regarding social facts as supervening on facts about individuals. They can affirm that while a social kind gives us a rule for carving up the world that is not equivalent to any rule provided by a kind of relation between individuals, no matter how complex, specified in nonsocial terms, any group instantiating a social kind will have a set of nonsocial properties such that any other group of individuals possessing those properties will instantiate that social kind as well. For every riot, there is a description of the behavior of

[8] I mean the notion of kinds being equated with one another to encompass both analytic reductions claiming that statements using kind-terms of one sort have the same meaning as statements using kind-terms of the other sort, and contingent type-identities such as "water = H_2O."

[9] Thus, those interested in extraterrestrial life sometimes maintain that life could be based on silicon-based compounds rather than carbon-based compounds as it is on earth.

the individuals involved that does not employ social terms and which is such that any other set of individuals satisfying that description would be rioting too.[10]

Moreover, there seems to be no barrier to taking this same line with more ambitious forms of social predication that ascribe biological or psychological attributes to groups. We need experience no metaphysical discomfort in describing organizations as goal-directed organisms of a certain sort, or as rational agents (thus implying that they have a variety of psychological attributes in their own right), since such facts can be regarded as supervening on nonsocial facts about individuals. Organizational organisms need be no more metaphysically problematic than biological organisms, and group minds need be no more metaphysically problematic than an individual mind.

The second argument that we can decide between the various ontological theses regarding organizations without assessing their explanatory potential stems from the claim that comprehending the behavior of social entities is not a matter of causally *explaining* it but rather of *understanding* it, for instance, as rational or irrational. But the contention that social phenomena are to be understood rather than explained does not by itself reduce the set of competing hypotheses: It does not entail that social entities are organisms of a certain sort, for example. Although understanding behavior as rational or irrational usually involves relating it to certain goals, the best way of understanding a particular social phenomenon may not be to relate it to the goals of some distinct social organism, but rather to see it as arising from the rational or irrational attempts of the associated individuals to promote their goals in the situation that they face. Even if social phenomena are to be understood rather than explained, then, we must still consider which of the competing ontological hypotheses yields the best way of understanding them.

The Alternatives

We cannot, then, avoid considering the relative explanatory merits of the competing hypotheses regarding the ontological status of

[10] It might be useful to distinguish weakly social terms from strongly social terms. Weakly social terms describe relations between individuals, but relations that cannot be reduced to relations specifiable in nonsocial—for example, psychological—terminology. An example would be a relation between individuals arising from the fact that they occupy certain offices in an institution. Strongly social terms describe social phenomena without mentioning individuals. "Riot" is a strongly social term. Although neither sort of term can be reduced to nonsocial terms, descriptions employing only weakly social terms will have a more individualistic feel.

social entities. Let us first see whether there are any reasons of a general sort for regarding some of them as preferable from the explanatory point of view.

Our main interest is organizations, understood as groups with internal decision-making procedures. Here the alternatives may be conveniently reduced to two. Organismic views treat organizations as goal-directed systems with a distinct ontological status like that of an organism. Views that regard organizations as real (rather than fictional) agents or persons form a subcategory of organismic views.[11] Associationist views, by contrast, treat organizations as nothing more than groups of individuals who have found certain relations between themselves to be mutually beneficial. Such views can maintain that some facts about organizations are not reducible to facts about the associated individuals, provided that they refrain from ascribing goals to organizations.

Some social theorists have found it useful to treat organizations as distinct goal-directed systems.[12] Since these organizational organisms cannot communicate with us directly, their goals must be inferred from other phenomena. In principle, this can be done in the same way the goals of animals are inferred. We consider what they seem to be trying to get, taking for granted that they have the same beliefs about their circumstances that we do. Once such judgments are in hand, we can proceed to try to formulate sociological laws governing the behavior of these entities.

We need not suppose that the goals ascribed to an organization in this way correspond to goals held by the individuals who comprise the organization. From the standpoint of the organization, its individual members are just so much functionally arranged material, analogous to the functionally arranged cells of a living body, and they need not be aware of their functional role at all, much less endorse it. Of course, the organization's actions supervene on the actions—or more broadly, behavior—of its members. But this argument claims that the behavior of organizations is best explained by regarding them as goal-directed systems in their own right, rather than by providing psychological explanations of the behavior of their members.

In the view of other writers, however, the organismic approach

[11] I assume that anything that is properly regarded as an agent or a person—in the sense that so regarding it best serves explanatory purposes—is also properly regarded as an organism (that is, as alive). Being alive encompasses such things as having a good and being in some respects self-directed, but need not involve the ability to reproduce. Thus, artifacts and even machines such as computers could be organisms in this sense. This is important for the organizational case, since organizations are plausibly regarded as artifacts. For discussion, see French (1984), chap. 7.

[12] For some references, see Keeley (1988), chap. 2.

does not explain organizational phenomena as well as approaches that view organizations as sets of persons who have come together for what they take to be mutual benefit. A recent statement of a view of this sort has been provided by Michael Keeley.[13] Keeley is a realist about social facts in the sense that he does not believe that all social kinds are reducible to kinds of relations between individuals specifiable in nonsocial terms. But he rejects organismic models of group behavior that regard groups as distinct organisms with goals of their own because he believes that associationist views have more explanatory power. This is not to deny that the members of organizations can be regarded as playing functionally specified roles, but the goals by reference to which these functions are specified are not those of some superindividual organism. Rather, they are the particular, possibly overlapping, goals of the members of the organization and other individuals. As Keeley puts it, we should not speak of the goals *of* an organization, but rather of the goals *for* an organization of various individual human beings.

Associationist views can accommodate the distinction between what an organization does and what its individual members do as the distinction between what the members of a group do collectively and what they do individually. Associationist views can regard organizational actions as events collectively produced by the members of the organization. The simplest case in which the members of an organization create an organizational action by acting collectively is the case in which their goals for the organization coincide. If they all agree on the desirability of the existence of some event or state of affairs, they can coordinate their actions to produce it. The analogy here would be the construction of a house or, perhaps better, the performance of a ballet or a symphony. The playing of the symphony is an action of the group. But it is not an action of the group understood as an superindividual organism with a goal of its own; it is an action of the group that is created by the coordinated pursuit of a goal shared by the individual members of the group.

As Keeley points out, however, to ascribe actions to groups on the associationist view we do not need to suppose that the goals for the organization of the individual members coincide. A given collective product might serve equally well the different goals for the organization of each of its members; it might be agreed to for that reason. An organizational action is also possible if a given collective product serves the different goals for the organization of the individual members unequally, but well enough for all to participate.

These points apply to the question of how the issuing of a direc-

---

[13] See Keeley (1988).

tive can be attributed to an organization on associationist views. On such views, an organization's issuing a directive can be regarded as an event that is produced by the collective action of the organization's members. This is so whether the directive is issued by a single member or generated by a vote among some or all of them. In both cases, the actions count as directives of the organization by virtue of the organization's constitution; and the maintenance of the constitution, viewed as a set of constitutive conventions, is something to which all (or at least most) members contribute.[14]

It might be argued that associationist views cannot accommodate the commonsense distinction between those who are members of an organization and those who are not. Such views are willing to speak only of mutually beneficial relations among individuals. But while the individuals whom common sense would regard as members of the organization participate in such relations with each other, some of them also enter, in their capacity as members of the organization, into mutually beneficial relations with people who are not, intuitively, members of the organization. For example, they purchase items for the organization or sell its products. If all that is relevant is mutually beneficial relations, then, it would appear that customers and suppliers must be regarded as belonging to the organization as well. Indeed, some associationist writers adopt this line.[15]

The associationist view easily captures the intuitive distinction between members and nonmembers. The members of an organization are those who are parties to the authority relations associated with it. Individuals who are not parties to these authority relations are not members of the organization, even if they perform functions without which it could not exist. Those holding authority could be either single individuals or groups of individuals that generate directives collectively, and a group possessing authority could be either distinct from or identical with the group of subordinates it directs. An example involving distinct groups would be an agency relation where the principal is a group that exercises its authority collectively over a separate group of agents. An example involving a single group would be the picture usually associated with contractarian theories of government, in which a group acts collectively to

---

[14] Copp (1979) argues that in certain circumstances the actions of an individual or group of individuals can be regarded as constituting an action of a collective. Copp's larger view is that collectives are spatially discontinuous concrete wholes that have person-stages as parts. See also Copp (1984).

[15] "Let us view the organization as a coalition. . . . In a business organization, the coalition members include managers, workers, stockholders, suppliers, customers, lawyers, tax collectors, regulatory agencies, etc." (Cyert and March [1963], p. 27).

create an authority whose directives are binding on each of its members.

This approach to the question of who is a member of an organization sheds light on whether shareholders are members of corporations. If the shareholders are appropriately regarded as forming a collective principal that has created a hierarchical structure of agents to carry out its purposes, they will be parties to the authority relations associated with the corporation and thus members of it. By contrast, if they are appropriately regarded as a group of investors—understood simply as suppliers of something the organization needs, namely capital—they are not parties to the corporation's authority relations and thus not members of it.[16]

If the foregoing discussion is sound, there do not in fact appear to be any general grounds for regarding either organismic or associationist views as incapable of providing satisfactory explanations of organizational phenomena. The decision between them must, then, be made by actually constructing explanatory theories and considering which are most satisfactory. This is done by the social sciences. They seek to explain social phenomena, and we should accept whatever ontological commitments are made by the theories that they ultimately find most satisfactory. Approaches that are broadly individualistic have achieved a good deal of explanatory success in many fields, especially economics, but as far as I am aware, there is no consensus among researchers on the best approach. I propose, then, to leave the question of the ontological status of organizations open.

The Moral Status of Organizations

Both organismic and associationist views allow us to speak of organizations as performing actions in general, and the action of issuing a directive in particular. Being a legitimate authority is not, however, merely a matter of being able to perform the action of issuing a directive; it is also having a right to do this. Thus, we must consider whether organizations are the sorts of things that can have rights, and more generally what their moral status is. I argue that even if there are no metaphysical reasons for denying that organizations are persons—that they have in their own right the properties that we normally take to be definitive of personhood—there are moral

[16] As we saw in Chapter One, the law of corporations gives shareholders the right to elect boards of directors, but it does not regard the directors as their agents. Further, it is difficult for shareholders to exercise this right of elective appointment effectively. Regarding them as mere investors may, then, be appropriate.

reasons for denying them the moral status that personhood usually brings with it.

To be more precise, I argue for what I call "moral individualism." Moral individualism is a view about which beings deserve moral consideration. It is often said that all moral theories are based on some view of what constitutes equal consideration of moral persons. To use Ronald Dworkin's terminology, each theory is based on some view of what it is to treat moral persons as equals. [17] Different moral theories do this in different ways. But however equal consideration is understood, the doctrine of moral individualism holds that organizations and other social entities—viewed as distinct from their members—are not appropriately accorded moral consideration in their own right. That is, they are not appropriately accorded any consideration over and above that accorded to the human beings who are their members. To put the point another way, a living organism can be said to have a good, in the sense that things can be said to go well or badly for it. But according to moral individualism, even if there are no metaphysical objections to talking about the good of an organization or other social entity, it can have no bearing on what morality requires. [18]

The import of the thesis of moral individualism can be made clearer by noting the kinds of moral principles it rejects. If organizations are understood not as mere groups of individuals, but as entities in their own right, there could in theory be the following four types of moral principles.

1. Principles governing how individuals should treat individuals.

2. Principles governing how organizations should treat individuals.

3. Principles governing how individuals should treat organizations.

---

[17] See R. Dworkin (1977), pp. 179–83. Dworkin is specifically concerned with the political case, where what is at issue is being treated as an equal by the government, but (with the possible exception of contexts shaped by central personal concerns) morality in general can be said to require equal consideration.

[18] For a similar view, see Hamlin and Pettit (1989b). Moral individualism constitutes a rejection of the view of Peter French. He regards corporations as "full-fledged members of the moral community, of equal standing with the traditionally acknowledged residents, human beings." And he says, "Corporations as moral persons will have whatever privileges, rights and duties as are, in the normal course of events, accorded to all members of the moral community" (1984, p. 32). Gilbert (1989) came to my attention too late to be taken into account, but I believe that the arguments I shall give for denying moral citizenship to social entities apply to her plural subjects as well.

4. Principles governing how organizations should treat organizations.

The thesis of moral individualism is that the moral theory that makes the best overall sense of the various particular judgments it is plausible to make about the goods and actions of organizations and of individuals in organizational contexts—the theory that is in reflective equilibrium with these judgments—will not contain any principles of the latter three kinds.

Let us begin by considering the claim that a plausible moral theory will not contain principles of Types 3 and 4. To give organizations moral consideration over and above the consideration accorded to their members is to entertain the possibility that the good of an organization could, morally, conflict with the good of its members. We must be clear about what this means. Utilitarianism is the view that maximizing the total aggregate welfare of all the humans—or perhaps, all the sentient creatures—in the world is the ultimate moral good. One can also imagine various group-relative versions of this principle according to which maximizing the total aggregate welfare of the individuals in some group is the ultimate moral standard for these individuals.[19] As is well known, principles of this sort can call for sacrificing the interests of some individuals when this will maximize total aggregate satisfaction, and it is natural to describe this as sacrificing their interests for the good of the group. It would be a mistake, however, to understand this as sacrificing the interests of individuals for the good of some superindividual organism whose good consists in the maximization of total aggregate satisfaction within it. Utilitarianism is best understood as articulating a particular interpretation of what it means to give equal consideration to all of the individuals within a group, namely, to count each as one and none as more than one in an additive calculation. Thus the sacrifices that utilitarianism can require of individuals are just sacrifices required by a particular Type 1 principle.[20]

Promoting the good of an organization, understood as a distinct entity, could involve acting contrary to what is required to give equal consideration to all of its members on any interpretation of this notion. As we have seen, the good of an organization is most plausibly viewed as some function of the attainment of the goals that can

[19] Lyons (1973), pp. 24–27 notes that there is evidence that Bentham intended his utilitarian standard as a parochial principal, applying only within the community of the agent.

[20] For a related distinction between two interpretations of utilitarianism see Kymlicka (1990), chap. 2.

be ascribed to it. But promoting the good of an organization, so understood, could involve failing to maximize total aggregate satisfaction within the set of members of the organization. Or, if equal consideration of individuals is best interpreted as a matter of justice or fairness, promoting the good of an organization could involve allowing some individual members to gain unfairly at the expense of other members.

There are several reasons for rejecting the idea that the goods of organizations, understood as distinct organisms, deserve moral consideration. One problem is that it is unclear how the good of a organization is to be interpreted. To be sure, as was just noted, if groups can be regarded as having goals of their own, the good of an organization will be some function of the attainment of these goals. But the particular function depends on the sort of life an organization, understood as a distinct organism, has; and organizations, so understood, have lives that are very different from those of natural persons.

In the first place, organizations have no normal life span. There is no reason in principle why an organization could not exist forever. But then there might be no urgency about meeting its claims. Further, if organizations are distinct organisms, they must have the basic interest in survival that all organisms have. But it is unclear what counts as promoting or frustrating this interest in the case of a organization. It may be possible to bring defunct organizations back into existence, in which case causing an organization to go out of existence might not constitute maleficent treatment of it. Organizations also readily undergo those processes so beloved of philosophers investigating personal identity: fission and fusion. An organization can divide into two or more organizations, or two or more can merge into one.[21] Are we to regard such processes as contrary to the survival interest of the organizations that cease to exist as a result, or not?

This, then, is the first objection to the idea that morality requires us to consider the goods of organizations, understood as distinct organisms. We have no clear sense of what the good of a organization, understood as something distinct from its members, is. The second objection is that principles dictating how organizations, understood as distinct entities, are to be treated seem pointless unless they can sometimes outweigh the principles that state what equal consideration of individuals requires. It is hard, however, to find a

---

[21] Werhane (1985), p. 35 notes that a similar point has been made by Richard Konrad.

case in which such outweighing is intuitively plausible. Suppose that an organization is threatened with nonexistence because all of its members have discovered more worthwhile ways to spend their time, and no other people are interested in replacing them or would be interested in replacing them in the future. For example, suppose that the only members of a corporation are its employees and they all receive more attractive job offers. It seems absurd that there could be any moral objection to the departure of the members on the ground that the organization will cease to exist if they leave.

We can consider another dimension of the problem. If an organization deserves moral consideration in its own right, its good must be taken into account not only by its members, but also by nonmembers. Further, it may sometimes be appropriate to sacrifice the interests of a nonmember for the good of the organization, that is, so that it can achieve its goals, even when no such sacrifice would be required by equal consideration of all the individuals involved (the nonmember and the members). Here, too, we seem to have absurdity. The good of an organization, understood as a distinct entity, seems to have no moral significance for nonmembers. This, however, strongly suggests that when the good of an organization is invoked by its members, they are really alluding to the fact that the organization benefits all of them, and that each has a reason for maintaining this mutually beneficial state of affairs.[22]

It might be argued that we should nevertheless accord equal moral consideration to organizations because they have the same properties—self-consciousness, memory, rationality—that confer the status of moral personhood on individuals. Even if this claim were conceded, however, it would have virtually no practical significance. It is most plausible to regard organizations as entities distinct from their members when they are large. Yet the larger an organization is, the smaller the relative weight of its moral "vote" will be, as compared with that of its members taken together. Consider an organization with ten thousand members. Here, giving equal moral consideration to the organization, understood as a distinct moral person, would mean adding one moral subject to the ten thousand whose interests must be considered in any decision affecting the group. This would rarely alter the moral conclusions that would be reached if the members alone were given moral consideration.

To resist this line of argument, it must be claimed not that organizations deserve *equal* consideration but rather that their goods

---

[22] This is not to deny that sometimes a nonmember may have a reason to contribute to the benefits the members of an organization receive by virtue of their membership.

should be given *more* weight in our moral calculations than the goods of individuals. We cannot, however, say that organizations deserve greater consideration because they possess the properties constitutive of personhood to a much higher degree than humans. We do not regard natural persons who are more intelligent than average as deserving greater moral consideration than those who are less intelligent. We think that the attributes that underlie moral personhood constitute people as deserving equal consideration when they reach certain threshold levels. Even if organizations are enormously more capable than natural persons, then, they can still only claim equal consideration with natural persons. The idea that the good of an organization should be given more weight than that of an individual is plausible only if it is understood as a claim to the effect that organizations contain (and serve) many individuals, and the interests of a large number of individuals outweigh the interests of a small number. This, however, is a point about what equal consideration of individuals requires.

Before moving on, it may be useful to consider what the rejection of principles of Types 3 and 4 means in a particular case. Suppose that the goals of two corporations would be best served by merging, but that five thousand employees would lose their jobs as a result. By the arguments above, even if we can make sense of talk of the goods of the two corporations, we should forget about these goods in deciding whether the merger is morally permissible. Rather, we should consider only which individual human beings will gain as a result of the merger, which will lose, and whether it is fair (or utility maximizing) that the winners gain in this way at the expense of the losers—bearing in mind that the individuals whose interests should be taken into account may include nonmembers of the two organizations who might be affected. Talk of the goods of organizations, understood as a distinct entities, is a red herring that diverts attention from these, the only morally important, issues.

Now let us turn to the question of whether a plausible moral theory will contain principles of Type 2, principles identifying requirements on organizations in their treatment of individuals that are different from the requirements that the individual members of the organization face. Again, we must be clear what is being asked here. It is compatible with an associationist view of organizations that the individuals who comprise an organization could collectively produce some event or state of affairs that is morally unacceptable because of its effects on individuals. It is also natural to speak of this as the organization's doing something wrong. But the question regarding principles of Type 2 is not whether individuals acting together can produce morally objectionable events and states of affairs that no individual acting alone could produce. Of course they can. The question is rather whether there are any moral principles governing the behavior of organizations, understood as distinct entities, that require or permit them to treat individuals in ways that the individuals who make up the organization are not required or permitted to treat individuals.

Let us begin with the hypothesis that organizations are permitted to do things that individuals acting alone or collectively are not permitted to do. One argument that organizations are permitted to do what individuals may not is an "ought implies can" argument to the effect that organizations cannot be held to the requirements that apply to individual humans because they are not capable of complying with them. Here the idea is that organizations, considered as organisms of a certain kind, have only limited rationality. They are like relatively simple animals with set ends that are not open to deliberative reconsideration. The only thinking they can do concerns the best means to their ends, and the only actions they are capable of performing are those deemed optimal in light of these calculations. Thus, it is no more appropriate to hold organizations to moral standards than it would be to hold animals to such standards. A view of this sort has been proposed by John Ladd. He suggests that we cannot legitimately hold organizations to moral standards because the language game that governs how we think and talk about them regards them as capable only of the single-minded pursuit of the goals that define them.[23]

For present purposes, the main thing to note about claims of this sort is that they make sense only if organizations are viewed as entities distinct from their members. Clearly, the human individuals associated with an organization are capable of deliberating about their ends, and thus of taking account of any moral objections there may be to the events or states of affairs that they produce collectively. So even if talk about organizations is governed by a distinct language game, it cannot be used as a shield by the members of the organization, a license to adopt certain ends or certain means of achieving them, simply because they have formed themselves into, or joined, an organization that has these ends.

If this is so, however, then talk about what organizations as distinct entities are permitted to do is otiose. As we have seen, even if organizations are distinct entities, their actions still supervene on the behavior of individuals. And from the standpoint of the individ-

---

[23] See Ladd (1970). For criticism of Ladd's view, see Goodpaster (1979).

uals in the supervenience basis, an organizational action is just an event that they collectively produce. So, they must consider whether morality allows them collectively to produce this event. But if the individuals associated with an organization may not pursue, collectively, certain ends, it does not matter if the organization, understood as a distinct entity, is permitted or even required to pursue them. It will not be able to act on the principles that apply to it because its human "cells" will not be morally free to do what they must if it is to achieve its goals.

This point deserves special emphasis. The central fact about organizational morality is that even if organizations are distinct moral agents, their actions supervene on the behavior of beings of another sort *who are also moral agents*. But the direction of necessitation in a supervenience relation is from the bottom up. What happens at the lower level determines what happens at the higher level. The moral analogue of this is that what ought to happen at the lower level determines what ought to happen at the higher level. If there is a clash between the moral principles that apply at the two levels—so that what is permitted at the higher level is not permitted at the lower level, or what is required at the higher level is not required at the lower level—the principles that apply at the lower level determine how the system as a whole should or may behave. This is because the individuals in the supervenience basis are appropriately guided by the principles that apply to them, not by principles that apply to beings of a different kind, and what they do determines what the organization does.

The issue of the feasibility of Type 2 principles turns, then, on an "ought implies can" argument, but one that is different from Ladd's. We cannot say that organizations, understood as distinct agents, face moral requirements that are different from those faced by the associated individuals because organizations could not act on such requirements (if the individuals behaved as they were required or permitted to). This means that any case that we are tempted to describe as one in which an organization does wrong even though no associated individual does wrong must, if the claim is to be sustained, be redescribable as a case in which individuals acting collectively do wrong even though no individual's action taken in isolation is wrong. Organizational "wrongs" that cannot be redescribed in this way have no moral significance. Similar points apply to cases in which it is said to be permissible for an organization to behave in a certain way. Given moral behavior by the associated individuals, it cannot do what it is permitted to do unless these individuals are permitted to produce collectively the event that constitutes the organizational action in question. So principles of Type 2 are otiose and can be disregarded.

Even if the sociological theory with the most explanatory power treats organizations as distinct organisms with goods of their own, then, it will still be inappropriate to give these entities citizenship in the moral realm, either in the sense of taking their goods into account when determining what morality requires, or in the sense of supposing that distinct moral principles govern their actions.

What are the implications of these results for whether organizations can have authority over individuals? It might seem that they force us to conclude that while organizations can be de facto authorities—believed, falsely, to have a right to issue binding directives—they cannot be legitimate authorities that actually possess such a right. If organizations deserve no moral consideration, they can have no rights of any kind. That is, it might seem that while general ontological considerations do not force associationist views on us, moral considerations do, since only individuals can have a right to direct. As we noted in Chapter Two, however, the right to direct required for authority need not be understood as a personal right: a claim to moral protection for a personal interest or choice. It can simply be a normative power to issue binding directives that arises from the fact that obeying these directives is the right thing for those to whom they are issued to do in the circumstances. Thus, as long as organizations, understood as distinct organisms, can perform actions, there is no barrier in principle to their having at least some kinds of authority. Still, if the above arguments are sound, the content of their right to direct cannot differ from the content of the right that can be ascribed to the associated individuals acting collectively. Let us then examine in more detail the Type 1 principles that determine how individuals should act.

The Morality of Individuals

For our purposes the most important question regarding Type 1 principles is how the existence of organizations, on either organismic or associationist assumptions, alters judgments about what the directive-independent reasons applicable to individuals require. Before we consider this question, we should examine in more detail the moral principles that apply to individuals outside organizational contexts.

Several taxonomic schemes provide useful ways of classifying the principles governing relations between individuals. One important distinction has already been alluded to. This is the distinction between what individuals acting alone have reason to do and what individuals acting collectively in groups have reason to do. Principles of both sorts are principles for individuals. The principles governing collective action are not principles that say what some super-individual organism must do. The distinction rather reflects the fact that when the outcome of an agent's actions depends in certain ways on what other agents do, the principles that normally govern how individuals should act to attain their ends no longer apply. The best-known example of this phenomenon is the so-called prisoner's dilemma. Here, if each of two agents acts in the way that would ordinarily maximize the attainment of his goals, both do worse than they could by cooperating. The principles governing collective action by individuals direct them to cooperate in such situations. I consider this distinction in more detail in Chapter Four. For the time being, the important point is that principles of both sorts tell individuals how to behave in their dealings with other individuals, and are thus Type 1 principles.

It can be argued that all moral principles are in some sense principles governing what individuals acting collectively should do. But common sense does not formulate most of its principles this way. The principles of commonsense morality prohibit or enjoin such things as committing murder and giving to charity. One way of classifying principles of these sorts is to make a distinction between what have traditionally been called perfect duties and imperfect duties. Perfect duties are requirements to do—or more usually not do—certain things to other people in the course of pursuing the various morally permissible ends that one may have. These principles prohibit employing certain means to one's ends, either because these means use people in morally impermissible ways or affect them incidentally in morally impermissible ways. Perfect duties identify ways in which the interests of others constrain what one may do to attain one's permissible ends. Perfect duties can also be regarded as duties of fairness. Unfairness is a matter of gaining inappropriately at another's expense, and the perfect duties prohibit various salient kinds of unfairness. Lying about the repair record of one's car to someone to whom one is trying to sell it violates a perfect duty.

Imperfect duties, by contrast, are requirements to promote the interests of others simply because they are in need, irrespective of whether having any dealings with them is conducive to the attainment of one's permissible ends. These duties, too, constrain what one may do to attain one's ends, but they do this by identifying competing ends that have a claim to one's attention as well. The requirement to throw a life ring to a drowning man is an imperfect duty.

Some normative moral theories try, in effect, to reduce one of these kinds of duties to the other. Contractarian moral theories try to account for all duties as in some sense duties of fairness, and utilitarian theories try to account for them as arising from a requirement that each promote the welfare of all. The difficulties encountered by both projects suggest that it may be better to accept two irreducibly basic kinds of moral duties.

Recently, another way of dividing up the considerations of commonsense morality has been proposed. This involves a tripartite classification, identifying (1) morally valuable goals, (2) permissions to refrain from promoting these goals in ways that would require large personal sacrifices, and (3) deontological constraints on the means that may be adopted to attain both these goals and permissible personal ends.[24] This scheme has some advantages over the last for the purpose of giving an account of how organizations affect the moral requirements that individuals face. From the moral point of view, one of the most basic facts about organizations is that individuals acting collectively within an organization can affect, for good or ill, large numbers of people. This is rarely true of the actions of isolated individuals, unless they are able to influence what an organization does. It is natural to describe this fact about organizations as their being able to promote or damage certain desirable social states of affairs. The concept of an imperfect duty, however, does not adequately capture this dimension of moral assessment. The reasons that we have to promote certain social states of affairs do not always present themselves, at least on the surface, as deriving from the needs of others. In order to account for such judgments, we must admit a broader category of morally valuable goals. Once this is done, we can regard the imperfect duties as one kind of requirement derived from such goals.

The deontological constraints associated with this way of viewing the moral landscape can be equated with the perfect duties, or duties of fairness, of the previous scheme.[25] The category of permissions, however, requires further explanation. The sense of permission involved here is permission to pursue personal ends. If there were no morally important goals, the deontological constraints alone would yield a satisfactory account of this sort of permission. We would be

[24] This tripartite distinction plays a role in much of Thomas Nagel's work on ethics. See, for example Nagel (1979).

[25] I describe deontological constraints as identifying salient kinds of unfairness in McMahon (1991).

permitted to promote our personal ends in any way that was not prohibited by the constraints. But this sort of *negative* permission cannot prevent a potentially unwelcome consequence of admitting morally valuable goals. There is always more that each of us can do to promote most of these goals. Thus, the requirement to promote them can create a situation in which one never has any free time to pursue personal ends. If room is to be made for the pursuit of such ends, we need *positive* permissions, permissions that take the form of a moral license to forego efforts to promote morally valuable goals when the personal costs would be too great. These positive permissions form the third component of the present taxonomic scheme. They can be regarded as playing a role in the previous scheme as well, since the imperfect duties are usually taken to require only such efforts to meet the needs of others as can be undertaken at modest cost to oneself.

There is one more useful way of dividing up moral considerations. Earlier, I posed the question of the moral status of organizations by asking whether organizations deserve equal consideration, and I mentioned that different conceptions of the requirements of morality can be associated with different ways of understanding the idea of giving people equal consideration. But we can divide conceptions of equal consideration into two broad kinds, *output-criterion* conceptions and *input-criterion* conceptions, where "output" refers to the actions an agent performs or their consequences and "input" to the antecedent process of deliberation.

Since giving people equal consideration is something that is done in the process of deliberation, both conceptions are concerned with how deliberation is conducted, but they differ in the way they understand the goal of deliberation. Deliberation guided by an output-criterion conception of equal consideration is guided by a concern to make people's lives equal in some morally valuable respect—for example, by giving them equal welfare, resources, or capabilities, or insuring their equal relative benefit from some cooperative endeavor or their Aristotelian proportionate equality. Deliberation guided by an input-criterion conception of equal consideration, by contrast, is guided by a concern to treat people equally in the process or procedure used to decide among the available alternatives (where this is understood in some way that does not involve reference to outcomes). One input-criterion conception of equal consideration is that associated with utilitarianism, which calls for counting each as one and none as more than one in the calculations that determine which course of action will maximize aggregate satisfaction. Another is that associated with using a fair lottery—one that gives everyone an equal chance of winning—to determine who is to have something that more than one person wants. Equal consideration of this latter sort does not aim to make the actual standing of people equal on any dimension of assessment.[26]

Lying behind these conceptions of equal consideration are the fundamental values of fairness and welfare-maximization. All of the forms of equal consideration can be regarded as displaying some sort of fairness. Utilitarianism, for example, treats people fairly in the process of aggregating satisfactions. But some conceptions of equal consideration seem to capture the value of fairness more fully than others. In general, output-criterion equal consideration, where it is available, seems to realize the value of fair treatment more fully than input-criterion equal consideration alone. Thus, procedural fairness by itself may not be sufficient to meet the demands of fairness.

If we are to account adequately for the conceptions of equal consideration we employ, however, we must supplement the value of fairness with the value of welfare maximization. Some conceptions of equal consideration that are inferior from the standpoint of fairness may nevertheless be judged appropriate in a situation because they give expression to the value of welfare maximization. In the case of this latter value, it is important to distinguish between welfare maximization that is compatible with fairness—making *fair shares* as large as possible—and maximizing *aggregate* welfare—which may involve treating some people unfairly. Typically, welfare maximization is a more compelling value when it is understood as calling for the maximization of fair shares than when it is understood as calling for the maximization of aggregate welfare. I consider these matters further in Chapter Five.

If all legitimate moral considerations reflect some understanding of equal consideration, and conceptions of equal consideration are themselves judged more or less suitable by how well they realize, in a given case, the fundamental moral values of fairness and welfare maximization, then all legitimate moral considerations can be regarded as grounded in one or the other of these values. Earlier, it was suggested that the deontological constraints correspond to salient kinds of unfairness. Thus, it might seem that morally valuable

---

[26] Ronald Dworkin (1985), pp. 190–91 makes this point by saying that treating people as equals may not involve treating them equally. But it is hard to see how treating people as equals is to be understood if not as treating them equally in some respect. My suggestion is that those forms of equal consideration that Dworkin regards as having no necessary connection with treating people equally should be understood rather as calling for equal treatment in the process of deciding.

goals should be understood as identifying states of affairs that contribute importantly to, or constitute important aspects of, the value of welfare maximization. But the value of fairness need not be restricted to the "microlevel" employment associated with the deontological constraints. It can also be given a "macrolevel" employment in which it characterizes the overall distribution of valued items in some group as fair or unfair. Thus fairness can be a goal—or underwrite certain goals—as well.[27]

Morally Important Social Values

Now that we have surveyed the main kinds of moral considerations governing the actions of individuals, we must investigate how the assumption that human communities contain organizations affects their application. As we have seen, organizations, understood as entities distinct from their members, have no moral status. Their presence can have moral significance only by affecting what individuals acting in organizational contexts have reason to do. In general, two cases can be distinguished. A single individual may act through an organization, or a group of individuals may act collectively within an organization.

The possibility of acting through an organization or collectively within it is of moral interest to the extent that individuals are able to produce in this way results that they could not have produced alone. These results could have moral significance by virtue of the operation of any of the considerations mentioned in the previous section. The requirements associated with perfect duties or deontological constraints comprise one set of these considerations. These requirements can be regarded as identifying certain salient kinds of unfair treatment. Unfair treatment is a matter of gaining inappropriately at someone else's expense, and individuals acting through, or collectively within, organizations can certainly gain inappropriately at the expense of others.

Similar points apply to morally valuable goals.[28] Utilitarians characterize the good that is to be maximized as the total or average level of desire satisfaction that prevails in a community. Other consequentialists have advocated pluralistic conceptions of the good, in which several different aspects of individual lives—autonomy and the development of talents, for example, as well as desire

[27] Libertarians can be regarded as claiming that the only legitimate employment for the concepts of fairness and justice is at the microlevel.

[28] The effect of the existence of organizations on the operation of positive permissions is examined in Chapter Six.

satisfaction—are taken as goods to be maximized. These goals, too, can have a bearing on what individuals acting through or collectively within an organizations should do.

When we move to the level of organizational action, however, other considerations of a clearly consequentialist nature are often cited as being of moral importance as well. This is easiest to see in the case of that most comprehensive of organizations, the state. We typically regard the legitimate goals of the state as including the defense of national territory, the maintenance of the rule of law, or, more generally, the maintenance of social peace, the development of culture, the advancement of knowledge, the fostering of community, the promotion of social prosperity, the protection of public health, and other goals which have as their object the production or maintenance of certain social states of affairs. Promotion of social justice is also a goal of many of the actions of the state. Affirmative action programs, for example, can be regarded as justified by their consequences for social justice. Let us call these considerations "morally important social values." How should the role of these considerations in moral thinking be understood?

One possibility is to view them as conditions of the flourishing of a society understood as a distinct superindividual organism. Just as one might suppose that the good of a person did not consist entirely in the maximization of personal desire satisfaction, so one might think that the good of a society, understood as a distinct organism, did not consist entirely in the maximization of total aggregate desire satisfaction within it. Rather, such an organism flourishes when it comes, as on organism, to know more or to develop a more fully articulated culture.

If we are to remain true to the tenants of moral individualism, however, we cannot take this line. The morally important social values must be understood as identifying components of the flourishing of individual humans, who are the only proper recipients of moral consideration. One way this could be done is to regard these values, or those tied to welfare, as intermediate goals in an act utilitarian moral theory. For present purposes, utilitarianism may be understood as a way of giving expression to the fundamental value of welfare maximization that (1) understands welfare as the satisfaction of desire and (2) employs an aggregation interpretation of the value of welfare maximization, as opposed to one that calls for the maximization of fair shares.

Utilitarian theories often hold that individuals can promote total aggregate satisfaction more effectively if they do not aim at maximizing it, but instead conform their behavior to certain rules, such as a rule prohibiting lying. Similarly, individuals acting through or within organizations may better promote total aggregate satisfaction if they do not aim directly at it, but rather at the production of certain social states of affairs—identified by the morally important social values—which are usually correlated with increased desire satisfaction. The reason such considerations play a role at the organizational level but not at the individual level is simply that only individuals acting through or within organizations have the opportunity to affect significantly these social states of affairs.

Another, nonutilitarian, possibility is to regard the morally important social values as identifying social states of affairs in which the sorts of things that pluralistic conceptions of the individual good find important are more fully available to individuals. Thus, those who think it important that individuals develop their talents even at some cost to individual desire satisfaction could be expected to think as well that a society should foster the development of culture even at some cost to total aggregate desire satisfaction. But given moral individualism, this must be because individuals benefit in some way not reducible to desire satisfaction when a society's culture is highly developed.

So far, I have been proceeding on the assumption that the value of the morally important social values is instrumental. The connection between the social state of affairs identified as morally important and the aspect of the flourishing of individual humans to which it contributes is contingent. It happens to be the case that the good in question can be promoted in this way, and it is logically possible that it could be promoted in some other way. We need not restrict ourselves to this view, however; for some components of human flourishing may be *constituted* by social states of affairs or relations. To put it another way, some components of the good life for an individual may be internally related to certain social states of affairs, so that these states of affairs are logically necessary conditions for the goods in question.[29] For example, if certain anarchists are right, the maintenance of the rule of law has only contingent, instrumental value since humans could in principle live just as well without government. But the value of the development of culture may be different, for it may be that individuals cannot receive the benefits that this social process creates otherwise than by being related to each other through a common culture. If so, any form of human life in which the social state of affairs identified by the value of the development

[29] See Moore (1959). For Moore, a relational property of some item A is internal to it if and only if a thing's lacking that property entails that it is not A.

of culture was missing would necessarily be one in which a certain component of a flourishing life for individual human beings was also missing.

It bears repeating that the morally important social values need not all be understood as identifying aspects of the foundational value of welfare maximization. When the concept of fairness is given a macrolevel employment in which it characterizes the overall distribution of valued items to the individuals in some group as fair or unfair, it can be regarded as identifying a morally important social value, or as underwriting other goals that constitute morally important social values, such as the goal of eliminating discrimination. The morally important social value of fairness usually identifies social states of affairs that are intrinsically good, but fairness can also have instrumental value, say, as promoting social stability.

The morally important social values can, then, be understood in a way that is compatible with moral individualism. They identify social states of affairs that contribute in some way to the flourishing of individuals. This does not, however, entail that an individualist—in the sense of reductionist—account of these states of affairs is appropriate. As we saw earlier, even if organismic views are mistaken, we still may not be able to reduce statements about some social phenomena, such as riots, to statements about individual humans. Similarly, there may be no nonsocial states of affairs to which the states of affairs identified by the morally important social values can be reduced. The states of affairs identified by these values may exist only at the social level.

The upshot of this is that if we approach the question of what we need to live well as individuals entirely in terms of effects of actions that can be described in nonsocial terms, we may not be able to account for important components of human flourishing. There may be certain irreducibly *social* conditions of the good life for *individual* human beings. But these conditions, identified by the morally important social values, are of moral importance because individuals need them, not because they are constitutive of the flourishing of some superindividual organism: an organization, community, state, or whatever.

The morally important social values do some of the work, I think, that those who have wanted to speak of group rights have invoked this latter concept to do. Given moral individualism, there are no group rights, in the sense of rights of groups understood as entities over and above their members, since such entities have no moral standing. They cannot be treated unfairly. When we speak of group rights, we must have something else in mind.

One case where we might find it useful to speak of group rights is the case where a group of individuals, all of whom have a right of a certain kind, agree to exercise this right collectively, that is, in accordance with a collective decision. We could speak of a group right here because actions that prevented a group that had decided on such policy from acting on its collective decision would treat the whole group unfairly. But this unfairness would be reducible to unfair treatment of each group member as an individual, to the violation of her rights.

There is also, however, another case where it would be natural to speak of group rights. There may be states of groups that are (1) not reducible to states of the individual members of the group, and (2) important for the flourishing of the individual members of the group. If so, the members of these groups may have a legitimate moral claim—a right—to the maintenance of these irreducibly social states of affairs. This, too, would not entail the rejection of moral individualism. The right in question would be a right of each individual member of the group that the group as a whole be a certain way; it would not be a right of the group, understood as a distinct entity, that it be a certain way.

Liberalism and Communitarianism

Since the concept of a morally important social value is unfamiliar, it may be helpful to illustrate it by using it to provide an account of a prominent current debate, that between liberalism and communitarianism. Communitarianism is associated with the view that a good society is one that is organized around the promotion of a single, shared conception of the good, while liberalism is associated with the view that a good society is one in which each individual pursues the good, as he or she understands it, within some framework of rules designed to insure everyone a region of action free from the interference of others. How is the choice between these two social forms to be understood?

On one interpretation of communitarianism, the shared conception of the good, the promotion of which is to be the focus of social effort, is a conception of the good of the community understood as an organism distinct from its members. But while communitarians sometimes speak as if they are sympathetic to such a view, it runs afoul of our earlier arguments against giving moral consideration to social entities. There is no moral basis for the subordination of an individual's interest to that of a group (understood as a distinct entity). Let us then seek an interpretation of communitarianism that is compatible with moral individualism.

Another common theme in communitarianism is that our identities are constituted by (certain of) the social relations in which we participate.[30] Thus the liberal view of the self that regards people as choosing their ends must be rejected. The appropriate posture of a self toward its ends is rather one of understanding; a self should try to understand the socially given ends that constitute it as what it is. This quest for self-knowledge is not to be pursued alone, but cooperatively with others who share the same commitments.

This claim, however, does not warrant the rejection of the liberal view of the good society. Virtually everyone will be constituted in part by commitments to a variety of associations smaller than the society in which he or she lives, and different people will be involved with different such associations. Thus the pluralism that justifies a liberal view will remain. Different members of a given society will have different selves constituted by different commitments, and the best social form will be one that allows them some space to develop these selves without interference from others. Of course, this result could be avoided if everyone in a society had only one commitment to an end or set of ends common to the society as a whole, but it is hard to see such a totalitarian vision as appealing.

If this is right, we must reject the suggestion that community is the only virtue a society needs. Justice is indispensable. But the possibility remains that community is a morally important social value in the sense outlined earlier. That is, the possibility remains that the social state of affairs that exists when everyone in a society shares at least some common ends and devotes at least some time to promoting them contributes in an important way to the well-being of the individuals who are members of the society. This social state of affairs would be either a means to, or constitutive of, a certain aspect of the flourishing of the members of a society. The criticism of liberalism associated with this moderate form of communitarianism is that in a liberal society, the morally important social value of community is inadequately promoted.[31] To assess the force of this criticism, we must consider in more detail why community is valuable.

The value of community points to certain respects in which the lives of individuals are better when the society in which they live is organized around a common end. For example, desirable forms of fellow feeling are likely to be found where people are acting jointly to promote some common end. And the attitude to those who have

---

[30] See Sandel (1982). A similar view can be found in Gould (1988), pp. 110–13.

[31] I take the contrast between radical and moderate communitarianism from Buchanan (1989). For a similar view that communitarian values should be regarded as supplementing rather than supplanting basic liberal values see Gutmann (1985).

fallen on hard times is also likely to be desirably different in a society committed to a common end. They will not be regarded as having a claim to charitable assistance, or as people who have paid with previous labors for insurance protection, but as fallen comrades who must be helped up so that they can resume their contribution to the common project. Similarly, the fact that an individual identifies with others in his society makes it easier for him to accept sacrifices for their sake, for he will regard those who benefit from his sacrifices as extensions of himself, and thus there will be a sense in which he is compensated for these sacrifices. Of course, these benefits would also accrue to those who participated in subsocial endeavors organized around common ends, but they would be more fully achieved if the society as a whole had some common ends.[32]

That the quality of human life could be improved in these ways seems beyond dispute, but the value of community, so understood, may clash with other moral considerations thought important by the members of a society. One of these is respect for rights. Organizing society around the pursuit of a common end might entail the abridgment of certain generally accepted rights. But there is another, in some ways more interesting, possibility. Certain morally important social values *other* than community might be more effectively promoted in a liberal society—that is, more effectively promoted if individuals were encouraged to adopt their own conceptions of the good and do what they could to promote these conceptions (within a certain social framework). Thus, liberals could plausibly claim that the advancement of knowledge, the development of culture, and the promotion of social prosperity are all better served if individuals pursue the good as they see it.

We can be more precise about why the promotion of these morally important social values in a liberal society would clash with the value of community. The mechanism by which individual pursuit of personal conceptions of the good promotes these values is competition. Knowledge is promoted by free (competitive) debate—that is, debate between people advancing competing arguments—culture

---

[32] It is worth noting that many of the benefits of community, so understood, can also be generated by shared cooperative activities, in the sense of Bratman (1992). Such activities are characterized by mutual assistance and responsiveness, but do not presuppose a common *ultimate* end. Each acts to promote a shared end, but each may regard the attainment of this end as a means to some further end (which may be different for each). Since the maintenance of a liberal social order could be a shared cooperative activity in this sense—for example, if there was an overlapping consensus of a Rawlsian sort on the desirability of its maintenance—there may be less of a conflict between liberalism and the value of community than communitarians claim.

by free competition for recognition, and prosperity by free (competitive) markets.[33] But competition can undermine the beneficial social relations identified by the value of community. This enables us to explain, I think, why the communitarian critique of liberalism has found a receptive audience. It is not because the arguments of Michael Sandel and others that liberalism carries with it unacceptable metaphysical commitments have been judged compelling. Rather, it is because the communitarian objections to liberalism have been taken as objections to the promotion of social goals by competitive means.

The view that competition between people seeking to promote different goals effectively realizes certain morally important social values can be called "social liberalism" to distinguish it from the political liberalism that justifies liberal institutions as the best way to insure equal concern and respect for individuals with different conceptions of what is valuable. Of course, there is room for disagreement about whether the claims of social liberalism are true in a given case. The debate between liberalism and traditional socialism was in part a debate about whether the value of social prosperity is best promoted by competitive or cooperative processes.[34] But let us suppose that it is true that the values mentioned above are best promoted by competitive processes. Communitarians can then be regarded as objecting to social liberalism that: (1) competitive processes are destructive of the value of community, and (2) the incremental moral gains that can be realized by promoting knowledge, culture, prosperity, and other values by competitive rather than cooperative processes are not sufficient to offset the reduction in the value of community that results.

It is not my purpose here to decide who is right in the debate between communitarianism and liberalism, but simply to show how morally important social values can be regarded as playing a role in it. Clearly there is room for disagreement about the relative importance in current circumstances of the morally important social values engaged in the debate, and a variety of positions are possible. Some might regard the value of community as of such paramount importance that they would be willing to live in any society organized around a single conception of the good. Others would want the underlying view of equal consideration to be congenial and the

[33] Liberals also believe that adversarial judicial proceedings are more likely to give people what they deserve.

[34] By contrast, contemporary socialists are more likely to defend socialism by arguing that prosperity is not the only good and that socialist institutions are better able to give all relevant considerations their due.

81

remaining morally important social values to be promoted as effectively as possible within a communitarian framework—that is, they
would want the common conception of the good around which
society was to be organized to have a certain content.[35] Similarly,
some liberals might be willing to accept certain curbs on the competitive processes that most effectively promote development for the
sake of a fuller realization of the value of community, while others
might think that we should be content with however much community is compatible with the optimal functioning of these competitive
processes.

The Moral Good

The moral considerations that bear on what people acting through,
or collectively within, organizations should do are various. They
include both the traditionally acknowledged components of commonsense morality and the consequentialist considerations that I
have called morally important social values. In deciding what to do,
moral agents must determine what all of these considerations taken
together require.

It will be useful to have a term for the understanding, not necessarily explicitly formulated, that each agent has about the relative
importance of the moral considerations that she acknowledges. Let
us call this her "conception of the moral good." In deciding what she
or others should do in a particular case she brings to bear her conception of the moral good, determines which of the considerations it
contains are applicable to the case at hand, and decides what course
of action they support (given her understanding of the relations
between them and their relative importance). I shall often refer to an
individual's seeking to promote her conception of the moral good in
a situation. By this I shall mean her doing what in her judgment she
has the best reason to do in that situation, given the moral considerations that she acknowledges. No commitment to consequentialist
views is presupposed, although for anyone who accepts morally

[35] A communitarian of the first sort would be willing to activate a machine that
would give everyone in his society an overriding commitment to some shared end but
would choose this end at random. Most communitarians seem rather to be what
might be called "hyphenated communitarians." They are, say, feminist-, or Marxist-,
or environmental-communitarians, depending on the conception of the common
good around which they think society should be organized. Few communitarians in
the United States, one suspects, would be willing to transformed into committed
members of an Islamic fundamentalist society provided that everyone else in the
country was too. When we raise the question of how hyphenated communitarians
are to live together while they are sorting out whose conception of the good will be the
common one, however, we seem to be driven to political liberalism.

important social values, consequentialist considerations will be among those consulted.

A conception of the moral good is not a conception of the common good in the sense of a conception of what would be in everyone's nonmoral interests. Nor is it a common conception of the good in the communitarian sense. A conception of the moral good need not be shared. It is a particular individual's conception of what morality enjoins and permits, and different people will usually understand this differently. Considerations thought to have moral force by some will not be thought to have it by others. And even those who agree on the relevant moral considerations may disagree about which have greater weight in a given situation.

In making these points, I do not mean to commit myself to some form of moral relativism. The different conceptions of the moral good that people hold could reflect their different perceptions of an objective moral reality, and some conceptions could be mistaken. Of course, the judgments that each individual makes about what morality requires or permits will be determined by the conception that she holds, not the conception that she ought to hold.

Political disputes are often characterized not as disputes between people with different conceptions of the moral good, but as disputes between people with different interests. This is misleading, however. The parties to a political dispute must try to enlist the support of others. And while this might involve logrolling—that is, the trading of favors—each will usually try to present the courses she favors as right for the group. But this must involve an appeal to considerations thought to be valid for all, and considerations having this feature are, functionally, moral considerations. Thus, even if the parties to a political dispute do not initially construe it in moral terms, they will typically develop conceptions of the moral good in the course of it. Moreover, these conceptions will not simply be rationalizations for what those holding them want. In responding to the moral arguments of others, individuals are often led to modify their views about what would be right, which means changing their minds about which of their interests they can appropriately try to advance. Although the fact that people have different interests may be part of the explanation of why they have different conceptions of the moral good, then, political disputes are best characterized not as disputes between people with different interests but as disputes between people with different conceptions of the moral good.

Conceptions of the moral good play a role in the acceptance of authority in two ways. As we saw in Chapter Two, to accept authority is to accept the preemption of one's judgment of what the applicable directive-independent reasons require, and what one regards as the applicable directive-independent moral reasons will be determined by one's conception of the moral good. One's conception of the moral good may also, however, contain considerations that justify the acceptance of certain authorities—that is, considerations deemed capable of justifying the preemption associated with authority. We turn to the justification of authority in Chapter Four.

C H A P T E R   F O U R

THE JUSTIFICATION OF AUTHORITY

Legitimate authority is authority that can be justified to those over whom it is exercised. I understand doing this as establishing that there is good reason, from the point of view of each subject, for him or her to accept the authority in question. The subjects need not, however, be aware of the justifying arguments. De facto authority based on false beliefs about what justifies it can still be legitimate, and a source of directives that coerces compliance can be a legitimate authority as well.

In Chapter Two, I distinguished three main species of authority. E-authority is authority based on relatively greater expertise in a given area; P-authority is authority based on a promise to obey; and C-authority is authority based on the authority's role in facilitating cooperation. We may take it for granted that there are legitimate authorities of each of these kinds, but we need to know more about the way the justifying arguments work and how strong they are.

Using the terms introduced in Chapter Two, we can say that a given source of directives is a legitimate subordinating authority for B if the reasons that support complying with its directives establish them as appropriately preempting the directive-independent reasons that would otherwise determine B's actions. Similarly, a given source of assertions is a legitimate E-authority for B if the reasons that support accepting its assertions establish them as appropriately preempting the assertion-independent reasons that would otherwise determine B's beliefs. Authority is stronger the more often it is justified in this sense.

Any source of directives or assertions having the presumptive status of an authority usually has it only over certain actions or in a certain subject matter, which allows us to speak of the scope of its implied authority. The strength of authority is relativized to scope. There are two dimensions of strength: robustness and reach. Robustness is defined for each person to whom directives are issued. The robustness, for a subject B, of the authority possessed by a given source of directives A, is a function of the variety of situations in which there would be sufficient reason for B to comply with any directive issued by A within the scope of its implied authority. Reach is defined for each occasion on which directives are issued to a group over whom A claims authority. The reach, on an occasion, of A's authority is a function of the percentage of the members of the group to whom a directive within the scope of A's implied authority is addressed on that occasion who have sufficient reason to comply with it. The robustness and reach of E-authority may be understood similarly, with "assertion" replacing "directive." We can derive a measure of the overall strength of an authority by combining considerations of robustness and reach. An authority will have a high degree of overall strength within a group if it has a high degree of robustness for a large percentage of the members of that group.

Strictly speaking, these measures apply to individual sources of directives or assertions. Here, however, we are mainly concerned with the relative strength of the three different forms of authority that have been distinguished, and especially with the relative strength of P-authority and C-authority. For the most part, then, I consider how the various factors that can reduce the strength of authority affect these three forms of it.

E-Authority

The Varieties of E-Authority

As we saw in Chapter Two, the general distinction between de facto and de jure or legitimate authority can be applied to E-authority no less than to the other forms. A de facto E-authority is someone whose assertions are taken as true by the members of a given group. When it is common knowledge within a group that all accord de facto authority to an individual or a set of individuals sharing a certain method, the E-authority of this individual or set of individuals can be said to be conventional within the group. The usual processes by which individuals become socialized to the conventions of a group can explain how this conventional status is perpetuated.

The utility of E-authority is clear. Most of us have reliable epistemic access to relatively mundane facts in our local environment, but modern life also requires us to act on the basis of a great deal of specialized knowledge that we lack the time or ability to acquire for ourselves. Our access to such knowledge thus depends on a division of labor. Some people are accorded the status of experts in particular fields, and nonexperts regard as true whatever the experts say (about the topics on which they are experts). Almost all of the beliefs that each of us has were acquired by accepting the word of someone regarded as an expert rather than by assessing the evidence ourselves.

E-authority is, then, indispensable. But how do we tell whether a given de facto E-authority is legitimate, or whether someone who does not now have the status of an E-authority should have it? To keep what is required clearly in mind, it is useful to take as a paradigm of deferring to an expert the case in which one believes what he says even though one has assessed the evidence oneself and come to a contrary conclusion. That is, although we do not usually bother to assess—to the extent that we can—the evidence relevant to the pronouncements of experts, the question of how E-authority is established is best formulated by considering the case in which we make such an assessment. What can justify deferring to the judgment of another when we have assessed the evidence ourselves?

E-authority is standardly justified inductively. That is, one notes that a certain individual's assertions regarding matters of some kind have usually proved true in the past and infers from this that his present assertions are likely to be true as well. One thereby acquires a reason for assenting to these assertions that takes precedence over one's own judgment of what the applicable assertion-independent reasons support. One acquires a good reason for believing what the authority says even though one is unable to follow his reasoning (if he offers any) or one's own reasoning continues to yield conflicting conclusions.

There are important differences between E-authority and subordinating authority. To accept the assertion of an E-authority is to revise one's assertion-independent judgment about what is right. One might say that E-authority is a device that enables one to acquire better judgments without acquiring better judgment. To accept subordinating authority, by contrast, is to act contrary to one's directive-independent judgment of what is right without revising it. These differences are reflected in the justification of these two sorts of authority. In a case involving subordination, the reason that justifies compliance with the directive is not a reason for supposing that what is directed is, independently, the right thing to do, that is, what one ought to have done even in the absence of the directive. Rather, it is a reason for complying with the directive even though one does not regard what is directed as, independently, the right thing to do. In the case of E-authority, however, the reason that justifies accepting an authoritative assertion is a reason for supposing that it identifies what is—and would be even in the absence of the assertion—the truth about some matter. The fact that the assertion of a justified E-authority purports to identify what is independently true has an important implication. Even though E-authority is genuine preemptive authority, we can, and do, reject it when we can plainly see that an authority is mistaken.

An E-authority is like an instrument that has proven in the past to be a much more reliable detector of something than common sense. Thus, what she says is not simply an additional piece of evidence to be added to the rest. Rather one does better if one is guided solely by it, disregarding one's own assessment of the evidence entirely. This remains true even if one thinks only that she is somewhat more likely to be right than one is. One still does better by accepting her assertions as made than one would by weighting them by the probability that they are right and balancing them against one's own (inferior) assessment of the evidence.[1]

It should also be noted that typically we take those whom we regard as experts as having succeeded in the past because they were trying to make correct judgments, and thus our expectation that they are correct in the present case presupposes that they are trying here as well. It presupposes that they are saying what they believe, that their assertions are sincere. We defer, then, not merely to the assertions of experts, but to their judgment.[2]

The inductive justification of E-authority can take a variety of forms. One of the most important involves the confirmation of predictions. One notes that the predictions that a given individual has made in the past have always or usually proven true, and infers from this that her present prediction is probably true as well. Alvin Goldman has recently noted some other methods of expert identification, and these, too, have an inductive structure.[3] Experts can be identified by their command of a factual record (every time one checks E's assertion against the record, it proves true), their ability to repair things the proper functioning of which nonexperts can detect (every time it has broken, E has been able to fix it), and their ability to design things to execute tasks the performance of which nonexperts can discern (every time E has said she could provide such a device, she has).

---

[1] See Raz (1986), pp. 67–69.

[2] Harman (1965) argues that since the inference that the present assertions of an authority are true assumes that she is saying what she believes, it is not strictly speaking inductive. But as far as I can see, if the authority's past successes were cases of saying what she believed, inferring her present success on inductive grounds would involve supposing that she was saying what she believed in this case as well.

[3] Goldman (1991), pp. 128–30.

As these examples show, expertise is not just a matter of superior propositional knowledge. It can also be practical. Someone can be an expert by virtue of her superior knowledge of how to do something as well as her superior knowledge of what is the case. Superior know-how can play a role in either of two ways. When the action necessary to solve a practical problem that one faces can be performed by another, the expert can perform it. And when the action cannot be performed by another—or one wants to perform it oneself—one can still benefit from expertise by complying with the expert's directives or imitating her. The directives of a practical E-authority have, however, a different status from those of a subordinating authority. They are, in effect, ought-judgments *reporting* what there is good reason for the person to whom they are addressed to do, rather than orders (which, when authority is justified, *create* a good reason for doing something). The author of a cookbook from which one has obtained good results in the past would be an example of an inductively justified practical E-authority.

In all of the above cases, the criterion on the basis of which expertise is discerned is external to the species of expertise involved. Nonexperts need not have even a rudimentary level of the competence possessed by the expert to judge her to be an expert, that is, to recognize her performance as successful. Other cases, however, lack this feature. Nonexperts need to possess, to at least some degree, the sort of competence the expert has in order to recognize her success. In both cases, expertise is established by inductive reasoning, but in cases of the latter sort, the criterion of success is internal to the particular form of competence on which authority is based.[4]

One important genus of E-authority established by an internal criterion is found when superior reasoning ability is displayed in a history of successful argument. That is, an individual may acquire the status of an expert in some area where the truth is determined by argument by establishing a record of success in supporting her assertions with compelling arguments. Such a history would generate an inductive reason for those who had found her arguments persuasive in the past to accept her present assertions even when they had not heard the supporting arguments—or were incapable of following them. They could infer from the fact that they had found her arguments compelling in the past that they should believe what she says now. The criterion in such cases is internal because to judge

---

[4] Thus, we can say that while E-authority in general is based on differences in expertise, when the criterion that establishes it is external, the difference can be a difference in kind, while when the criterion is internal, the difference must be difference in degree.

success one must have been able to follow at least some of the expert's arguments. Expert authority in mathematics is of this sort, and a similar phenomenon can be found in the practical domain to the extent that the expertise involved is established by argument. Thus, someone might win acceptance within a certain group as an authority on the right thing to do by being able to support her practical judgments with arguments that others in the group found convincing.

Another genus of authority established by an internal criterion is authority based on superior perception. Perhaps the simplest example would be the case of someone with twenty-twenty vision in a car full of nearsighted people. The person with twenty-twenty vision could acquire within this group the justified status of an E-authority on what distant road signs said by virtue of the fact that the others could see for themselves, on closer inspection, that her perceptual judgments were usually correct. Similarly, someone might be able to make perceptual judgments under nonideal epistemic conditions that others could verify when conditions were ideal. In these cases, the criterion is internal because success is judged using the same sensory modality on which the expert relies. It might seem that the use of the word "authority" is inappropriate here since E-authority presupposes access to a body of knowledge acquired through some process or learning or training. But the epistemic structure of the situation is the same as in the paradigm cases; there are good inductive reasons for supposing that someone has greater competence to make certain judgments. And when superior sensory discernment is a result of special training—as when one has the ability to name the note played by a musical instrument—we do not hesitate to speak of expertise.[5]

Authority based on superior perception also has an analogue in the practical or evaluative domain. Here the superior perception is superior discernment of the good or the right. When someone wins acknowledgment as a superior judge of the market value of paintings by being able to predict what they will sell for, we have a case of authority established by an external criterion. But someone might also win acknowledgment (within a certain group) as an expert discerner of the aesthetic value of paintings. This would happen if others found that with further exposure, they usually received

[5] Heda Segvic has suggested to me that we would not call someone an expert unless we thought she had knowledge of the presumed area of her expertise. This is a weaker requirement than a requirement of training, but I think we can be justified in deferring to the judgment of someone who is merely more likely to be right than we are.

greater satisfaction from contemplating the objects that he pronounced more valuable than those he pronounced less valuable, even when they initially found nothing to choose between them. Similarly, someone might win the status of an expert on good manners if he established a history of producing what others recognized as fitting or appropriate responses to problematic situations. This latter form of expertise would be practical—based on superior know-how—but identified by an internal criterion. As with forms of practical authority identified by an external criterion, one could make use of someone possessing such know-how to a superior degree by retaining him as an agent or by following his directives or imitating his behavior.[6] The superior perception of such an expert could be either intuitive apprehension of independently existing evaluative facts or superior taste (relative to a certain sensibility).

We should be clear about what is going on when evaluative expertise is established by an internal criterion. In such cases there could easily be E-authority established by an external criterion as well. The person acknowledged as an expert on value within a certain group would be able to predict what the members of that group would like, and this would be a form of expertise that anyone could appreciate. But someone who was an expert on what people who had a certain sensibility would find satisfying could also be an expert in another sense for these people. If he shared the sensibility about which he was an expert and made sincere value judgments based on it, he could come to be regarded by them as an expert on what was good (of a certain kind).[7]

Finally, it should be noted that there can be hierarchies of justified expert authority, in which those at lower levels defer to the judgment of those above them, who in turn defer to the judgment of those above them. These arrangements, too, admit of inductive justification. Thus, an individual might regard himself as knowing some of what he knows because it has been communicated to him by someone whom he acknowledges, for inductive reasons, as an expert. Armed with this knowledge, as well as knowledge that he had acquired himself, he might win the status of an expert in some population of people less competent than he by establishing within this group a record of reliable prediction, compelling argument, discerning perception, or whatever. Among other things, he would then be an expert for this group on who the (topmost) experts in the

---

[6] Cf. the discussion of exemplary authority in De George (1985), pp. 45–46.

[7] The ability to articulate what others feel in some inchoate way is a form of expertise that does not, I think, establish an authority relation. For there is assent only after the recipients have had the confirming experiences.

field were. Such hierarchies constitute an integral part of the division of labor associated with the authority of expertise. They are however, informal and fluid arrangements. The inductive evidence that establishes one individual as relatively more expert than another is constantly being updated, and the positions that people occupy in hierarchies of expertise change as their knowledge, or that of others, grows.

Moral Authority

In the previous section, I noted that contemporary society is built on a division of epistemic labor. Most of what we regard ourselves as knowing we have learned from experts. But many people in contemporary societies regard moral thinking as lying outside this division of labor. Of course, they may acknowledge experts on the sociological question of what moral conventions prevail in what communities or on the philosophical question of what normative moral theories have been proposed and how they might be criticized or defended. They may also solicit moral advice. But they are not prepared to defer without argument to anyone's judgment about what course of action would be morally right in a particular case. What is the explanation for this?

One possibility is that morality—in the sense of morally appropriate conduct—is not a topic about which it is possible to make statements that are true or false, and thus not a topic about which anyone can acquire knowledge. One of the principal problems of metaethics is whether moral judgments are the sorts of things that can be true or false. Some writers take the grammatical appearance that such judgments present—that is, the fact that they are expressed in the indicative mood—at face value and regard them as reports of normative facts, facts about what ought to be done. Others, motivated by the metaphysical and epistemological difficulties associated with the acknowledgment of moral facts, regard this grammatical appearance as misleading. These noncognitivists hold that moral judgments do not represent a kind of fact but rather express the speaker's desires or aversions. This suggests that moral expertise is not acknowledged in the contemporary world because noncognitivism is the correct account of moral judgment, and thus there is nothing about which anyone can be an expert.

Even if noncognitivism is true, however, there is still room for expert authority on moral matters. As we saw in the previous section, some people can become recognized as better than others at determining what is good from the standpoint of a particular sensibility. This is true if the sensibility has the character of a perceptual faculty, and thus gives rise to judgments that are cognitive in character, but it is also true if the sensibility is grounded in certain desires or attitudes. Those sharing a sensibility could find that a particular individual performed actions that struck them as especially fitting in situations that presented moral problems, and on this basis conclude that it would be appropriate to accept her directives or imitate her.[8]

These points can be illustrated with Aristotle's theory of moral education, as it might be applied to the case of moral learning by adults. For Aristotle, virtues of character are acquired by habituation—by repeatedly performing virtuous actions—and this in turn is a matter of imitating the actions of virtuous people. Virtuous people thus have the status, in Aristotle's scheme, of experts whose actions are worthy of emulation. But how can the nonvirtuous identify the virtuous?[9] The mechanisms discussed above provide an answer. The virtuous could be regarded as possessing a certain kind of know-how, practical wisdom, that consists in being able to act appropriately in a particular case, especially a case in which humans are tempted to act wrongly. This knowledge is revealed not by their arguments in support of certain courses of action, which the nonvirtuous might not be able to understand, but by the perceived fittingness of what they do. That is, even those who are not virtuous, and are not able to determine what would be fitting by deliberating themselves, could recognize fitting actions when performed by others and be led by this perception to take these others as models. In this way, they could acquire the ability to live a life that is satisfying to the human sensibility. Aristotle probably regarded the perception of objective values as playing a role in the superior sensibility of the virtuous, but a noncognitivist reading of his theory is also possible.

If the truth of noncognitivism is not the explanation for the fact that our society contains no generally acknowledged moral experts comparable to experts on physics, what is the explanation? An important clue is provided by the fact that the method of demonstrating moral expertise that we have envisaged makes use of an internal criterion. It consists in the demonstration to those who have a certain competence to a lower degree that others have it to a higher degree. There will, however, be general acknowledgment of exper-

---

[8] For a somewhat different account of how normative authority is possible within a noncognitivist framework, see Gibbard (1990), esp. chap. 9.

[9] G. Dworkin (1988), p. 43, notes that the virtuous have the status of experts in Aristotle's theory, but he does not say how they are to be identified.

tise established by an internal criterion only to the extent that the competence displayed is generally possessed (to some lower degree). This is not the case in the moral and evaluative domains.

If noncognitivism is true, this point can be put by saying that different people have different moral desires and aversions, and thus moral expertise can be established only within groups of people whose underlying moral motivations are similar enough to enable them to judge the same actions fitting. But the point remains sound if we opt for a view according to which moral judgments report truths and are thus vehicles for the communication of knowledge about some realm of normative facts (about what ought to be done). Even if this is so, the possession by some of greater knowledge must be established by an internal criterion. There is no external standard comparable to reliable prediction by which moral experts can be identified. The identification of such experts depends on perceived fittingness and, especially, on the presentation of compelling arguments. But the presentation of arguments can establish expertise only for those who find them persuasive. Sometimes, the underlying basis of assent to arguments of a certain sort is virtually universal, with the result that there is wide agreement on who the experts are. Mathematics, in which there are generally acknowledged experts, provides an example. We do not find the same phenomenon in assessing morality, however. It is simply not the case that there are some people who can present moral arguments that everyone finds compelling. This results in a situation in which no generally acknowledged moral experts can be expected.[10]

These points can be summed up as follows. The problem of moral authority is not a problem about whether there are normative facts about which some individuals can have superior knowledge. It is a problem that arises because moral expertise can only be established by an internal criterion. Even if there are moral facts, and some people can know them, it does not follow that these people can acquire the status of moral experts. For judgments identifying moral experts are conditioned by judgments about what is right. It is by doing something that we perceive to be right in a particular case, or presenting arguments that convince us that something is right, that certain individuals win acknowledgment as moral experts. Where there is disagreement about what is right, then, there will be dis-

---

[10] Estlund (1993), secs. 7–10, rejects what he calls normative epistemic authoritarianism (the idea that those with greater practical wisdom should rule) on the ground that reasonable people can disagree about who the knowers are. That is, disagreement about this is possible without anyone being guilty of epistemic negligence. Estlund's explanation for this is different from mine, however.

agreement about who the moral experts are. The obstacle to moral authority is not the nonexistence of moral knowledge but the existence of moral disagreement.

At least this is the obstacle to generally acknowledged moral authority on a par with authority in mathematics. To a certain extent, talented individuals may be able to reduce moral disagreement by winning acceptance as moral experts within a group of people who initially disagree. A society may be able to form itself into subgroups based on the acknowledgment within these groups of relative moral expertise. This phenomenon is found today. Especially within certain religious traditions, some people are prepared to defer to the moral judgment of people they acknowledge as moral experts, and this deference may be justified by the perceived fittingness of the experts' judgments. But many find no one to whom they think it justified to defer. They consult friends and acquaintances, but they make up their minds themselves.

The Strength of E-Authority

What are the implications of all of this for the strength of E-authority? Robustness is a function of the variety of situations in which acceptance of an authoritative communication is justified. In the case of E-authority, the justification in question is inductive, namely, a history of success as determined by either an external or internal criterion. Let us suppose that the inductive case for according someone the status of an E-authority on some topic is extremely strong: She has made many statements about this topic in the past and they have always proven correct. In this case, her assertions (or directives expressing ought-judgments, in the case of practical E-authority) will appropriately preempt almost all of the relevant assertion- or directive-independent reasons. In a wide range of possible evidential situations, it will be appropriate for others to accept what she says about what the relevant evidence is and what it supports. The only exception is the case in which others can see clearly that what she says is false. For those who have strong inductive reasons to regard a particular individual as an E-authority on certain matters, then, her authority will be quite robust.

The reach of an E-authority depends on how many of the people who have occasion to form beliefs about matters on which the individual in question is said to have greater expertise find that good inductive reasons justify them in regarding her as an E-authority. Again, let us suppose that her record of success, for those able to discern success, is extremely strong. Where the criterion of success is external, virtually everyone who has occasion to form beliefs of the relevant kind will be capable of discerning her success, and the reach of her authority will be extensive. When the criterion of success is internal, however, the reach of her E-authority will be determined by how widespread her sensibility, or susceptibility to her arguments, is. Since it is a fact of contemporary life that people differ in their moral judgments, the reach of the authority of someone who has the status, for some people, as a moral expert is not likely to be great. Most will not regard her as routinely more adept than they are (or the authorities that they acknowledge are) in determining what morality requires.

P-Authority

Now let us turn to authority justified by a promise to obey. Here again, our main concern is not whether authority can be justified by a promise, but rather how a promise justifies authority, and how strong authority justified by a promise is.

The Ground of Promissory Obligation

Two main accounts of how promises create reasons for action can be found in the literature on promising. According to one, which I call the "reliance view," promises create reasons for action by virtue of the operation of a broader principle which states that when one intentionally induces someone to rely on one's performing a certain action—that is, acts with the intention of inducing reliance—and succeeds, one creates a reason to perform the action relied upon. According to the other account, which I call the "communication view," promises create reasons for action by virtue of the operation of a principle that states that one can create certain sorts of moral reasons for action by simply communicating one's intention to create them.[11]

I have spoken of promises as creating reasons for action, but the language that is customary here is that of obligation. Promises are said to create obligations. Following Joseph Raz, we may understand the difference between obligations and other reasons for action in terms of preemption. A reason for action has the status of an obligation if it preempts some of the considerations with which it

[11] For an account of the reliance view, see MacCormick (1972). For an account of the communication view, see Raz (1977). I discuss both, and defend a reliance view, in McMahon (1989).

competes.[12] Alternatively, a reason for action makes a particular action obligatory if it works by preempting some of the other reasons that might count against performing this action. Preemption thus enables us to capture the element of bindingness or constraint that is part of the etymology of the word "obligation." There is constraint because something prevents the agent from taking into consideration, and thus acting on, all the reasons that would normally have a bearing on what to do. In a sense, however, this constraint is self-imposed because it arises from the agent's acknowledgment of a consideration having preemptive force.[13]

Either of the two views mentioned above can explain how promises create obligations, for both can be regarded as grounding promises in intermediate-level moral rules that can themselves be regarded as having preemptive force. This is easiest to see in the context of act consequentialist moral theories.[14] These theories often advocate acting on, and even inculcating, rules compliance with which will sometimes be wrong on act consequentialist grounds. Acting on such rules will be appropriate from the standpoint of these theories if the rules in question (1) identify act-types the instantiation of which is almost always the best thing one can do in any situation in which they can be instantiated, or, in the case of prohibitions, almost always suboptimal in any situation in which they can be instantiated; and (2) the situations to which the rules apply are situations in which agents are likely to be tempted by self-interest to misjudge the balance of consequentialist considerations. For example, although consequentialists armed with a certain theory might admit the possibility that the balance of good moral reasons could sometimes justify theft, they might also feel that self-interested considerations could easily tempt us to exaggerate the force of these reasons, with the result that an agent would do better in the long run by accepting a general prohibition on theft than by referring directly to ground-level consequentialist considerations.

The intermediate-level rules employed in this way by consequentialist moral theories have the status of preemptive reasons for action because (1) they exclude and replace reasoning based directly on consequentialist considerations, and (2) there is a good reason for

[12] Here "obligation" is being used broadly, so as to encompass both what would ordinarily be called obligations and what would ordinarily be called duties.

[13] The term "obligation" typically suggests stringency; obligations are thought to be strong reasons for action. But it would be a mistake to regard this as a defining feature of obligations. As Raz (1977), p. 223, notes, obligations can be trivial if the reasons preempted would in any case have had little force in the situation.

[14] Cf. Raz (1977), pp. 219–23.

giving them this status, namely, that better compliance with the underlying consequentialist considerations is likely to result.

Both the principle of reliance and the principle of communication can be regarded as intermediate-level moral rules of this sort, and thus both can ground the obligatory character of promises. Moreover, neither need be limited to working in conjunction with a utilitarian theory. Raz has suggested that the value that underlies the principle of communication is the intrinsic value of certain relationships the creation of which is facilitated by promising.[15] And although it is customary to regard the principle of reliance as identifying a utilitarian consideration—namely, the frustration of desire occasioned by the nonoccurrence of something that someone was relying on—this is not necessary. A foundational concern to minimize unfairness is also capable of justifying the acceptance of the principle of reliance as an intermediate-level rule, since disappointing reliance usually involves gaining inappropriately at someone's expense. It should be noted that when intermediate-level moral rules function as preemptive reasons, they are reasons to act against one's judgment of what the balance of reasons requires, not against the real or actual balance of reasons. If they prevent one from being led astray by one's own calculations, they secure action in accordance with the actual balance.

This is not the place to discuss the relative merits of the two views of promising, and thus I leave open the question of which of them is preferable. When one or the other has special implications for my argument, I shall point this out.

The Strength of P-Authority

Showing that promises can be preemptive reasons for action does not by itself give us P-authority because the general form of preemption involved in intermediate-level moral rules does not involve replacement by directives. It is more like a decision. One acts not on the balance of reasons as one sees them at a particular time but on the basis of some previous deliberation that one—or one's society— has engaged in. Indeed, Raz refers to rules as general decisions.[16] But since a promise can create a moral reason to do something that there was formerly no moral reason to do, the obligatory force of the

[15] Raz (1977), pp. 217–18. The classical view of this sort is provided by Rousseau, who regards the social contract as bringing into existence a new form of life and new goods that are superior to those replaced. See Raz (1986), p. 80.

[16] Raz (1978), p. 139.

moral rule requiring the keeping of promises is easily transferred to complying with someone's directives. One need only make such compliance the content of a promise. That is, one can create a pre-emptive reason to comply with someone's directives, and thus confer the status of preemptive reasons on the directives, by promising to comply with them.

Although this shows that P-authority can be genuine authority, serious questions arise about its strength. The difficulties here can be brought out by considering what the situation would be if promises did not create preemptive reasons for action, but rather reasons that had to prevail by outweighing others. In this case, we could not, strictly speaking, regard a promise to comply with someone's directives as creating an authority relation, for the mark of authority is preemption. Let us call the relation created "quasi–P-authority." Despite the fact that quasi–P-authority is not P-authority, a given quasi–P-authority would have moral powers virtually equivalent to those of a P-authority if the promise to comply with his directives routinely outweighed the directive-independent considerations counseling noncompliance. How likely would this be?

When the competing considerations are nonmoral, a quasi–P-authority will indeed have moral powers virtually equivalent to those of a genuine P-authority. Moral reasons for action almost always outweigh nonmoral reasons, and a promissory obligation is a moral reason for action. When the competing considerations are moral, however, the moral powers of a quasi–P-authority will be significantly diminished. The promissory obligation that provides a reason for the subordinates of such an authority to comply with his directives will have to outweigh other considerations of the same type, and will frequently be unable to do so. A promissory obligation is, after all, only one moral consideration among many, and the others may be sufficient, alone or in combinations, to prevail against it. So quasi–P-authority will have considerably less strength when the competing considerations are moral.

Ordinary P-authority is, however, in the same predicament. The preemptiveness of promissory obligation is the preemptiveness of intermediate-level moral rules, and such rules do not typically preempt competing moral considerations. This can be seen in ordinary cases not involving authority. One's duty to care for a sick child, for example, would usually outweigh a promise to give a lecture. But there is no reason why a promise to comply with someone's directives should be any different. So it appears to be possible to regard promissory obligations to obey as preemptive only when the competing considerations are nonmoral. When they are moral, P-authority is no better than quasi–P-authority. Indeed, P-authority just is quasi-P-authority.

Let us examine why this is so in more detail. It is true that the point of intermediate-level moral rules is to prevent us from being swayed not only by nonmoral considerations that might tempt us to act inappropriately but also by moral considerations that are tainted by self-interest, in the sense of being given excessive weight because they coincide with self-interest in the case at hand. But in the first place, the exclusionary force of the reasons associated with a particular intermediate moral rule does not apply to other moral reasons grounded in intermediate moral rules. Reasons grounded in these rules must simply be weighed against each other. And second, intermediate rules can be bypassed, so that moral deliberation takes place directly in terms of the foundational considerations that support the rules. Writers who make a place for intermediate rules typically provide that one may ignore them and consider directly what the underlying reasons support "in a cool hour," that is, when one has time for reflection and is not at the moment experiencing any temptations. This gives rise to talk of two levels of moral thinking.[17] When one rises to the higher level, however, one simply assesses the weight of the values that underlie a rule relative to all of the other moral values acknowledged as having foundational significance. In the case of promising (on the reliance interpretation), for example, one considers the weight of considerations of reliance or fairness relative to the other values regarded as foundational by the particular theory that one accepts. When one has time to reflect on whether to keep a promise, then, the exclusionary character of the intermediate rule that justifies keeping it evaporates.

It might be argued that if promises did not preempt moral as well as self-interested considerations, they would be useless for the purpose of inducing reliance. For we can never be sure that moral considerations will have no bearing on whether an agent should perform a particular action in the future. In fact, however, we can often predict with a great deal of confidence that the promised action will be permissible at the time it is to be performed, and thus that the promise will be a decisive consideration in favor of performing it. The promised action might be permissible because no other moral considerations are relevant to its performance, or because the other applicable moral considerations cancel each other out.

There is another point to mention. We may suppose that on nei-

---

[17] For a two-level view, see Hare (1981).

ther interpretation of the rule of promising can a promise obligate the promisor to do something the wrongness of which is common knowledge between him and the promisee. If, however, the promised act is one that there will be (exclusive of the promise) sufficient moral reason not to perform, yet at the time of the promise neither party knows this, the fact that it was promised can count as a reason for performing it that may be able to tip the balance in favor of performance. If one intentionally induces someone to rely on one's acting in a certain way, unaware that there will be (exclusive of this induction of reliance) sufficient moral reason against acting in this way, and he relies on one's performance not knowing this either, the fact of his reliance must be taken into account in reaching a conclusion about what morality requires one to do. That is, innocent reliance can create a moral reason for doing something that there would otherwise be sufficient moral reason for not doing, and this reason may be able to tip the balance of all applicable considerations in favor of doing it. Similar points apply to the communication view of promising.[18]

Promises need not, then, be able to preempt competing moral considerations to play an important role in our lives. Nevertheless, there are serious questions about the strength of P-authority when the directive-independent considerations that bear on the appropriateness of some action that one has been ordered to perform include moral considerations. A promise to comply with someone's directives is a promise to perform whatever action in some set of actions, usually roughly specified in advance, the person to whom the promise is made may choose. Since the set is specified in advance, it seems that one could consider whether there will be decisive moral reasons against performing any of the actions one might be called on to perform and modify the promise accordingly. To do this, however, one must be able to anticipate what the situation will be at the time one is called on to perform a given action. And although this may be relatively unproblematic in the case of simple promise—so that only rarely will one discover later a good reason to break a promise to give a lecture at a particular time—it poses a

---

[18] A couple of other points are worth noting. First, the claim that a promise to do something known to be wrong cannot be binding is true only if we speak of what is wrong, all things considered. A promise to do what is presumptively wrong, for example, lie, may be binding if it is not wrong, all things considered. One might, say, promise to lie to a murderer about the whereabouts of his intended victim. Similarly, when other moral reasons are involved, false promising may be justified. An example would be a case in which one falsely promises to contribute to an immoral enterprise because one knows that if one does not the promisee will find someone whose cooperation can be relied upon.

substantial epistemic challenge when one may be called on to perform any of a variety of actions at any time in the indefinite future. When one has promised to obey someone's directives, then, the likelihood that decisive contrary considerations unanticipated at the time the promise was made will become evident at the time performance is required is significantly greater than with an ordinary promise.[19]

The upshot of these observations is that both the robustness and the reach of P-authority will often be diminished when the directive-independent considerations that support not complying with a P-authority's directive are moral. They are diminished relative to what they would be if the directive-independent considerations were exclusively self-interested. In such circumstances, somebody whom one has promised to obey (in a certain area of one's life) will have the status of a legitimate P-authority only intermittently. And at any given time, a significant percentage of the members of a group all of whom have promised to obey directives emanating from a certain source may find that they cannot regard this source as a legitimate P-authority. This latter result is especially likely if, as I am supposing, the members of a society hold different conceptions of the moral good.[20]

C-Authority

The General Basis of C-Authority

The third species of authority that we have distinguished is C-authority, authority justified as facilitating mutually beneficial cooperation. People can often improve their situation *by their own lights* if they cooperate with others. This is because by acting together the members of a group can produce an event or state of affairs that each values but that none of them could have produced alone. Authority can facilitate such cooperation.[21]

---

[19] To say that the considerations are decisive is to say that they would outweigh even innocent reliance.

[20] These observations have obvious relevance to the feasibility of deriving a reason to obey the law from a promise to obey. Discussions of this way of underwriting political authority, which is associated with consent theories, usually focus on whether most of the members of a given society can plausibly be regarded as having done anything that has the force of a promise to obey the law. Even if they can, however, there will often be moral reasons against complying with a given law that are capable of outweighing a promissory obligation to obey. This topic receives further discussion in Chapter Eight.

[21] The possibility of justifying authority in this way is discussed by R. Friedman (1990). Finnis (1990) emphasizes that when it comes to organizing cooperation, groups have only two options: unanimity or authority.

To see this, we must first be more precise about the rational structure of mutually beneficial cooperation. Let us call the event or state of affairs produced by cooperation X. Looking at cooperation to produce X from the standpoint of an agent A who is contemplating contributing to this effort, we may distinguish three evaluative quantities. There is the incremental increase in the value of X (from A's point of view) that A's contribution will create. There is the total value that X will have for A when her contribution is added to those of the others who have contributed or who will contribute. And there is the cost to A of her contribution. Cost is to be understood as opportunity cost, the value to A of the best alternative she could realize with the resources she is contemplating contributing. It must be emphasized that we are looking at all of these quantities from A's standpoint, not from a standpoint that takes everyone's interests into account. In mutually beneficial cooperation, each agent participates to advance her own aims.

With these distinctions before us, we can divide the cases in which mutually beneficial cooperation is possible into two kinds. In the first, the incremental increase in the value of X that an agent's contribution will produce is greater than the cost to her of contributing. In such cases, a principle of rational action, which I call the "principle of individual rationality," justifies contributing to the production of X. In cooperative contexts it reads:

> *The Principle of Individual Rationality.* One has reason to contribute to a cooperative venture that produces something that one regards as good if the incremental increase in the value of this good that will be created by one's contribution exceeds the cost to one of contributing.

In the second kind of case, the incremental increase in the value of X that an agent's contribution will produce is not greater than the cost to her of contributing, and thus individual rationality does not justify contributing.[22]

This is not the end of the matter, however, at least when cooperation takes the form of the production of public goods, goods that cannot be provided to any of the members of some group without being provided to all of them. In many, perhaps most, such cases, while the incremental increase in the value of X that each individual's contribution will create does not exceed the cost to her of contributing, the value that X will have for each when her contribution is added to those of the others who have contributed, or will contrib-

[22] For a discussion of when individual rationality justifies contributing to the joint production of a good, see Olson (1971), pp. 22–36.

ute, is greater than the cost to her of contributing. This is possible because, since X is a public good, the contribution that each makes does not benefit her alone. There are, to use the technical economic term, positive externalities associated with contribution. The incremental increase in the value of X that each contribution produces is an increase for everyone in the group, and if many contribute, the aggregate value for each of all these increases may exceed the cost to her of her contribution.

In cases of this sort, conformity to the principle of individual rationality by everyone in the group brings an avoidable loss for all, since it dictates not contributing. But if enough people in the group ignore individual rationality and contribute anyway, the benefit that each contributor receives will exceed the cost to her of her contribution. To provide everyone with a reason for contributing in such situations, we need to introduce a second principle of rationality, which I call the "principle of collective rationality." It may be formulated as follows:

> *The Principle of Collective Rationality.* One has reason to contribute to a cooperative venture that produces something that one regards as good if its total value to one when one's contribution is added to those of the others who have contributed or will contribute exceeds the cost to one of contributing.

Collective rationality is not the rationality of a group understood as a distinct entity. It is a different way for individuals to process the rational import of the considerations that they acknowledge as reasons for action, a way different from the way provided by individual rationality. It exists only because individual rationality has collectively disadvantageous consequences for individuals in certain situations where each would benefit from cooperation. For the purposes of the principle of collective rationality, an action counts as a contribution if it increases the value of the good produced (which, since this good is public, increases the benefit to each contributor) or reduces the cost to each contributor of producing it.

The principle of collective rationality provides a reason to contribute to a cooperative effort only if enough others will cooperate to create a good that has a total value for one which exceeds the cost of contributing. When a cooperative endeavor meeting the conditions specified by the principle of collective rationality is not already in place, then, the principle will underwrite mutually beneficial cooperation only if the *assurance problem* can be solved, that is, only if there is good reason for each to believe that enough others will contribute. It should also be noted that some cases in which the principle of individual rationality alone can underwrite mutually beneficial cooperation also require that an assurance problem be solved. These are cases in which the incremental increase in the value of X produced by one's contribution will exceed its cost to one only if it is made in combination with contributions by others. We consider these matters in more detail in the next section.

There is one case of cooperation justified by the principle of collective rationality that deserves special mention. This is the case where a cooperative project producing a public good is already underway, and thus individual rationality dictates being a free rider on the contributions of others. Here the assurance problem is solved trivially; others are already making their contributions. Thus, the justification for contributing as well proceeds straightforwardly from the principle of collective rationality. As was noted earlier, the principle of collective rationality is meant to cover not only the case in which one's contribution will increase the value to one of the good produced but also the case in which it will merely reduce the cost that each contributor has to bear. Of course, the total value of X for each must still exceed the cost (the opportunity cost) to each of her contribution.

For the principle of collective rationality to yield these results, the benefits that one could reap as a free rider must be disregarded in calculating the opportunity cost of contributing. The opportunities considered in calculating this cost must be restricted to those that would still be available if the cooperative project did not exist. This is, in effect, to make the benchmark for rational cooperation the noncooperative outcome. One has reason to contribute to a cooperative scheme if the benefit that one receives from it exceeds the maximum benefit one could have obtained, using the resources one would have contributed, had the scheme not existed. The opportunities by which the value of the noncooperative outcome is assessed, however, need not be restricted to opportunities to benefit by unilateral action. They can also include opportunities to benefit by participating in some alternative cooperative scheme. The principle of collective rationality will not justify cooperating in the production of X if one could instead contribute the resources involved to the production of some good Y with greater benefit to oneself.

The rationale for the principle of collective rationality is as follows. Reason is general, and treats like cases alike. From the standpoint of reason, then, if all the members of some group find themselves in a situation where the value of some collectively producible good would exceed the cost to each of her contribution, it must be the case either that all have sufficient reason to contribute to its production (if the assurance problem can be solved) or that none have. Thus, to take a case where the assurance problem is solved, if all are already contributing—perhaps because a habit of contributing was inculcated in childhood—it must be the case either that each has sufficient reason to continue (that reason endorses the habit of each) or that each has sufficient reason to desist (that the habit of each is contrary to reason). But only the former alternative yields the result that individuals have sufficient reason to reap fully the benefits deriving from the positive externalities associated with the production of public goods. So if, as Kurt Baier has said, the point of practical reasoning is to enable us to get more of what we want or to avoid more of what we want to avoid, contributing must be what practical reason requires.[23] Similar reasoning justifies interpreting the opportunity costs of contributing so that they do not include the benefits obtainable by free riding.[24]

The principle of collective rationality is not a moral principle, and it identifies what *there is* good reason for agents to do, regardless of their beliefs about the situation they are in. Thus, the justification for contributing to cooperative ventures that it provides is different from those provided by the natural duty of justice or the principle of fair play. I say more about this later in the chapter. It might be thought that the principle of collective rationality could be dispensed with, since if a group finds itself confronting the indefinite repetition of a game having a prisoner's-dilemma structure, individual rationality alone can often justify each member in cooperating. In particular, a strategy of initial cooperation followed by mimicking the opponent's previous move (tit-for-tat) will often be individually rational. But I do not want to tie my argument to the possibility of repetition. Some groups may routinely confront situations that are novel from the game-theoretic standpoint. Indeed, as we shall see, it is precisely when what would constitute rational cooperation changes often that authority has a distinctive role to play.[25]

Given this account of the rational structure of mutually beneficial

[23] See Baier (1958), p. 301.

[24] The argument in this paragraph assumes that all rational agents will do whatever practical reason is understood to require in a situation. That is, it is meant as a contribution to what might be called the full-compliance theory of practical reason. It combines this assumption with a further assumption about the point of practical reasoning. It is not intended as a justification of collective rationality to individual rationality. For an argument of the latter sort, see Gauthier (1986). For a discussion of some related issues, see McClennen (1992).

[25] An anonymous reader pointed out the need for clarification here. For an account of the strategy of tit-for-tat see Axelrod (1984). For another limitation of tit-for-tat, which is applicable to many of the cases involving incremental goods that we shall consider, see Pettit (1986).

cooperation, what is the role of authority in facilitating it? I consider this question in more detail shortly, but for the time being we may take its principal role as solving the assurance problem. Suppose that there exists within a community an individual who is able to secure general compliance with his directives by threatening to punish anyone who does not comply with them. This sort of directive power could be used to give the members of the community sufficient reason under the principle of individual rationality to contribute to a cooperative scheme contribution to which was supported by the principle of collective rationality. Its use for this purpose would be welcomed even by those who were prepared to comply with the principle of collective rationality. It would provide assurances that others would make their contributions, since it would create a situation in which they experienced no conflict between the dictates of collective rationality and the dictates of individual rationality.[26]

Of course, punitive sanctions could also justify contributing to a cooperative effort that was not supported by the principle of collective rationality, so we must distinguish cases in which such sanctions make mutually beneficial cooperation possible (and are justified by this fact) from cases in which they are used to force people to do things that do not benefit them. Although someone whose directive power derives solely from his ability to apply coercive sanctions is not a de facto authority, I call any individual or group that uses any kind of directive power to facilitate mutually beneficial cooperation by solving the assurance problem a legitimate C-authority.

An effective source of coercion could, then, count as a legitimate C-authority if its coercive power was used to solve the assurance problem associated with rational cooperation. The results described in the preceding paragraph can be secured more economically and more effectively, however, if there exists in a community a source of directives whose directive power takes the form of de facto authority. Where there is de facto authority, people are prepared, without the threat of punishment or the hope of reward, to comply with the authority's directives. And since the directives of a de facto authority are taken as preemptive reasons for action, it will be possible for each member of a group that receives directives from a source whose status as a de facto authority is common knowledge within the group to have more confidence that the others in the group will comply with them than he could if they were supported by coercive

---

[26] As has been noted, cooperation that could be justified by the principle of individual rationality may also require that an assurance problem be solved, which means that authority could play a role in such cases as well, but for the time being I shall ignore this complication.

sanctions, which must outweigh competing considerations. Of course, like coercion, de facto authority could be used to secure the performance of actions that did not benefit those performing them. On the model of the coercion case, we can call de facto authority that facilitates mutually beneficial cooperation by solving the assurance problem justified or legitimate C-authority, and de facto authority that does not facilitate mutually beneficial cooperation unjustified or illegitimate, unless it can claim legitimacy as P-authority or E-authority.[27]

The Game-Theoretic Structure of Cooperation

We have just considered in a general way how authority can be justified as facilitating cooperation, but we need to be more precise about how such justifications work. The first step is to characterize more accurately the situations in which C-authority can play a role. Game theory provides a useful tool for doing this. Two main kinds of games are relevant here. A coordination game provides a paradigm of a situation in which the principle of individual rationality alone can justify contributing to a cooperative venture, and the prisoner's dilemma provides a paradigm of a situation in which the principle of collective rationality is necessary to justify contributing.

A simple example of a coordination game is the case in which two people want to meet and do not care where they meet. Let us suppose that there are two possibilities, they can meet at the flagpole or at the pier. Thus, each has two strategies, to go to the flagpole or to go to the pier. The situation they face is illustrated by Figure 1, with each getting a payoff of 1 if they meet and 0 if they do not.[28]

An outcome of a choice of strategies is an equilibrium if no party could have done better by acting differently, given what the others have done. It is a coordination equilibrium if no party could have done better if any one person, himself or another, had acted differently. In the case illustrated above, meeting at the pier and at the flagpole are both coordination equilibria because neither would have been better off if either alone had acted differently. A coordination problem arises when there are two or more coordination equilibria and one must be made the basis of cooperation. Figure 1 illustrates a simple coordination problem.

---

[27] Because the function of C-authority is to solve the assurance problem, a given source of directives can be vindicated as a legitimate C-authority only if it has de facto authority or some other form of directive power. Cf. Raz (1986), p. 56.

[28] A's payoffs are indicated by the number in the lower left corner of each box, and B's by the number in the upper right corner.

B

	Flagpole	Pier
Flagpole	1 1	0 0
Pier	0 0	1 1

A

Fig. 1. A Simple Coordination Problem

Some established social practices are coordination equilibria; they are solutions to coordination problems. The most familiar is the practice (in the United States) of driving on the right. The principle of individual rationality is sufficient to maintain such practices, but we should note the role played by assurance. Each has sufficient reason, under the principle of individual rationality, to contribute to the realization of the particular coordination equilibrium the practice realizes because each believes that the others will contribute to its realization as well. When a group faces the task of establishing coordination, however, some way must be found to provide this assurance. Still, this is often easily done. Since each wants to contribute if the others do, it is enough if one of the equilibria can somehow be made *salient* within in the group.

Since authorities can make coordination equilibria salient by directing their production, there is a role for authority in solving coordination problems. Indeed, the existence of coordination problems enables us to broaden the account offered earlier of how authority facilitates cooperation. It may do this not only by solving the assurance problem when there is just one strategy by which mutually beneficial cooperation can be accomplished but also by choosing among different available cooperative strategies.

The familiar prisoner's dilemma is named for a problem of cooperative action involving two prisoners who are known by the authorities to be guilty of two crimes, a lesser offense and a greater offense. The authorities want a conviction for the greater offense, but only have evidence sufficient to convict the prisoners of the lesser offense. They thus confront the prisoners with the payoff matrix found in Figure 2, where the negative payoffs represent years in jail, and confessing is understood to involve implicating the other.

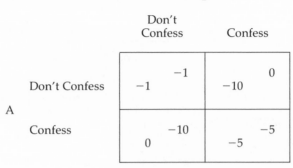

Fig. 2. The Prisoner's Dilemma

This situation differs from a coordination problem in that the cooperative outcome, neither confessing, is not an equilibrium of any kind. Each does better by defecting from it given that the other does not. Indeed, defecting is a dominating strategy. The payoff that each agent receives from his action depends on a factor over which he has no control, what the other does. But no matter what this is, confessing will be best for each. If both follow this course, however, both will be worse off. Thus, there is good reason for them to cooperate even though individual rationality dictates noncooperation.

When there is more than one cooperative strategy available in a prisoner's dilemma situation, individuals who accept the principle of collective rationality face a coordination problem. That is, a coordination problem can be embedded within a prisoner's dilemma problem. The matrix in Figure 3 provides a simple illustration. "C1" stands for cooperative strategy 1, "C2" stands for cooperative strategy 2, and "NC" stands for the noncooperative strategy. Those who accept a reason to cooperate will avoid the noncooperative strategy, but will need some way to make either (C1,C1) or (C2,C2) salient if they are to realize fully the benefits of cooperation.

Now that we have considered these representative two-person games, let us turn to multiperson cooperation. Here individuals cooperate to produce a public good. Sometimes multiperson cooperation can be justified by the principle of individual rationality alone, and sometimes collective rationality must play a role. But the rational structure of such cooperation is more complicated than in the two-person case.

B

		C1	C2	NC
	C1	6 6	2 2	9 −5
A	C2	2 2	6 6	9 −5
	NC	−5 9	−5 9	0 0

Fig. 3. A Coordination Problem within a Prisoner's Dilemma

These matters have been explored in detail by Jean Hampton.[29] She makes a distinction between cases where the public good produced by a cooperative effort is an *incremental good* and the cases where it is a *step good*. In cases of the former sort, each cooperative act makes some incremental contribution to the good to be produced, augmenting its value for the agent (although perhaps by only a tiny amount). Contributing to clean air by installing pollution control equipment is an example. In the case of a step good, by contrast, the contributions do not create any value until a certain threshold number of contributions have been made, at which point a good having a certain value for each comes into existence. Further contributions may either add no additional value, add it in another step after a further threshold is crossed, or augment it incrementally. An example of a step good of the first sort is a bridge. A partially completed bridge produces no benefit, and after it is completed, continuing to "build" it is a waste. As Hampton notes, the distinction between incremental and step goods is not sharp. As the steps become smaller, a good produced in a number of steps turns into an incremental good.

As we have seen, when the increase in the value of some collectively produced item created by a given agent's contribution exceeds the cost to her of contributing, individual rationality justifies contributing. Typically, however, the production of an incremental good does not satisfy this condition. Each contribution adds some-

[29] See Hampton (1986, 1987).

111

thing to the value of the good, and since it is a public good, everyone in the relevant group benefits from each contribution. But for each increment, the cost to the producer usually exceeds the augmentation in the value of the good that results. Thus, from the standpoint of individual rationality, contributing to its production is not rational, and ceasing to contribute if one has been doing so is rational. If a group is to produce such a good, and incentives of some kind are not available, its members must accept the principle of collective rationality. Since noncontribution to the production of an incremental good is a dominating strategy—at least when the incremental increase that one could effect is less than the cost to one for all levels of contribution by others—the production of such goods resembles the prisoner's dilemma. It should be noted, however, that here, too, this prisoner's dilemma structure can contain within it a coordination game (for those who accept the principle of collective rationality) if there are several different incremental goods a group could rationally produce and one must be chosen.

On the face of it, step goods seem to be similar. If there have been enough previous contributions so that one's own action will result in the crossing of the threshold and the production of the good, individual rationality will dictate contributing. But if not enough contributions have been made (or more than enough have), the cost to a given agent if her contribution will exceed the incremental benefit that she receives from making it and contributing will thus be irrational. And it is so unlikely that one's contribution will cause the threshold to be crossed that this possibility can apparently be disregarded. Once again, then, it seems that a source of reasons for action independent of individual rationality is required if a group is to produce the good.

As Hampton has shown, however, individual rationality often has the resources to underwrite a collective effort to produce a step good. This can be seen when it is noticed that it is not just the person who finds that exactly enough previous contributions have been made to render his contribution decisive in bringing the good into existence who is given a reason to contribute by the principle of individual rationality. Cooperation will also be individually rational for those who have an opportunity to contribute earlier, if they know that exactly enough others will contribute so that when all the contributions are added together, the threshold will be crossed. Within such a minimally sufficient set of agents, contributing is rational for everyone because producing the cooperative outcome is a coordination equilibrium. None does better if any fail to contribute. But this means that if some way can be found to select a minimally sufficient

112

set of producers from the larger set of those who could contribute, and to make their membership in it common knowledge among them, individual rationality will suffice to secure the production of a step good.

The problem facing a group that would benefit from the production of a step good is not, then, getting people to contribute to a plan that divides the group into a minimally sufficient set of producers and a set of nonproducers. Any such plan will identify a coordination equilibrium for the group as a whole. For no one member, either one of those designated as a producer or one of those designated as a nonproducer, will do better if anyone alone departs from the plan. The problem is rather generating (and making common knowledge) a plan that divides the group into a minimally sufficient set of producers and a set of nonproducers. This is a coordination problem, a matter of choosing between different ways of assigning behaviors to the group each of which has the status of coordination equilibrium. As we have seen, individual rationality can solve such problems if some way can be found to make one of the equilibria salient.

The problem of making one of the equilibria salient, however, must not be minimized. In many situations where a group faces a coordination problem, agreement suffices to make one of the equilibria salient. But in cases of the sort we are now concerned with, agreement will be difficult because the members of the group will have conflicting preferences among the various possible equilibria. Each will prefer an equilibrium in which he is a nonproducer to an equilibrium in which he is a producer. The situation the group faces is thus a multiperson analogue of another two-person game discussed in the literature, the so-called battle of the sexes game—after the paradigm case in which a husband and wife want to do different things, but each would rather do what the other wants with her or him than do what he or she wants alone. Their situation is represented by the matrix found in Figure 4, in which A prefers to go sailing and B prefers to go riding. As can be seen, there are two coordination equilibria, but each ranks them differently.

In a battle of the sexes problem, there is no difficulty securing compliance with a cooperative scheme that has somehow been made salient and, a fortiori, with a scheme that is already in existence. Even those who find the scheme suboptimal do better by contributing than they would by not contributing. But there can be serious problems about selecting a scheme to implement, since each will try to make salient a scheme in which his preferred coordination equilibrium is realized.

Indeed, the situation individuals trying to create a step good face

B

	Sailing	Riding
Sailing	1 \\ 2	0 \\ 0
Riding	0 \\ 0	2 \\ 1

A

Fig. 4. The Battle of the Sexes

in making a particular scheme salient itself has a characteristic game-theoretic structure, that of the game of chicken. Each will agree to be one of the producers if the only alternative is the nonproduction of the good. But each would prefer to be a nonproducer. Thus, each will judge it rational to stall, hoping that a sufficient number of others will find the prospect of nonproduction threatening enough to join the set of producers before he finds this prospect threatening enough. The matrix for a game of chicken resembles the prisoner's dilemma except that in the prisoner's dilemma, each finds unilateral contribution the worst outcome and general noncooperation the next worst. In a game of chicken, it is the other way around. Thus, each can be induced to contribute unilaterally by the threat of general noncooperation. A representative matrix is found in Figure 5.

Given that it has the character of a chicken game, the problem of dividing the group into a set of producers and a set of nonproducers can be solved by individual rationality alone if there is some dead-

B

	Cooperate	Do not Cooperate
Cooperate	5 \\ 5	8 \\ 3
Do not Cooperate	3 \\ 8	0 \\ 0

A

Fig. 5. A Chicken Game

line by which a decision must be made. As the deadline approaches, the threat of the outcome that each prefers least, namely, the good's not being produced at all, becomes more tangible, and some people start to "chicken out" in the face of this threat. That is, they agree to become producers. When enough do, the group as a whole is divided into a minimally sufficient set of producers and a set of nonproducers.

Chicken games can arise not only in the process of designating a set of producers of a step good but also in the process of implementing the plan that organizes the actions of the producers. The designation of a minimally sufficient set of producers will usually be relative to some understanding of how much work can reasonably be expected of any individual. The minimum number necessary is the minimal number that can produce the good if each does that much work. Often, however, it is physically possible for each of the members of the set of producers to do more. Thus it is rational for each member of this set to shirk, trying to get the others to do more than their allotted share of the work. This shirking will have the character of a chicken game since each will be willing to do more than his share if necessary to prevent the project from collapsing.

This point can be generalized to the case where the designated set of producers of a step good is larger than minimally sufficient, including the case where everyone in the larger group is designated as a producer, perhaps because it is thought that fairness requires that each do a little bit (as opposed to a few doing a lot). Any such group of designated producers will face a chicken game created by attempts to shirk. Still, individual rationality alone will suffice to get the good produced because as the threat of noncooperation becomes more tangible, some will chicken out and start contributing. The resulting division of labor will not, however, retain any fairness the initial plan may have had.

This picture of how step goods can be produced by individually rational agents may seem to have an air of artificiality about it because the idea of dividing a group into a set of producers and a set of nonproducers seems strange. But it can be seen as cogent if we suppose that those who are designated as nonproducers of a particular step good are put to work producing a different one, or that a group seeking to produce a step good is divided into a number of subgroups each of which is responsible for a part (which itself has a step structure) of the larger good. In such cases, chicken games of the sort just discussed will arise if there is a certain redundancy in the assignments, so that those assigned to each task do not actually constitute the minimum number necessary to perform it.

The Justification of C-Authority: Incremental Goods

Now that we have a more precise understanding of the kinds of situations in which individuals might cooperate, we can return to the question of how facilitating cooperation justifies authority. Let us begin by considering cooperation to produce an incremental good. It has already been suggested that the principal role for authority when cooperation is justified by either the principle of collective rationality or the principle of individual rationality is to contribute to the solution of the assurance problem by lending its directive power to particular mutually beneficial cooperative strategies. In the simplest case, such directives merely direct what everyone in the group already understands to be required to achieve mutually beneficial cooperation. But when a group that accepts the rationality of cooperation could implement any of several mutually beneficial schemes, authoritative directives can also perform the task of making one of the plans salient.

For two reasons, however, it might be claimed that playing this role does not actually justify authority. The first is that while a given source of directives may facilitate cooperation, the mere fact that it does this does not justify us in regarding its directives as preemptive reasons for action, and thus does not establish it as a genuine authority. The second is that while de facto authority can facilitate cooperation, it is not the most effective or efficient social mechanism for doing so.

Let us begin with the first objection. As we have seen, contribution to the production of incremental goods is often rational only under the principle of collective rationality. But we are supposing this to be a valid principle of practical reason. We may, then, take it that there is good reason for all of those who satisfy the conditions specified by the principle in a particular case to contribute to the production of an incremental good, as long as the assurance problem is solved. Moreover, the directives of a de facto authority can solve the assurance problem even better than coercive sanctions because they will be regarded as preempting competing considerations. The problem we face, then, is to show how the fact that the directives of a de facto authority make action on the principle of collective rationality possible *justifies* regarding them as preemptive reasons for action.

The solution can be found in the fact that the reasons that justify compliance with a directive that would create an optimal level of an incremental good are reasons of collective rationality—by complying, one acts as collective rationality requires in the situation—while the directive-independent reasons that justify noncompliance are reasons of individual rationality. In general, the principle of collective rationality preempts the principle of individual rationality. Only if the requirement that it articulates excludes and replaces the judgment deriving from individual rationality will the cooperative benefits associated with compliance with it be achieved. If collective rationality were merely a source of reasons that had to be weighed alongside those deriving from individual rationality, it would not always prevail. And every case in which it failed to prevail would be a case in which individuals failed to achieve the benefits of cooperation.

Given this understanding, we can regard the directives of an authority that facilitates cooperation to produce an incremental good as acquiring preemptive force vis-à-vis the directive-independent reasons that counsel noncompliance by riding piggyback on the preemption of individual rationality by collective rationality. That is, the reason to comply with the directive is that collective rationality justifies the action that results, and since collective rationality preempts individual rationality, the directive does too. Moreover, the reason that the principle of collective rationality provides to comply with the directives of a C-authority is a directive-dependent reason, in the sense of a reason that comes into existence with the directive. The reason for action provided by the principle of collective rationality only becomes active when the assurance problem is solved, and it is the promulgation of the directive that provides the required assurance.

This means that we can regard C-authority that makes it possible for a group to produce an incremental good as satisfying Raz's normal justification thesis. To be sure, when the situation is viewed through the lens of individual rationality, the members of the group may better comply with the reasons that apply to them by rejecting authority and acting as free riders. But when the situation is viewed through the lens of collective rationality, they will better comply with the applicable reasons by accepting authority. And collective rationality takes precedence over individual rationality.

Now let us turn to the second objection to regarding the facilitation of cooperation to produce incremental goods as justifying authority. This is that a society whose members accept the principle of collective rationality need not make use of an authority to solve the assurance problem since they could solve it in other ways.[30]

---

[30] Green (1988), p. 147, puts this point as follows. A de facto authority that enables the members of a group to produce at an optimal level various public goods is itself a kind of public good. But this public good cannot have been produced with the benefit

The most important of these alternatives to de facto authority is reliance on conventional social norms dictating cooperative action. To know that such a norm is in place is to know that others are disposed to act cooperatively. Thus, if one accepts the dictates of collective rationality, one will have a good reason to act cooperatively as well. Since even individual rationality dictates encouraging such dispositions in others, it is easy to explain how norms of this sort could become established in a society. And they provide a mechanism for solving the assurance problem that requires fewer social resources to maintain than de facto authority.[31]

As it happens, however, there are good reasons for relying on authority rather than norms to solve the assurance problem in an important class of social situations, namely, those in which a scheme of cooperative action must be put into place quickly, or there are frequent changes in context of action that in turn alter what scheme of cooperation would be most beneficial for the members of a group. Norm formation is a slow process, and once norms are in place, they can be hard to change. But groups must often be able to make quick changes in their cooperative actions. At the level of societal action, this is one important reason for relying on laws, understood as authoritative directives applicable to the populace generally, rather than conventional social norms. The importance of authority is even clearer in such organizations as armies or corporations, however. These organizations must be able to change cooperative strategies rapidly, and norm formation is simply too slow a process for solving the assurance problem, even assuming that everyone accepts the priority of collective to individual rationality. When some source of directives is commonly known to be a de facto authority, by contrast, all in the relevant group can be assured of general compliance with any cooperative strategy it directs, even a novel one.

The Justification of C-Authority: Step Goods

The production of a step good presents a battle of the sexes problem, which is a kind of coordination problem. One of the coordination equilibria that consists in the division of the group into producers

---

of authoritative directives, and if one public good can be produced in this way, why not others? Green regards this argument as establishing that authority cannot be justified as facilitating cooperation. The discussion that follows explains why I do not agree.

[31] For an account of the role of norms in solving prisoner's-dilemma problems, see Ullman-Margalit (1977), chap. 2; and for an account of norm formation, see James Coleman (1990), chap. 11. Finnis (1990) notes that the authority of rulers complements norm-formation.

and nonproducers must be chosen. The earlier discussion suggests that authority would be useful here. The principle of individual rationality alone can provide the parties with a reason to contribute to any such scheme that gains salience, but authority can play a important role in making one of them salient.

Here, too, it might be objected that a source of directives that plays this role is not a genuine authority, and unlike the parallel objection to authority that facilitates the production of incremental goods, this objection has some force. For if, in coordination games, individual rationality alone justifies contributing to the realization of a coordination equilibrium that has been made salient, individual rationality alone justifies complying with a directive that makes a given equilibrium salient. But it would be misleading to characterize its doing this as its providing a reason to contribute that preempts reasons of some other sort for not contributing. Rather, the situation is one in which individual rationality supports one course of action prior to the issuing of the directive and another after. In this case, the principle of individual rationality does not establish the directive as a preemptive reason for action.[32]

Despite this, however, it will still usually be possible to regard a source of directives that facilitates the production of step goods as a genuine authority. For the principle of individual rationality will not be the only source of reasons underwriting compliance with these directives.

In the first place, collective rationality will often play a significant role in such cases as well. As we have seen, the implementation of a plan to produce a step good that designates a set of producers will often be accompanied by chicken games if the producers act on the principle of individual rationality. This will happen if the set of designated producers is not actually minimally sufficient, and shirking is thus possible. To be sure, individual rationality can usually secure the production of the good in such cases because eventually some will chicken out and take on the role of producers. But the members of the group as a whole might find this process undesirable. Although each may acknowledge a reason deriving from the principle of individual rationality to try to shift his burden, each may also feel that he would do better if all accepted their assigned burdens than if all tried to shift them. That is, each may feel that in the long run he would do better under such a scheme than he would playing (sometimes winning and sometimes losing) chicken games to determine who contributes. Cooperation of this sort, however,

---

[32] I make this point in McMahon (1987), p. 326. See also Green (1988), pp. 111–17.

can only be justified by the principle of collective rationality. Thus, this principle can contribute to the justification for complying with the directives of an authority that organizes cooperation to produce a step good by assigning each member of a group a task.

There is another reason why individuals or groups that organize the production of step goods—or more generally that solve coordination problems—can be regarded as genuine authorities. Their doing so often involves the exercise of E-authority, since expertise of certain kinds often contributes to the ability of a source of directives to solve coordination problems. As Raz has noted, the business of solving coordination problems is not simply that of creating or maintaining a coordination equilibrium when everyone in a given group is aware that they face a given coordination problem, that is, when the matrix describing the outcomes of the various possible combinations of action is common knowledge within the group. Often those who in fact face coordination problems do not know that they do.[33] E-authority can play a role here in two ways. It can inform the members of the group that a coordination problem exists, sketching its structure, or it can simply issue directives general compliance with which will realize one of the equilibria. In the latter case, the group members' (uninformed) judgments of what the applicable directive-independent reasons require are preempted by the authority's directives.

If the authority's assertion alone is taken as a good reason for believing that a coordination problem exists, it is functioning as an E-authority on the existence of coordination problems.[34] The justification for regarding it as such will be the inductive one that its assertions have proven correct in the past. Similarly, if it simply issues directives, the justification for accepting them will be that doing so has in the past led to more satisfactory results. The authority in question will thus be practical E-authority of the sort discussed earlier—one whose directives express ought-judgments. Just as one could acknowledge somebody as having good judgment about what one should do in situations of a certain kind because in the past acting on her judgments had proven more satisfying than acting on one's own, so a group can acknowledge somebody as having good judgment about what it should do because in the past collective implementation of her directives resulted in outcomes that each group member regarded as successful coordination.

This suggestion by Raz seems to accord well with the way C-

[33] See Raz (1990b).
[34] This is noted by Raz (1990b), p. 10.

authorities actually work. Typically those over whom C-authority is exercised regard it as having the job not merely of providing them with a reason to do what they can see clearly needs to be done but also of determining what needs to be done when this is not clear. To the extent that mutually beneficial cooperation is at issue, this involves determining when mutually beneficial cooperation is possible. This point holds true for cooperation to produce not only step goods but also incremental goods.

C-authority, then, may sometimes involve E-authority. Yet there are good reasons for regarding C-authority as a distinct species of authority. As we have seen, cooperation can take a variety of forms, and thus most de facto authorities that facilitate cooperation will sometimes, or with respect to some of the projects that they make possible, be functioning in one of the ways that we have distinguished, and sometimes in the others. That they facilitate mutually beneficial cooperation is a more important feature of such authorities than how they do it on a particular occasion.

The Strength of C-Authority

Armed with these points, we can address the question of the robustness and reach of C-authority. To the extent that C-authority functions as E-authority, the answers are those we reviewed earlier. Recall that E-authority can be quite robust and, when the criterion of success is external, it can have extensive reach as well. When C-authority is justified by the principle of collective rationality, its robustness and reach can also be quite extensive. It preempts not particular kinds of reasons but a whole way of processing these reasons into practical judgments, namely, that provided by individual rationality. And although C-authority justified by the principle of individual rationality alone is not actually preemptive, it, too, can be said to have a great deal of strength. For when a group faces a coordination problem, there will be sufficient reason for everyone in it to comply with any directive that makes one of the equilibria salient.

This is not, however, to say that there are no limits on legitimate C-authority. Collective rationality and individual rationality both dictate contributing to a cooperative venture only when what one will receive from it exceeds the cost, including the opportunity cost, of contributing. Those who would prefer the noncooperative outcome—either in itself (they prefer conflict to peace, say) or because they think it would be an effective means to further ends, including the establishment of a new authority more to their

121

liking—will have no reason to comply with the directives of a C-authority.[35] The robustness and reach of C-authority will be curtailed accordingly.

This matter deserves further discussion. When a de facto authority whose legitimacy as a C-authority we wish to ascertain is well established, we have a choice about how we understand the noncooperative outcome by reference to which we determine whether cooperation to implement a particular directive is mutually beneficial. It may be understood either as the outcome that would obtain if there were a complete collapse of authority—the state of nature, relative to this source of directives—or the outcome that would obtain if the particular project that the directive was intended to promote collapsed. Refusal to comply with a given directive will more often be in accordance with reason on the latter interpretation of the noncooperative outcome than on the former; for it is more likely that a group member will judge the collapse of one project to be preferable to its implementation than that he will judge the collapse of all the projects the authority in question organizes to be preferable to the implementation of all of them—including the one project at issue.

It might be objected that either interpretation, and especially the one that justifies cooperation in a wider variety of cases, proves too much since it could justify compliance with the directives of a repressive government. But as we have seen, in calculating whether the benefits of cooperation exceed the costs, costs are to be understood as opportunity costs. Thus, there is no good justification for complying with the directives of a repressive government if the establishment of a more beneficial alternative is possible. By contrast, if a repressive government is indeed the only feasible alternative to a noncooperative outcome that would be worse, it is arguable that there is good reason to comply with its directives, for the time being at least. Of course, cases in which all the members of a group would find the same alternative authority preferable to the existing one are rare. More likely, they would disagree about which alternative would be preferable. These issues are discussed more fully in Chapter Five.

It is important to note that C-authority can be justified in the ways I have suggested even when the goals that the members of a group seek to promote are moral. One might suppose that individual rationality is self-interested rationality and collective rationality

---

[35] Recall that we are understanding the opportunity cost of contributing in such a way that the benefits one could receive by being a free rider are excluded.

is the voice of morality. But actually both are just ways of processing the force of whatever reasons for action an agent acknowledges; they place no limit on the content of these reasons. Thus, one can take an individually rational approach to the implementation of one's conception of the moral good. Similarly, the concept of mutually beneficial cooperation can be understood by reference to conceptions of the moral good. One might find that one could promote one's conception of the moral good most effectively by cooperating with others who were trying to promote their own, different conceptions. In such cases, collective rationality would justify cooperating.

These points are not affected by the possibility that our moral views—or for that matter our identities as persons—are socially or historically conditioned. Whatever has constituted us as the kinds of beings we are has obviously constituted us (or at least members of developed societies) as people who hold conflicting moral and political views, and thus as people who can benefit from C-authority. The quasi-Hobbesian story (with conceptions of the moral good taking the place of self-interest) that I have told to justify C-authority is not committed to "abstract individualism." To be sure, the common institutions in and through which C-authority is exercised must contain roles, paradigmatically that of citizen, that are not defined in terms of any of the conflicting conceptions of the moral good. But the abstraction from substantive commitments that this involves is not a matter of supposing the occupants of these roles to lack such commitments. Rather, it is what might be called "disjunctive abstraction"; it regards citizens has having one or another of a variety of substantive conceptions of the good.

Political Obligation

The foregoing account of C-authority has been meant to be general, applying to any source of directives that facilitates mutually beneficial cooperation. But since this includes governments, which make it possible for the individuals that reside in the territories they govern to cooperate in the production of the rule of law and other public goods, political authority is an important instance of C-authority. It may, then, be useful to conclude by comparing the justification for accepting political authority associated with the above account of legitimate C-authority with the justifications that some have sought to provide using the principle of fair play and the natural duty of justice. Because I have argued that when a group wants to avoid chicken games, the principle of collective rationality will play a role in justifying cooperation to produce step goods as well as incremental goods, I shall focus on it.

The principle of fair play is usually interpreted as making the existence of a reason for an individual to contribute to a cooperative scheme conditional on his voluntarily acceptance of its benefits. The mere fact that he receives benefits from some scheme—whether newly created or, as in the case of the state, long established—does not suffice. So the feasibility of using the principle of fair play to justify political authority depends on whether the members of states can be regarded as voluntarily accepting the benefits of political society, and this is controversial.

The principle of collective rationality, however, allows contributions to be demanded from those who simply receive benefits, at least in certain circumstances. Suppose that a cooperative scheme S, based on some schedule that determines what those who benefit must contribute, benefits me. The principle of collective rationality says that there is good reason for me to contribute, as dictated by the schedule, if the benefit S confers on me is greater than the alternative benefit I could obtain by using the resources the schedule calls on me to contribute in any of the ways that would be possible if S did not exist. As I have noted, here we must include the benefits I could receive from alternative cooperative schemes to which I might contribute instead.[36]

In this respect, the principle of collective rationality resembles the natural duty to uphold just institutions.[37] Unlike the natural duty of justice, however, and indeed the principle of fair play as well, the principle of collective rationality is not intended as a moral principle, identifying one moral reason among many. It enables individuals to do better by their own lights in certain situations, those in which mutually beneficial cooperation is possible. If their concerns are

[36] In his discussion of the principle of fair play, Simmons (1979), pp. 131–36, argues that benefits that cannot be avoided without inconvenience can be regarded as having been voluntarily accepted only if the person in question knows that they have been cooperatively produced and regards them as worth the cost of his contribution. To say this is to say that *there is* a reason for an individual to contribute to a cooperative scheme only if he *believes* that certain conditions obtain. This subjective feature is the remnant of "acceptance" for such benefits, and Simmons thinks it is usually absent in the case of the benefits conferred by governments. The principle of collective rationality, however, does not tie what there is reason for the recipients of benefits to do to their beliefs. Klosko (1992) argues that when a cooperative venture provides goods of a certain important kind, the principle of fair play can be understood as working this way to. See esp. chap. 2.

[37] As Waldron puts it: "Can an organization simply *impose* itself on us, morally, in this way? There comes a point when the theorist of natural duty must stop treating this question as an objection and simply insist that the answer is yes" (1993, p. 27).

moral, the benefit each receives from cooperating is that the world looks better from her moral standpoint, but the reason the principle provides is not itself a moral reason. Thus, although the principle of collective rationality can explain why we should normally accept the authority of the government (or governments) of the territory in which we reside, it is not, strictly speaking, a source of political obligations.

What is at issue here can be illustrated by reference to Immanuel Kant's account of the benefits of political society. Kant says that in the state of nature each does what morality *seems* to her to require, which creates conflict. And he appears to hold that the way moral agents benefit from entering political society is that they come to act on true, as opposed to merely apparent, moral requirements.[38] When accepting political authority is justified by reference to the principle of collective rationality, however, the way moral agents benefit from political society is rather that each can regard social life as morally improved in light of her conception of the moral good.

These points continue to hold if an individual's moral conception is, wholly or in part, a conception of justice. In this case, she will usually regard the result of general compliance with the directives of a legitimate C-authority as an improvement (over the noncooperative outcome) from the standpoint of justice as she understands it— although possibly not as much of an improvement as that she could effect by riding free on the cooperative efforts of others and promoting her conception of justice as individual rationality dictates.[39] We cannot, however, make the stronger claim that C-authority is legitimate only if it organizes cooperation that is in fact just. The justice of a scheme of cooperation is not a condition of the application of the principle of collective rationality. Just as the principle of individual rationality can justify purchasing an item from a price-discriminating seller who unfairly charges one more than others if buying it is still the best use of one's resources, so the principle of collective rationality can justify contributing to an unfair scheme if the benefit one receives exceeds that one could receive by using the contributed resources in the best way that would be possible if the scheme did not exist. This does not mean that one must simply accept an existing scheme that meets this condition. One can use

---

[38] See Kant (1991), pp. 123–33. Kant's theory is obscure, but his claim that there can be no right of resistance to established authority seems to depend on some view to the effect that the state is a condition of the possibility of genuine right.

[39] I say "usually" since if an individual's conception of the moral good allows other moral considerations to take precedence over justice, gains on these dimensions might suffice for mutually beneficial cooperation.

any bargaining power one may have to alter the distribution of benefits and burdens it provides for. But the principle does not require that the distribution that ultimately emerges from this bargaining process be just.

Raz's Service Conception

It is useful to note a distinction between P-authority on one hand and E-authority and C-authority on the other. In Chapter Two, I pointed out that E-authority and C-authority both satisfy Raz's normal justification thesis. This states that the normal justification for authority is that the subordinate better complies with the assertion- or directive-independent reasons that apply to her by accepting authoritative directives.[40] The discussions earlier in this chapter can be regarded as spelling this out in more detail.

Raz also mentions another thesis that legitimate authority often satisfies: the dependence thesis. This states that an authority's directives should be based, in the main, on the same reasons that apply to the subjects in the situation, in the sense of being reasons that the subjects would take into account if they were capable of reasoning effectively for themselves. Together with the normal justification thesis, the dependence thesis leads to what Raz calls the service conception of authority, according to which the function of legitimate authority is to serve those who receive authoritative communications by helping them better to comply with the reasons that apply to them.[41]

This latter notion places both E-authority and C-authority in sharp contrast with P-authority. The central case of P-authority is the authority of a principal in an agency relationship. But the service conception implies that those holding authority are, in a way, the agents of—or perhaps, better, trustees for—the subjects. An authority of

[40] As Raz (1986), pp. 70–78, notes, whether people would do better by complying with authoritative directives depends on how well they could do on their own. Thus, we cannot conclude that the normal justification thesis will yield the same results regarding the legitimacy of a given authority for all those over whom it claims authority.

[41] For both of the above points, see Raz (1986), pp. 42–52. Here Raz also takes pains to state that the dependence thesis does not imply that authoritative communications make no difference to what the subjects ought to do. Soper (1989) suggests replacing Raz's service conception of authority with a "leader conception" that sees it as resolving disputes with a zero-sum aspect. Since the service conception views authority not as improving performance incidentally, but as aiming to help subjects do better by their own lights, it may defuse feminist criticisms of authority as antithetical to the ethic of care. More broadly, it is plausible that a nonpatriarchal society would need preemptive authority. For it would need people who were 'good team players,' and this involves a willingness to implement policies that one thinks mistaken.

this sort does not act under the direction of the subjects, but it must act for their benefit, in the sense of enabling them to do what they have good directive- or assertion-independent reason to do. Otherwise, it is illegitimate. This contrast plays an important role in the discussion of managerial authority in Part II.

CHAPTER FIVE

DEMOCRACY

In Chapter Four, we saw how the three kinds of authority that I have distinguished can be justified. In the cases of E-Authority and of C-authority, the justification involves showing that the subordinates better comply with the directive- or assertion-independent reasons that apply to them by accepting authoritative communications.

The reference point for these judgments has been a situation in which the authority in question does not exist. That is, a particular authority is legitimate for a given individual only if she does better accepting its communications than she would if it did not exist. In the case of C-authority, this includes joining other cooperative schemes that might be more beneficial to her. This latter point has the following consequence. An existing C-authority will lose its legitimacy for a given individual if it becomes possible to establish an alternative authority that would organize the cooperative enterprise in question in a way that would be more beneficial to her—in the sense of enabling her to realize a greater improvement in her performance relative to the considerations that she regards as reasons for action.

This account of legitimate C-authority conceals an important problem, however. Establishing an alternative C-authority requires securing the cooperation of others. If all agree that some particular alternative would be preferable to the existing authority, establishing it is unproblematic. From the standpoint of the principle of collective rationality, the situation presents a simple coordination problem. But what happens if the members of the group disagree about which alternative authority would improve their performance the most, or some think improvement is possible and others do not? It seems that they might all have to judge the existing authority legitimate, despite the fact that many could do better with a different one. For they will not normally be able to achieve the coordination required to establish one of the alternatives.

It is useful to discuss this problem in a different form. Instead of considering competing C-authorities, let us consider a single C-authority that could issue any of several directives. If there is one directive general compliance with which everyone in the group would regard as better than general compliance with any other possible directive, they could all appropriately regard the authority as deficient, from the standpoint of legitimacy, if it did not issue that directive. The members of the group would then have a prima facie reason to replace the authority, which would gain strength the more it issued directives that all regarded as suboptimal.

More often, however, the members of a group guided by an authority will disagree about which directive would provide the best basis for organizing cooperation. If cooperation on the basis of any of these directives would nevertheless be regarded by each member of the group as preferable to the noncooperative outcome, this situation has the structure of a battle of the sexes problem. The different possible directives correspond to different coordination equilibria that could be realized, but the members of the group disagree on their ranking.[1] Since a battle of the sexes problem is a coordination problem, any de facto authority can bring about cooperation in such a situation by simply issuing a directive that makes one of the equilibria salient. Thus it can retain its legitimacy, as we have been approaching legitimacy so far, no matter what directive (within the feasible range) it issues. Whatever choice it makes, the members of the group will judge that they could do better by complying than they could if coordination was not achieved.

Yet it seems to matter how the authority makes its decision. If its procedure were always to choose whatever directive was preferred by member Smith, the others in the group could justifiably complain. But if its following this procedure would not undermine its legitimacy as an authority—if the principles of collective and individual rationality would continue to justify compliance—what could provide the basis for such a complaint? Intuitively, what grounds the complaint is that the procedure followed is unfair and possibly inefficient, in the sense that it frustrates more people than it satisfies. This raises the question of what would constitute a fair or welfare-maximizing procedure for generating directives when there are conflicting preferences, within some group that could benefit from cooperation, regarding the directive on the basis of which cooperation is to be organized. The answer that comes immediately to mind is democracy. It seems that a vote within the group would be

---

[1] It should be borne in mind here that we are assuming that the individuals in question accept the principle of collective rationality. Thus, none regard free riding as an option.

a fair and welfare-maximizing way of deciding which directive to issue.[2]

The examination of this suggestion is the topic of the present chapter, but we should be clear at the outset about what is at issue. It is tempting to describe the claim that democracy is required in such a situation as the claim that only democratically exercised C-authority can be legitimate. As I have noted, on my account of the legitimacy of C-authority, we cannot say this. A dictator could claim legitimacy as a C-authority if his directives facilitated mutually beneficial cooperation as well as any feasible alternative. In justifying democracy by invoking the values of fairness or welfare maximization, then, we are moving beyond considerations of legitimacy and introducing moral considerations.

This is an important departure from my previous approach. On that approach, it was possible for people with diverse conceptions of the moral good to accept the legitimacy of a given C-authority. Each could regard general compliance as preferable, by his or her own moral lights, to the noncooperative outcome. But if moral values must be invoked to justify democracy, only those holding certain conceptions of the moral good, conceptions that give an important place to these values, will be able to perceive the appropriateness of democracy. Still, the values of fairness and welfare maximization are widely shared. So if these values do support democracy, it will be possible to make a case for the democratic exercise of C-authority that most can accept. When necessary to avoid confusion, I use the term "moral validity," as opposed to "legitimacy," to distinguish ways of exercising C-authority that are preferable in light of these moral values. Even if democratically exercised C-authority is no more legitimate than dictatorially exercised C-authority, it may still be able to claim greater moral validity.

Relatively specific moral values can be used to justify democracy. One might, for example, favor it because one regards the life of political activity—of participation in the decision making that governs the collective actions of a group—as intrinsically valuable, or perhaps even the highest form of life for animals of our species. As I noted in Chapter One, such participation is often regarded as a component of intrinsically valuable self-realization. Similarly, one might favor democracy because one regards it as fostering intrinsically valuable diversity or individuality. But these values are not as widely shared as fairness and welfare maximization, and thus do

---

[2] Kavka (1986. pp. 179–80) notes that democratic decision provides a natural way to solve battle of the sexes problems (which he calls 'impure coordination problems').

not provide as broad a platform on which to construct arguments for democracy.

It may be useful to compare my approach to the connection between fairness and democracy with that of John Rawls in his recent writings. His strategy is to derive principles of justice for the basic structure from the idea of a society as a fair system of cooperation, which he believes to be implicit in the public culture of democracies, rather than from substantive moral conceptions about which people will disagree. My approach is similar in seeing a connection between democracy and fairness. I use the value of fairness—as well as the value of welfare maximization—to justify democracy. My argument is intended to appeal to all whose conceptions of the moral good give a prominent place to fairness, but they need not understand it in precisely the same way. It is enough if there is agreement that fairness supports democracy, or to use a Rawlsian idiom, if there is an overlapping consensus on this.

Of course, Rawls has devised a distinctive way of working out the requirements of fairness for the basic structure, by asking what the people whose common life it constitutes would agree to when considered simply as occupants of the role of citizen (that is, in abstraction from their particular commitments).[3] This is not essential for my argument, however, nor, I think, for liberalism. The essence of political liberalism is that the common institutions in and through which authority is exercised be fair between individuals who hold different substantive conceptions of the moral good (or individuals whose conceptions can endorse a fair structure). The Rawlsian thought experiment is an especially vivid and powerful way of articulating the basic liberal requirement of fairness, but there is no reason in principle that the idea of a fair agreement between fully informed individuals, or the idea of a perfectly sympathetic and fair ideal observer, could not be used to articulate this requirement as well.

The values of fairness or welfare maximization play a role in many arguments for democracy. Arguments that justify democracy as promoting liberty constitute an important instance. Democracy, in the form of the popular election of leaders, has been defended as pro-

[3] As we noted in Chapter Four, although citizens will have substantive commitments, the role of citizen cannot be defined in terms of any of them—or at least any on which they differ. Thus, to determine what citizens qua citizens would choose, we must suppose them to have only motives that are appropriate to this role. Rawls now calls these "highest order interests" in maintaining a capacity for an effective sense of justice and a capacity to form, revise, and rationally pursue a conception of the good. See Rawls (1980).

moting negative liberty, the absence of external constraints on action, by providing a way in which the members of a group can defend themselves against despotism.[4] This argument is, however, incomplete unless it also invokes the value of fairness. The case for democracy as promoting negative liberty is strongest if the liberty that each enjoys is the maximum liberty compatible with a like liberty for all, which is to say, if liberty is fairly distributed.[5]

Arguments that employ fairness or welfare maximization to justify the democratic exercise of C-authority may present it as having purely instrumental value—that is, as having value solely because it reliably produces outcomes that are fair or welfare maximizing. To be sure, a dictator, too, might be able to realize such outcomes, especially if he was an expert on what fairness and welfare maximization require. But as I noted in Chapter Four, moral expertise is difficult to establish to the satisfaction of all the members of any large group—or indeed any group selected on some ground other than affinity of moral values. So it is plausible that the most effective way of realizing outcomes that are in fact fair or welfare maximizing is to employ democratic decision-making procedures.

Democracy may also be regarded as intrinsically valuable. Many writers have spoken of democracy as required to satisfy our interest in autonomy, and here it seems that it is simply exercising control over a group of which one is a member, rather than any consequences this may have, that is regarded as valuable. Of course, the autonomy of some can come at the expense of the autonomy of others. Each may find exercising such control in a way that excludes others more valuable than exercising it in a way that includes them—that is, each may find that dictatorship by him or her would be best from the standpoint of the value of autonomy. The values of fairness and welfare maximization must, then, be regarded as playing a role in establishing the intrinsic value of democracy as well. Democracy is justified as a fair or welfare-maximizing compromise between individuals each of whom wants to be a dictator.[6]

[4] Pateman (1970) contrasts participatory views of democracy with protective views that regard democracy mainly as providing a check on ruling elites.

[5] Democracy can also be defended as promoting positive liberty; see Gould (1988). Gould understands positive liberty as self-realization, so my earlier remarks about justifying democracy on this basis apply to her approach as well.

[6] For an account of democracy along these lines, see Singer (1973). If democratic decision making is intrinsically valuable for these reasons, a dictator who was an expert on what fairness required would have a good (although perhaps not decisive) reason to transform his dictatorship into a democracy. For related discussion see Copp (1993), sec. 4.

Direct Democracy: Preliminaries

As I indicated in Chapter One, I regard democracy as reflexive authority, a way of exercising authority in which those who are subject to authority collectively determine the authoritative directives that will guide them. Let us focus first on C-authority. Democratically exercised C-authority is distinguished from other forms of C-authority by the fact that the directives that make collective action possible are themselves collective products. They are decided upon, or adopted, collectively. When the action of generating a directive is itself a collective action, there is a danger of a regress since performing it may also present collective action problems. That is, authority may be necessary to facilitate the collective action of generating an authoritative directive. This would be procedural rather than substantive authority. It would generate directives designed to facilitate the process of deciding what to do, not directives on the basis of which cooperation would actually proceed.

Groups may, however, be able to dispense with such procedural authorities. As we saw in Chapter Four, collective action problems can be solved by norms as well as by authority if what constitutes optimal cooperation for a particular purpose is relatively stable over time. The problem of collectively generating a directive may have this feature even if what would constitute optimal collective action for the group changes often. A group may, then, simply come to use a particular procedure without its ever having been explicitly adopted, or it may continue to accept a procedure that was explicitly adopted in the past even though no authority dictates this.

This line of thought gives rise to a distinction between the constitution of an authority and its routine exercise. The constitution is not a written document but rather a set of conventions governing the process by which authoritative directives are generated.[7] A constitution need not be democratic, but when it is, it establishes a procedure that enables the members of a group to generate collectively the authoritative directives that guide them. What we wish to know is whether the adoption of a democratic constitution is supported by good moral reasons.

The democratic decision making found in the modern world is almost always representative. The collective action of generating directives is performed in two parts. First, a group collectively de-

---

[7] Consulting a written document may, however, be one of the things the conventions require.

cides on an individual to represent it in a legislative body, and then the members of that body collectively create the directives that will guide the further actions of all the members of the subject population, themselves included. In considering what fundamental moral values support the democratic exercise of authority, however, I focus first on the simpler case of direct democracy. Here, the collective action of generating directives for the group is performed in one stage. The members of the subject population decide for themselves the directives on the basis of which they will cooperate.

Democratic decision making typically involves choosing among alternative proposals by means of a vote employing the method of majority rule. In the standard case, voting is preceded by two prior stages. In the first, measures are proposed for consideration by the group, and in the second, they are discussed. Democracy is most fully realized—is most fully a process in which the generation of a directive for the group is a collective action of the whole group—when the procedures that guide the collective action of generating a directive give each member an equal conventional right to participate in each of these earlier stages of the process, as well as the right to vote. Democracy is most fully realized when all the members of the group have the right to make proposals for consideration by the group; the right to participate in the discussion of proposals, both in defense and criticism; and the right to vote, with each vote counting equally. In considering what justification there might be for democracy, I focus on what justifies according these rights equally to all.

The fact that democracy is being considered as a form of C-authority has a consequence that should be noted before we proceed. Authoritative directives have the status of preemptive reasons for action. Thus, if democracy is a way of exercising C-authority, the members of a group generating directives democratically must be prepared to comply with these directives even when their own judgments of what the applicable directive-independent reasons require dictate doing something else. This is worth emphasizing, since it is common in the literature on democracy to distinguish democracy from hierarchy, with the implication that democratic decision making is not hierarchical. As long as some group members have their judgment preempted, however, they will be in the same situation as subordinates in a hierarchy. They will be acting on directives different from those that they regard as justified by the applicable directive-independent considerations.

The only difference between the subordination associated with democracy and that involved in a typical hierarchy is that the subordination is not to a particular person. Those who are subordinated in a democracy are subordinated either to a subgroup within the decision-making body, the majority, or to the decision-making body considered as a whole. The latter interpretation is plausible to the extent that we can regard all as accepting the authority of the constitution, that is, as taking themselves to have a good reason to determine directives in this way.[8] For then it will not be the case that one subgroup directs the actions of another, but rather that all are on the receiving end of a directive capable of preempting their judgments of what the applicable directive-independent reasons require. The difference between the majority and the minority will consist solely in the fact that the directive-independent judgments of those who are in the majority on that occasion agree with the authoritative directive, while the judgments of those in the minority do not.

Democracy and Preference

One of the most important questions we face in considering what can justify democratic decision making is how we are to understand what a vote expresses. Basically there are two possibilities. A vote may express what might be called a simple preference—that is, a reason-generating consideration that is not itself susceptible to rational criticism or modification—or it may express a reasoned judgment about the relative desirability of the various alternatives. Let us consider first how democracy might be justified on the former assumption.

On this interpretation, the three stages of democratic decision making may be understood as follows. Various members of the group propose directives the adoption of which would be optimal from the standpoint of their preferences. The ensuing discussion does not take the form of trying to show that one's own preferred alternative is right and the others wrong, since preferences are not susceptible to such assessment. Rather, it takes the form of pointing out the consequences of the alternative proposals in the hope of bringing others to see that one's own proposal will satisfy their preferences better. Then people vote for what they most prefer after all of this instrumental information has been provided.

Most of the literature on voting treats it as a way of constructing a preference ranking for a group out of the rankings of the members of the group. This approach goes with a theory of rational action ac-

---

[8] Of course, the constitution does not issue directives, but it can be regarded as having authority to the extent that its provisions are taken as preemptive reasons for action.

cording to which rational agents act so as to realize their most preferred alternative. The assumption, apparently, is that a rational group will act so as to realize its most preferred alternative. So characterized, however, voting seems to be associated with a picture of the group as a distinct organism. Talk of a group preference is hard to divorce from the idea that groups are distinct entities, at least when unanimity is absent. We seem to be talking about a general will that is separate from the particular wills of the members. On the view of democracy that I propose, however, the emphasis is on group action rather than group preference. The group performs the collective action of generating a directive to guide its further collective actions. This directive need not be regarded as expressing a preference distinct from that of any individual. It can be seen as a way of resolving conflicts between individual preferences. That is, democracy can be viewed as a way of deciding, by aggregating votes, which of the different directives the individual members of the group would prefer will actually be put into effect.

It has been known since the eighteenth century that when the input to a majoritarian social choice procedure is a ranking of more than two alternatives, voting can result in a circular ordering at the societal level. A situation can develop in which there is no alternative that is preferred by a majority to every other in pairwise comparisons. Instead, for each alternative, there is another that a majority would prefer. Such circular preference orderings make rational action, understood as realizing the most preferred alterative, impossible. Kenneth Arrow has shown that no procedure for constructing a social preference out of individual preferences—or for generating a directive to guide a group's actions—that meets certain minimal formal conditions is immune to this problem.[9] Some voting systems also have the feature that how the agenda is set—in what order issues are considered—will affect the outcome, and this, too, seems to constitute a kind of irrationality.[10] These difficulties can be avoided if individual preferences are single-peaked, in the sense that the farther along some dimension of desirability a given alternative is from each individual's most preferred alternative, the less he prefers it.[11] But this condition is not met in many situations where voting is called for. Still, those who favor democratic procedures can be seen as regarding the risk of irrationality as preferable to dictatorship and thus as opting for democracy despite these difficulties.[12]

[9] See Arrow (1963), esp. chap 5.
[10] This is noted by Wolff (1970), pp. 61–63.
[11] See Black (1958), chap 4. See also Arrow (1963), pp. 75–80.

The question we must now address is what moral reasons support this choice.

The Fairness of Democracy

Democracy, in the sense of the three-stage process outlined above, can be said to be a fair way of resolving disputes, but this claim must be stated carefully. One respect in which democracy seems fair is that the conventional rights associated with it are equal rights. This can be seen as fair when it is contrasted with alternatives in which such rights are unequal. Relative to these alternative arrangements, democracy secures a kind of equality in the actual standing of people. They are treated equally by the procedure. But the equality conferred by equal rights to participate and to vote—that is, by procedural fairness—is only what I have called input-criterion equal consideration.[13] When the directive decided upon is put into effect, the majority gets what it wants and the minority does not. In this respect, democracy resembles utilitarianism.

In his discussion of democracy, Peter Singer suggests that the employment by a group of a democratic decision-making procedure is a form of fair compromise, comparable to dividing what is in dispute equally, or (when it cannot be divided) deciding who will get it by a lottery.[14] But the first of these methods employs an output-criterion conception of equal consideration, while the second employs an input-criterion conception. And the compromise involved in democracy, understood as deciding by the method of majority rule, is based on an input-criterion conception of equal consideration as well. Giving everybody one vote is a fair compromise within a set of people each of whom wants her preferences to count for more than those of other people—at the limit, people each of whom wants to be a dictator. But the output of democratic decision making is not typically a fair compromise among the alternatives preferred by each group member. The outcome is exactly what some people want and not at all what other people want.

In Chapter Three, I noted that in any given situation, some conceptions of equal consideration will be preferable to others from the standpoint of fairness; they will provide a better interpretation of what fairness requires in that situation. Typically, fairness prefers output-criterion equal consideration to input-criterion equal consid-

---

[12] For a discussion of the possibility that Arrow's logical result may not be empirically relevant, see Hardin (1993).
[13] See Chapter Three.
[14] Singer (1973), pp. 32–33.

eration. This means that when it is possible to strike a compromise between the competing alternatives, fairness favors striking it rather than resorting to a vote. Sometimes compromise is impossible, however, and groups can be so large that negotiating a compromise would take more time than the group has to make a decision. In such cases, fairness endorses the employment of some input-criterion conception of equal consideration. Still, we cannot automatically conclude that democracy is the fairest such procedure. The choice of which of the competing claims will find expression in authoritative directives can also, as was just noted, be made by a lottery, and this may be fairer than democracy.

The equal consideration associated with a lottery is also input-criterion equal consideration; a lottery is a procedure for deciding between competing alternatives that does not involve reference to any sort of outcome-equality. It is tempting to say that a lottery that gives everyone an equal chance of winning, or of being among the winners, is fairer than democracy because even a member of a tiny minority can win. But here, too, we must be careful. In certain situations the difference between democracy and a lottery is subtle.

Although a fair lottery to pick a dictator will give everyone an equal chance of attaining this position, external benefits will accrue to any others who share the dictator's view of what directives would be appropriate. And those whose preferences are widely shared are more likely to find themselves receiving such benefits than those whose preferences are not widely shared, since it is more likely that one of them will win the lottery.[15] So although we can say that a lottery gives every individual an equal chance to win, it does not give every individual an equal chance of getting what she wants. It gives her a chance of getting what she wants that is equal to the proportional size of the group that has the same view of the issue to be decided that she does. In a sense, then, a fair lottery favors a majority just as voting does. Still, a lottery appears to be preferable from the standpoint of fairness because it gives individuals in the minority some chance to get what they want, while voting does not. If this is right, the case for voting over a lottery must take the form of a case that welfare maximization is more important than fairness. For voting by the method of majority rule is guaranteed to satisfy more people than it frustrates, at least relative to the set of alternatives within which a majority is finally obtained, while a lottery is not.

It can be argued, however, that voting is not always inferior to a lottery from the standpoint of fairness. This point is best illustrated

[15] See Wolff (1970), pp. 44–45.

in another context. In his article, "Should the Numbers Count?" John Taurek argues that when we face a choice between saving five people and saving one, deciding whether to save the five or the one by flipping a coin is just as acceptable as following a rule that dictates saving the larger number.[16] This procedure, which is a fair lottery between interest groups rather than individuals, is often criticized, but to my knowledge no one has rebutted the claim, implicit in what Taurek says, that tossing a coin—and thus giving each individual involved an equal (.5) chance of being saved—constitutes a fair procedure for deciding who will be saved.

This might seem to imply that we must explain the intuitive unacceptability of flipping a coin in such a case by saying that the value of maximizing total aggregate welfare outweighs fairness. In fact we need not; saving the five can be regarded as dictated by a fair procedure, too. For nature's determination of who can be saved along with others and who can only be saved alone can be seen as a kind of lottery. In the case at hand, then, we can regard being guided by the value of welfare maximization as having the support of fairness as well. This allows us to conclude that the reason for saving the five is not that the value of welfare maximization outweighs fairness, but rather that saving them has the support of both values while flipping a coin has the support of only one. In Chapter Three, I said that while welfare maximization is a widely accepted value, there is controversy about whether it should be regarded as supporting making total aggregate welfare as large as possible or making fair shares as large as possible. In the present situation, however, where we are restricted to input-criterion conceptions of equal consideration and we face a choice between procedures both of which can claim to be fair, invoking the aggregation interpretation of welfare maximization to decide the issue is unproblematic.

Generalizing this result, we can say that counting each as one and none as more than one in a maximizing calculation is as fair a way of deciding what to do as employing a lottery when a single decision affecting a group must be made. For who is in the group that would be favored by such a procedure and who is in the group that would not can be regarded as, in some ultimate sense, a matter of chance. But this Benthamite conception of equal consideration is not always as fair as a lottery when many different decisions affecting the same group must be made. In a situation of the latter sort, the possibility of satisfying an output-criterion conception of equal consideration reemerges.

[16] Taurek (1977).

Let us return to the method of majority rule as our example of counting each as one and none as more than one in a maximizing calculation. Under certain conditions, democratic decision making, taken as an ongoing process, can fully satisfy an output-criterion conception of equal consideration. This will happen when the probability that any given individual will be in the majority on any of the issues to be decided is equal to the proportional size of the majority, for example, each individual has a .6 probability of being in the majority when the majority for an alternative is 60 percent. On this assumption, over time everyone will benefit equally from democratic decision making.[17] To take a simple case, if the majority in every vote is 60 percent, everyone will get what she wants 60 percent of the time. Sometimes, then, we can regard the method of majority rule as according the members of a group full output-criterion equal consideration.

When the probability that each group member will be in the majority on a given issue is not equal to the proportional size of the majority, however—and in particular, when there are entrenched minorities, groups that are consistently outvoted—the method of majority rule does not secure output-criterion equal consideration. In such a case, a lottery would be fairer than voting. The frequency with which each got what she wanted would be proportional to relative size of the interest groups of which she was a member, but this would be preferable from the standpoint of fairness to some never getting what they wanted, which is the result when the method of majority rule is employed in a context in which there are entrenched minorities.

When repeated decisions must be made and there are entrenched minorities, then, it is no longer possible to say that the Benthamite conception of equal consideration—counting each as one in a maximizing calculation or a vote—is as fair as a fair lottery. In such cases, democracy is supported only by the aggregation interpretation of welfare maximization, or at least this is so if what each winner gains from having her preferred alternative enacted equals what each loser loses.[18] Fairness rather supports making group decisions by a lottery, since a fair lottery will insure that even members of an entrenched minority get what they want some of the time. It follows that we can opt for democracy only if we regard the aggregation

[17] I take the general line of argument in this paragraph from Barry (1979). To make this assumption is in effect to assume that there are no stable interest groups, or that the contending interest groups line up in different ways on different issues.

[18] See Barry (1979), pp. 76–77. Riley (1990) argues that democracy can be regarded as the form that utilitarianism takes when only ordinal utility information is available.

interpretation of the value of welfare maximization as taking precedence over fairness. As we have seen, this is a more problematic employment of the value of welfare maximization than using it to decide between procedures that are equivalent from the standpoint of fairness. The important point, however, is that democracy is not supported by the value of fairness when there are entrenched minorities.

So far we have focused on voting, but these conclusions are only reinforced when take into account the preliminaries to voting. When votes express preferences, coalition formation is common. In this process, instead of proposing one's most preferred alternative and trying to convince the required number of people that it would be best from the standpoint of their preferences as well, one makes concessions, modifying one's proposal so that, while it is less than ideal from one's own point of view, it will be more attractive to others and ultimately to a majority. The rationale from the standpoint of each member of the coalition for participating in it is that half a loaf is better than none at all. But concessions are made only to the extent necessary to attain a majority, so those who would insist on the greatest concessions in any particular case will not be included in the coalition. If this is the same group over and over, the process can be criticized from the standpoint of fairness.[19]

A feature of how democracy actually works may seem to hold out some promise of viewing it as a fair procedure when there are entrenched minorities. This is the fact that minorities can be influential beyond their numbers by threatening to cause trouble for the decision makers if their views do not get adequate consideration, which is to say, if the outcome of the process is not fair (or fairer) to them. This phenomenon has been most discussed in connection with representative democracy, where it is noted that minorities within a population can secure outcomes that constitute fair compromises by pressuring elected officials after the vote that elected them. Indeed, it has been suggested that democracy actually works not as rule by a

---

[19] Christiano (1993) defends democracy as providing each member of a group with equal resources for determining its collective properties. But when it is employed in this way, equality of resources functions as an input-criterion conception of equal consideration. And even with vote trading, which Christiano allows, it is unlikely to achieve output-criterion equal consideration over time when there are entrenched minorities. Or at least this is so if people choose trading partners partly on the basis of how compatible with their own goals the programs to which they will be contributing when they keep the bargain are. Christiano explicitly states that the conception of justice on which he bases his argument is not outcome-oriented. But in my view, fairness cannot rest content with procedures that yield unequal outcomes over time when others are available that lack this defect, or like a lottery, display it to a reduced degree.

majority, but as a process in which governmental officials seek to give something to each of a variety of organized minorities.[20] But the influence groups have on the process is not determined by fair procedures, or indeed by formally established procedures of any kind. It is a matter of bringing to bear various kinds of social power. And there is no guarantee that all minorities will have enough power to secure an outcome that in fact satisfies an output-criterion conception of equal consideration.

Political Liberalism

These shortcomings of democracy from the standpoint of fairness bring us to another way of exercising C-authority, political liberalism, understood as acceptance by an authority of limitations on the content of authoritative directives. So characterized, this is merely the formal idea of limited authority, and there is no reason to apply the term "liberalism" to it. This term can be seen as appropriate, however, when we consider what sorts of restrictions on content are justified by basic moral values.

Political liberalism can be regarded as a response to the problem of the unfairness of making decisions by the method of majority rule when there are entrenched minorities. Ronald Dworkin has made familiar the idea that rights are "trumps" on utilitarian considerations,[21] and it is easy to provide a rationale for this in terms of output-criterion equal consideration. Utilitarianism can justify what is intuitively unfair treatment of some for the sake of maximizing total aggregate satisfaction, and thus supplementing utilitarian considerations with moral rights is a way of insuring a certain amount of output-criterion equal consideration. But since the aggregation interpretation of the value of welfare maximization justifies employing the method of majority rule even when there are entrenched minorities, there is role for trumps in this case as well. We can suppose that they have as their content certain rights of individuals that majorities may not abridge because to do so would be to treat minorities unfairly. Respect for them can be written into the consti-

[20] See Dahl (1956), chap. 5. In Dahl's view, it is not only interelection governmental decision making that is influenced by minorities. He also argues that elections give effect to the will not of the majority, but of minorities (plural), because office holders often win by proposing a set of policies each of which satisfies only a minority. A candidate can win by doing this if each minority feels strongly enough about the issue of concern to it that it is prepared to let its vote be determined by the candidate's position on this issue. Democracy is thus not system of majority rule, but a system of minorities rule.

[21] R. Dworkin (1978), p. 136.

tution of the democratic authority, as constraints on outcomes designed to insure that what the authority directs does not stray too far from the output-criterion equal consideration that fairness requires. Output-criterion equal consideration is promoted by guaranteeing each person the liberty to act in certain ways in pursuit of his or her preferences. Of course, instituting a particular liberal scheme involves deciding which states of the world are to count as protected parts of people's lives and which are to remain within the purview of authoritative decision making.

The combination of political liberalism and democracy can, then, be defended as a good way to satisfy both welfare maximization and fairness when there are entrenched minorities. If this is right, to suggest, as some recently have in the United States, that placing certain social decisions in the hands of an independent judiciary is contrary to democratic principles is to make a fetish out of democracy. There is nothing sacred about democratic procedures. They have value only because of the moral values that are more fully realized when they are employed. When there are entrenched minorities, however, there is only one such value, the utilitarian value of greater total aggregate welfare. The value of fairness does not support democracy in such circumstances; rather, it supports certain limitations on what the majority may decide. Thus, democratic liberalism—democratic decision making limited by constitutionally protected rights the elaboration of which is the job of an independent judiciary—represents a good institutional compromise between the two competing foundational moral values when there are entrenched minorities.[22]

Democracy and Judgment

Now that we have considered how democracy might be justified on the assumption that votes express simple preferences incapable of rational revision, let us turn to the hypothesis that they express

---

[22] These points shed light on current controversies about "judicial legislation" in the United States. The constitution is doing its job only if it protects minorities against unfair treatment now. Since not all of the ways that people can be treated unfairly now could have been foreseen in the past, a means of updating the understanding of unfairness that judges employ must be found. But if there are entrenched minorities, this updating cannot take the form of passing new laws for the judges to interpret. Democratic legislation in such circumstances would merely perpetuate the problem. Judges can do their job only if they have some other way of determining what fairness requires now. Having them simply rely on their intuitions would be undesirable, but educating them to a tradition of fairness-based judicial decision from which they can extrapolate what fairness requires now would seem to be workable solution.

judgments that can be revised upon rational reflection. Of particular interest here is the possibility that votes express judgments of what I have called the moral good. This notion is broader than that of the common good, interpreted either narrowly as what the personal goods of all the members of a group have in common or broadly as what would constitute a fair resolution of the competing claims of each group member's personal good. In some circumstances, morality may place other values ahead of fairness, and a group may have to take account of the moral claims of outsiders. Presumably the moral good encompasses the common good on either understanding of it.[23]

Epistemic Democracy

One possible interpretation of the hypothesis that votes express judgments capable of rational revision is that they express judgments capable of being true or false. This opens up the possibility of arguing for democracy not on the ground that it promotes fairness or welfare maximization but rather on the ground that democratic procedures yield judgments that are more likely to be true than those made by the individual members of the group. This would be, in effect, to regard the group as a whole as an expert on the matter to be decided; voting is the way that we learn what this source of expertise believes.

Views of this sort have recently been labeled epistemic conceptions of democracy. The *locus classicus* is Jean-Jacques Rousseau. He says:

When a law is proposed in the people's assembly, what is asked is not precisely whether they approve of the proposition or reject it, but whether it is in conformity with the general will which is theirs; each by giving his vote gives his opinion on this question, and the counting of votes yields a declaration of the general will. When, therefore, an opinion contrary to my own prevails, this proves only that I have made a mistake, so that what I believed to be the general will was not so.[24]

[23] Estlund (1990) argues that certain conditions that must be satisfied if a decision procedure is to be regarded as democratic can only be satisfied if votes are statements about the common good. Thus, he concludes that we should cease to regard democratic decision making as aggregating preferences and regard it instead as aggregating judgments about the common good. But Estlund's argument actually supports the less restrictive conclusion that votes must express non–agent-relative value judgments. Judgments of what would be conducive to what I have called the moral good—the set of all valid moral considerations that bear on a decision—may be regarded as of this sort.

[24] Rousseau (1968), part 4, sec. 2. See also Coleman and Ferejohn (1986) and Cohen (1986).

Here Rousseau claims that the group as a whole is more knowledge-able than any individual member about the general will.

On one way of interpreting Rousseau's theory, the general will is the will of a corporate body distinct from the individual members who comprise it. On this interpretation, his claim in the passage cited is that if the members of a group want to know what this corporate body wills, they should vote on this, with their votes registering their opinions. The opinion that gets a majority of votes can be regarded as true, or perhaps as closer to the truth than any other possibility of which the voters are aware. Even if the general will can be discovered in this way, however, the claim that the individuals in the society should be guided by it—should regard declarations of the general will as preemptive reasons for action—depends on the further assumption that it is appropriate for each individual to defer to the general will. And if the general will is the will of a distinct corporate body, this assumption violates the precepts of moral individualism. As we saw in Chapter Three, although the ontological claim that some groups are distinct from their members, and even that they have wills of their own, may be acceptable, the claim that these entities or their choices deserve any independent moral consideration is not.

If the members of a group are to defer to democratic decision making because of its epistemic properties, then, they must be able to regard it as a way of obtaining a better understanding of what they *as individuals* have reason to do. And if the result is to give them all a reason for acting, the reason that the vote identifies must be a reason that everyone can acknowledge. Moral reasons are usually regarded as aspiring to this general character. Ideally, then, democracy will be a way of discovering moral truths regarding how the members of the group should behave—a way of determining what the moral good, as it bears on the actions of the individual members, is.[25]

But how is the expertise of the group in this or any other matter to be established? This question is vital since one cannot decide to believe something. One has to suppose that there are good reasons for believing it—which includes good reasons for regarding any putative expert as right about it. There seems to be no reason in principal why an inductive criterion could not be used to establish a group's success. When the measures voted on are judgments, they

---

[25] One question that arises for epistemic conceptions of democracy is why what a group should do is to be determined by a vote of its members rather than the vote of some other, possibly larger group. This question is especially pressing if the vote is meant to identify the moral good. We often suppose that impartial outsiders are better able to determine what agents morally ought to do.

could have the character of predictions; and even when they do not have this feature, they could be perceived by each as more fitting than the judgments with which he or she began.[26] As it happens, however, in the case of groups, mathematics can also be employed to establish E-authority. The Condorcet jury theorem shows that if the individual judgments of the members of a group about some issue are more likely to be right than not, the group's decision, as determined by a vote in which each member expresses his opinion about this issue, is virtually certain to be correct if the group is large enough.[27]

This result may seem to fly in the face of common sense because it suggests that a vote is like an experiment in science. In the latter case, different researchers may advance competing hypotheses, but once the experiment is performed, all who made erroneous predictions change their minds. This is not, however, what happens when votes are held. Those in the minority do not change their minds; they do not suddenly decide that they were wrong all along.

It could be replied that this is simply a result of unfamiliarity with the jury theorem, but there is another explanation. One has a reason to regard the hypothesis that gets the most votes as true only if one has reason to regard the voters as more likely to be right than not. The voters must be established as having a certain amount of expertise for one to have a good reason to regard the winning hypothesis as true.[28] But one must use an inductive criterion to determine that the voters have this competence, and it may be difficult to get the required inductive evidence.

The difficulties involved here are especially acute when the issue to be decided has a moral dimension. As we have seen, moral expertise cannot be established by an external criterion. People can be judged likely to be right only by a history of compelling argument or fitting performance. This in itself does not rule out the application of the Condorcet jury theorem. But as was noted in Chapter Four, internal criteria work in such a way that when there is first-order disagreement about what is right, there is also second-order disagreement about who is an expert. So the epistemic virtues of voting cannot be realized when a group must decide moral issues about which its members strongly disagree, which is to say, these virtues cannot be realized in precisely those cases where a group would have the most use for a reliable source of moral expertise.

---

[26] It is less clear how the possession by a group, as opposed to the individual members of it, of a history of successful argument is to be understood.

[27] For an account of Condorcet's jury theorem, see Cohen (1986). An accessible proof of the jury theorem can be found in Estlund (forthcoming).

[28] See Estlund (1993), sec. 11.

There does not, then, seem to be much prospect of justifying democracy by reference to the epistemic virtues of voting when people's votes express their moral judgments. But voting is only the culmination of the democratic process; it is preceded by making proposals and, especially, by deliberation. So perhaps the claim that democracy has epistemic virtues can be made out by reference to these features of it, in particular to the judgment improving properties of deliberation. To view democracy as having this effect, we do not need to regard the judgments as capable of being true or false. As we noted in Chapter Four, we can distinguish between better or worse judgments—relative to some sensibility—even if noncognitivism provides the correct account of these judgments.

One way democratic deliberation could improve judgment is that in the course of such deliberation, each member of the group could discover that (relative to his sensibility) a particular member deserved to be acknowledged as an expert in moral matters of the sort under consideration. But the epistemic role of democratic deliberation, as opposed to ordinary E-authority, is clearest if we make two assumptions. First, while some people could, in principle, have greater competence in a matter about which the group is deliberating—either because of their sharper vision, or their superior taste, or their greater reasoning ability—no one has the sort of history of success that would warrant according her the status of expert on this matter. And second, on any given occasion, any of the members may have a better understanding of the matter being decided than the others in the group. Democratic deliberation can then be viewed as a device that enables the group to benefit from the occasionally superior judgment of its different members. The satisfaction of these conditions does not imply that the group is an expert to be deferred to. If disagreement remains after deliberation, a vote will not eliminate it. But actions by the members that, if repeated often enough, might justify conferring the status of expert on them—especially the provision of compelling arguments—enable others to subject their own judgments to rational revision.

It is important to see how the role of deliberation in improving judgment differs from the role that it plays when votes merely express preferences. In the latter case, discussion of the preconditions and consequences of certain acts may change one's mind about what actions one wants the group to perform. One may discover, when these matters are fully discussed, that one does not prefer what one thought one preferred. This happens, however, because one acquires a better understanding of the properties of the various means to one's ends. When votes express judgments, by contrast, reasoning about ends is a possibility. One may thus discover through shared deliberation that an end that one initially thought appropriate does not have the value that one initially thought it had.

On this way of understanding the epistemic benefits of democracy, each is educated by the deliberative process and can suppose others to have been as well. Thus, each can plausibly regard the result of a vote taken after shared deliberation as more likely to be correct—to be in accordance with reason in the matter at hand—than the result of a vote taken before. That is, *given that a decision is to be made democratically*, it is more likely to be correct if the vote is preceded by shared deliberation. It does not, however, follow that a group member has any reason to regard the result of a vote as more likely to be correct than the judgment *he* makes after observing and participating in the process of shared deliberation. So his compliance with it will still depend on his regarding democracy as a way of exercising legitimate C-authority, the ultimate case for which is moral rather than epistemic.

Although democratic *deliberation* could have epistemic virtues, improving the judgments of a group's members, the argument for *voting* must be the same as that which justifies it when votes merely express preferences. It is a fair or welfare-maximizing way of resolving disagreement about which directives are to give expression to C-authority. The only difference is that these disagreements are what might be called "informed disagreements," since they have been shaped by shared deliberation about what ends the group should adopt. When we first considered epistemic democracy, it seemed to promise a whole new way of justifying democracy. For the normal justification thesis alone—that is, without supplementation by moral values—can justify E-authority. But given that there is no reason to regard the result of a vote as revealing the judgment of some sort of expert, at least when votes register moral judgments and the group members disagree about moral matters, the epistemic virtues of deliberation do not relieve us of the need of viewing democracy as a form of C-authority justified by the values of fairness and welfare maximization.

Consensus

We must be careful, however, not to be too dismissive here. One important new element has been introduced. When people deliberate in a public forum, trying to justify their positions to each other, they may sometimes reach a consensus. Collective deliberation may make a vote unnecessary because it eliminates all disagreement. Or, a vote may reveal that a consensus exists. To be sure, this is also a possibility when votes merely express preferences that are beyond rational criticism. Consensus is more likely, however, when deliberation takes the form not just of pointing out to people how they can get what they want but also of rational assessment of ends.

It will be useful to consider why this is so. Given that one's aim is to convince enough others to vote for the measures that one regards as appropriate, one will not merely be using the debate to refine one's own judgment. One will also be trying to change the minds of those who disagree. But when one puts one's case in terms to which one thinks others will be susceptible, one makes it vulnerable to rebuttal in these same terms. Of course, one might choose argumentative ploys solely on the basis of their likely effectiveness in convincing others, without accepting their implications oneself, but this would involve a kind of unfairness. To put it another way, one's efforts to convince others of one's position make one susceptible to a requirement of fairness to deliberate in good faith regarding the matters under consideration, which is to say, to consider the arguments of others. This is an application of the value of fairness to the process of deliberation that goes beyond the requirements of procedural fairness that dictate such things as giving everyone a chance to speak. In light of this requirement to deliberate in good faith, the possibility of a consensus emerging is greater than when votes merely express preferences. In the latter case, fairness requires only that each get an equal opportunity to deliver causally efficacious remarks.[29]

Why is a consensus worth seeking? After all, consensus does not imply truth. Consensus is a matter of convergence of judgment, and there can be convergence on a falsehood. One important reason a consensus is worth seeking is that the emergence of a consensus has implications for the exercise of authority. Where there is consensus that a certain course of action should be followed, there is no need for preemption of anyone's judgment of what the applicable directive-independent reasons require, and thus no need for authority. This is important because, as we have seen, when democracy is a way of exercising C-authority, its justification depends on moral values. Although we have sought justifying values that are widely shared, there is no guarantee that they will be shared by all. So the fact that democracy may sometimes produce consensus is an additional factor in its favor.

---

[29] I have presented the requirement to deliberate in good faith as a requirement of fairness or reciprocity. But it could also be presented as a requirement of rationality itself. For not to consider the arguments of others is irrational as well as unfair.

It must be emphasized here that we are speaking of a genuine consensus, that is, agreement about what the applicable directive-independent reasons require, as opposed to a compromise in which people accept a course of action for all to pursue while retaining the conviction that some other course would be preferable. If a consensus is to have the authority-dissolving effect that has just been sketched, all must come to agree that one of the alternatives facing the group is the best thing the group could do. Conversely, putting a compromise into effect requires authority, or some other device that will insure that each of the parties to the arrangement has a reason to act contrary to his judgment of what the applicable directive-independent reasons require. It should be noted, however, that compromises can be assessed as fair or unfair, and thus there could be a genuine consensus on the fairness of a compromise.

Consensus is usually a feasible goal only in small groups, but the beneficial effects of deliberation in reducing the strains associated with the exercise of authority do not depend on actually reaching a consensus. To regard a given de facto authority as a legitimate C-authority one must be able to regard the collective implementation of its directives as preferable to the noncooperative outcome. But the less severe the disagreement among the members of the group, the less likely it is that any one of them will find noncooperation preferable. Even when consensus is unlikely, then, aiming at it can have a beneficial effect on a C-authority's authority.

It should be borne in mind, however, that if the group does not achieve a consensus, and voting is resorted to, there will still be the possibility of entrenched minorities. Even if we suppose that votes express rationally revisable judgments, then, we must provide for constitutional limitations on democratic decision making, limitations that protect certain individual rights in order to insure that the outcomes produced by implementing authoritative directives are not grossly unfair to any of the members of the group.

Democratic Legitimacy

What are the implications of the foregoing remarks for the legitimacy of democratically exercised C-authority? Since the normal justification thesis can support compliance with the directives of a dictatorial C-authority, we cannot say that those who accept the values of fairness and welfare maximization have no reason to obey other C-authorities. The conclusion can only be that such people will regard the democratic exercise of C-authority as possessing greater moral validity than any other way of exercising it. Each such person will want to do as well as she can consistent with everyone else also doing well, and thus will bring to bear some conception of the members doing well collectively. The basic values of fairness and welfare maximization provide such conceptions. Together they call either for the exercise of C-authority in a way that maximizes equal attainment of objectives (which democracy alone accomplishes over time when there are no entrenched minorities) or in a way that maximizes the aggregate attainment of objectives within constraints justified by fairness (which liberal democracy accomplishes when there are entrenched minorities).

This account of democratic legitimacy raises questions, however, about the status of moral convictions in a democratic society. Some people will regard their conceptions of the moral good as so important that they take precedence over fairness and welfare maximization, and thus will not view democracy as the most appropriate way of exercising C-authority. If such a person is able to get power, he will see no reason to accept demands for a transition to democracy, and if he lives in a democratic society, he will try to transform it into a dictatorship organized around his conception of the moral good.

The above account of the moral validity of democracy provides no way of refuting such people since it takes as axiomatic the supreme moral importance of fairness and welfare maximization. The scope of the challenge that they pose to democracy is, however, more limited than it might initially seem. An existing democracy need not tolerate the subversive efforts of such people on the ground that it cannot claim legitimate authority over them. For they remain susceptible to the basic justification of C-authority. It will usually be true for them as well that cooperation to implement any of a variety of directives is preferable to general noncooperation, and thus there will be good reason for them to obey the directives of any de facto C-authority, including a democratic C-authority, that meets this condition. The only exception would be a case in which they could plausibly suppose that the chaos that would result if C-authority collapsed would be quickly followed by a dictatorship more to their liking. In such a situation, they would be justified in trying to foment revolution. But this means that their rejection of fairness and welfare maximization would normally have significance only if they attained power.[30]

---

[30] There will rarely be good reason for supposing that the collapse of authority will be followed by better arrangements. In general, there would seem to be as good reason to expect a worse regime as to expect a better one. It should also be noted that while a democratic authority cannot legitimately force those who have no reason to comply with its directives to accept its authority—it must allow them to emigrate, for

The possibility of such zealots raises a question, however, about those whose respect for fairness or welfare maximization makes them accept democracy. If people can be led by their strong allegiance to a particular conception of the moral good to reject the democratic ideal, does this mean that only those who lack strong moral convictions can embrace this ideal? To put it another way, does this mean that the only values to which anyone who embraces the democratic ideal can have a strong commitment are those that underwrite the political morality of democracy itself—fairness and welfare maximization?

It will be useful to begin by considering political liberalism rather than democracy. It will be recalled that political liberalism is a way of securing, at least in part, the output-criterion equal consideration that fairness requires when there are entrenched minorities. Here there is not so much a weakening of substantive moral conceptions as a restriction of their scope. A conception of the moral good may be regarded as having two components, a personal ideal of morally adequate or exemplary conduct by oneself, and a social ideal of a morally adequate or exemplary social order, which may include conformity by everyone to one's personal ideal. Political liberalism has the effect of separating these two components, allowing agents to retain their personal ideals as genuine conceptions of the way a component of the world (namely, they themselves) ought to be. The fate of social ideals, however, is determined by the exercise of authority, and liberal constraints grounded in the value of fairness will sometimes block their enactment into law.[31] In a liberal social order, then, full moral status seems to be enjoyed only by (1) the fairness-based political morality of liberalism, and (2) each individual's personal ideal. Social ideals appear to have a diminished status.

To the extent that these appearances reflect reality, political liberalism cannot claim the allegiance of all regardless of their substantive moral views. The case for liberalism is basically a conflict avoidance case. When the members of a given society hold different and

---

example—it can defend itself against them if they refuse to leave. For it is in a state of nature with respect to them.

[31] For one view about when such ideals can be legitimately enforced by a majority see Nagel (1987), esp. sec. 7. The paradigmatically liberal position, exemplified by its treatment of religion (at least in the United States), is that there should be no official expression of the social ideals of any of the competing conceptions of the good, considered as such. But allowing official expression of the ideals of the majority to the extent that this does not infringe on the ability of minorities to pursue their personal ideals is a possible liberal position as well—although perhaps not as much in the fair spirit of liberalism as trying to give some official expression to each of the different social ideals held by the members of the larger society.

incompatible social ideals, there are essentially three possibilities: liberalism, segregation (into subgroups each of which is governed by a particular social ideal), and civil war. Liberalism claims to be the best of these on both fairness and maximizing grounds, but those holding some social ideals may prefer segregation, and some may judge conflict in a good cause preferable to what they regard as a morally corrupt peace.[32]

Now let us consider the situation when there are no entrenched minorities. Here, democracy alone suffices to secure the output-criterion equal consideration favored by the value of fairness. Voting to enact social ideals will result over time in each finding her ideal enacted equally often. But, abstracting from any commitment she may have to the values of fairness and welfare maximization, each will judge this outcome less desirable than dictatorship on her terms. Does this mean that the members of a democratically governed group cannot regard their conception of the moral good as articulating genuine moral requirements, as opposed to mere interests of theirs?

There is a sense in which the citizens of a democracy do view their substantive moral conceptions as mere interests, as claims the satisfaction of which is important in the first instance as satisfying them. This emerges most clearly when we invoke the value of welfare maximization in support of democracy when people's votes express moral conceptions. To speak of maximizing the aggregate satisfaction of different moral conceptions seems to be to treat them as interests. If democracy is a way of exercising C-authority, however, there is also a sense in which the citizens of a democracy can continue to regard their particular conceptions of the moral good as articulating genuine moral requirements. This can be seen by considering the so-called paradox of democracy.

It has been suggested that democracy generates a paradox.[33] Someone who accepts the appropriateness of democratic decision making will believe that she morally ought to comply with any directives that the majority enacts. But in proposing and voting for various measures, she expresses her convictions about what the group morally ought to do. Thus, if she finds herself in the minority, she will apparently be confronted with a situation in which she must judge both that she morally ought to comply and that she morally ought not to.

---

[32] Segregation, however, still implies that subgroups will follow a right-respecting, and thus liberal, "foreign policy" in their relations with other subgroups.

[33] See Wollheim (1962).

The zealot's posture toward democracy seems to reflect one response to this contradiction. The zealot appears to reject one of the conflicting ought-judgments; he denies that he morally ought to comply with democratically enacted directives. This suggests that a committed democrat must take the opposite course and reject the judgment that she morally ought to act on the concerns to which she gives expression in the process of voting—thus demoting them to the status of mere interests. In fact, both of these characterizations of the situation are mistaken.

The paradox of democracy is dissolved when we reflect on the preemptive character of all authority relations. To accept the legitimacy of an authority is to regard its directives as preemptive reasons for action, reasons that exclude and take the place of one's judgment of what the applicable directive-independent reasons require. But as we saw in Chapter Two, this "surrender of judgment" is solely a practical matter; the directive replaces the judgment for practical purposes only. One can continue to judge an authoritative directive mistaken as long as one does not act on one's judgment.

Preemption played a role in our earlier discussion of the zealot. There we saw that his judgment that his substantive conception of the moral good has greater moral importance than the values of fairness and welfare maximization does not buy him very much. It means that he will acknowledge no reason to accede to demands for democracy or liberal rights if he ever attains power, but it does not provide him with a basis for concluding that he need not comply with the directives generated by an existing democratic authority. For, unless conditions are favorable for a revolutionary change of government that would be to his liking, he must still accept such an authority as a legitimate C-authority because general compliance with its directives would be preferable, by his own lights, to the noncooperative outcome.

The status of democratic authorities as legitimate C-authorities also, however, shows that those who accord a preeminent position to the political morality of fairness and welfare maximization need not be regarded as demoting their substantive moral conceptions to the status of mere interests. To be sure, these conceptions are treated as interests in so far as it is thought necessary to give each a fair share of what he wants, or to maximize overall satisfaction of these claims. But democracy (that is; democratic C-authority) adopts this posture toward substantive moral conceptions only after they have been preempted. And as we have seen, preemption need not involve abandoning one's conviction of the rightness of the preempted judgments. So democracy, viewed as reflexive authority, is compatible with moral conviction. Similar reasoning shows that political liberalism, understood as a way of exercising authority, is compatible with moral conviction about social ideals.[34]

I believe that democracy is best viewed as reflexive authority, the collective exercise of authority by those subject to it, in all those cases (the norm in large groups) where deliberation does not produce a consensus. But it is possible to take the production of a consensus by deliberation—as opposed to the resolution of disagreements by voting—as the paradigm of democratic decision making. A recent example is provided by Joshua Cohen. Cohen understands democracy in terms of an ideal deliberative procedure that aims at consensus among those committed to free deliberation among equals. He suggests that a group's shaping of its common life by shared deliberation is valuable in its own right; and he asserts that democratic institutions are best justified as giving expression to this value, rather than by considerations of fairness.[35]

In addition to construing democracy less as a competitive game and more as a cooperative process, this view can be regarded as a response to recent developments in moral theory. A traditional theme in political thought holds that societies benefit when disputes are understood as conflicts of interest, as opposed to disagreements of principle, because interests can be compromised while principles cannot. With the recent flowering of normative moral theory, however, it has come to seem unsatisfactory to ignore the moral dimension of political disputes, and this raises the question of how the centrigual effects of disagreements of principle are to be avoided. The deliberative approach to democracy appears to embody the hope that since moral positions admit of deliberative modification, disagreements of principle can be overcome by shared deliberation

---

[34] To be more precise, one can retain moral conviction in the sense of retaining one's view of what individual rationality requires when applied to one's conception of the moral good. What the values of fairness and welfare maximization outweigh is one's preference, within the range of options that are acceptable from the standpoint of collective rationality, for the cooperative scheme that is most favorable to one's own conception.

[35] See Cohen (1989). Deliberative democracy is starting to receive a good deal of attention, but I shall discuss only Cohen's formulation. Cohen (1988) argues that the ideal of deliberative democracy can be more fully realized if socialist arrangements, in the form of social control of investment and worker self-management, are in place. I discuss the implications of democracy as reflexive authority for these questions in Chapter Nine. It may be noted here, however, that on my view, democracy will more fully satisfy the moral values that support it if all have fair access to the means of communication.

on the moral merits of the issues a society faces. The initially divergent moral convictions of the members of the group will be transformed into a shared conviction by the process of deliberation.

This view cannot be given detailed consideration here, but I believe that there are reasons for doubting whether the process of deliberation can, in the end, avoid the sort of compromising of principles that is inimical to moral conviction. I also believe that relying on authority to resolve disputes can accommodate moral conviction better than deliberation to the sort of consensus a group will usually have to settle for.

Consensus removes the need for authority, which means that it removes the preemption that protects moral conviction. This causes no problems if the members of the group can always reach what I shall call a "strong consensus" about what measures to adopt. A strong consensus exists when there is agreement on the substantive rightness of some course of action. To the extent that a group succeeds in reaching a strong consensus, fairness need play no role in justifying compliance with democratically generated directives. For if a group can reach a strong consensus, no one will have to subordinate his substantive moral views.[36]

Earlier, however, I noted that there can also be a consensus on what would constitute a fair compromise between the claims of the competing conceptions, that is, on what would constitute giving output-criterion equal consideration to these claims. Let us call such a consensus on what fairness requires a "weak consensus." A weak consensus stands midway between a strong consensus and a vote. A group that cannot achieve a strong consensus may still be able to avoid a vote by achieving a weak consensus. It is plausible that a group seeking to reach a consensus through collective deliberation will often have to settle for a weak consensus. Although the power of collective deliberation to generate a consensus on the substantive rightness of a course of action should not be underestimated, this process usually takes a good deal of time. When an issue is first perceived as confronting a society, positions on how to address it are likely to diverge greatly, and it is only after prolonged debate that any convergence can be detected. Often, however, a group must

[36] For a view of democratic decision making that regards it as appropriately aiming at a strong consensus and that sketches some principles that should govern relations between people seeking such a consensus, see Gutmann and Thompson (1990). It is worth noting that the exercise of authority may contribute to the emergence of a strong consensus. It is plausible, for example, that the enactment of the Thirteenth Amendment has contributed significantly to the present consensus in the United States that slavery is morally impermissible. This is another reason for doubting that authority can be replaced by deliberation to a consensus.

make a decision about how to address an issue before full convergence is achieved, so weak consensus will be the only sort of consensus that it can hope for.

The compromise that weak consensus entails can, however, be subversive of moral conviction. When fairness plays the role of grounding a weak consensus on what would be a fair compromise between competing claims, it has the effect of demoting other moral concerns to mere interests. This can be seen by noting the parallels between Cohen's deliberative conception of democracy and contractarian moral theories.[37] Thomas Scanlon's formulation of such a theory provides a good example. He defines the moral wrongness of an action as follows. "An act is wrong if its performance under the circumstances would be disallowed by any system of rules for the general regulation of behavior which no one could reasonably reject as a basis for informed, unforced general agreement."[38] The idea of reasonable rejection is tied to the desire to reach agreement. The standard is what one who desired to reach such an agreement could reasonably reject.[39] But this idea of reasonable rejection is very close to the idea of a fair compromise. What one could reasonably reject is, in an important respect, what one could reject as unfair to oneself given the total set of competing claims. To put it another way, the idea of agreement among people who want to reach an agreement that no one can reasonably reject is, in an important respect, the idea of agreement among people committed to offering reasons of fairness in support of their positions and considering with an open mind the reasons of fairness offered by others. In effect, then, Scanlon defines the moral point of view in terms of what would be agreed to by a process of ideal democratic deliberation that reached a consensus on what fairness requires. If moral right and wrong is understood as the *outcome* of this (ideal) process, however, any moral character that the concerns of the parties might initially have had must be lost in the course of it. And the same must apparently be said of the concerns brought to a process of actual democratic deliberation that achieves a weak consensus on a fair compromise between the competing views.[40]

[37] These parallels are noted in Christiano (1990).

[38] Scanlon (1982), p. 110.

[39] As we have seen, Cohen's view contains a similar provision in that consensus is sought among those committed to free deliberation among equals.

[40] It might be thought that there is no problem here if the moral standard appealed to in democratic deliberation is one like Scanlon's. For if morality is understood in this constructivist way, actual democratic deliberation that seeks a weak consensus can be regarded as a surrogate for morality, approximating its requirements. In fact, the problem remains. The members of the group will start with different views about

Viewing democracy as a fair and welfare maximizing way of exercising authority appears, then, to have advantages over viewing it simply as a process of deliberation. For the role that the values of fairness and welfare maximization play in justifying the democratic exercise of C-authority, unlike the role that fairness will often play in characterizing democratic deliberation that aims at a consensus, is not one that forces those employing democratic procedures to think of their substantive moral conceptions as mere interests. This is not to deny that, in many respects, the deliberated exercise of reflexive or democratic authority, the sort of exercise preceded by shared deliberation, is preferable to its undeliberated exercise. We saw earlier why this is so. The point is simply that given that the goal is to decide disputes between people holding different conceptions of the moral good—to determine a social response to them—deciding them by the reflexive exercise of authority may have a less corrosive effect on moral commitments than trying to decide them entirely through deliberation, and thus often settling for a weak consensus on what would be a fair compromise.

Democracy and Expertise

The foregoing argument for democracy presupposes that while, on any given occasion, some of the members of a group may produce more compelling arguments or judgments than others, no one has the sort of regularly superior competence in the relevant areas that would justify conferring upon him the social status of expert in those areas. Can democratic decision making play a role when some people do have the social status of experts? This question is especially germane for our purposes since as we saw at the end of Chapter Four, C-authority often involves E-authority on how best to achieve the benefits of cooperation.[41]

There are at least two separate questions here. One is whether there is any legitimate role for democracy in the exercise of expert authority per se. The other is whether there is a role for democracy in

---

what would constitute a fair reconciliation of their competing interests (or about the common good or the general will), and to the extent that democratic deliberation strikes a fair compromise among them, it will involve the demotion of their initial moral concerns to mere interests. Of course, this would cause no difficulty if all accepted that in striking a fair compromise between their different views of the common good, they were actually identifying the common good. But there is no reason to suppose this, and, it is not the idea behind epistemic democracy.

[41] Strictly speaking, the argument that the values of fairness and welfare maximization create a presumption in favor of the democratic exercise of C-authority covers only the case where expertise does not play a role.

choosing who is to exercise authority in certain situations where expertise is a qualification for being in authority.

Democracy and E-Authority

Can there be democratic exercise of E-authority? Suppose that, by virtue of a history of past success, one of the members of a group is appropriately acknowledged as an expert on an issue facing the group. Suppose further that each member of the group votes for the hypothesis that seems right in light of his own assessment of the evidence, so that the expert gets one vote along with everyone else. This way of combining democracy with expertise is not a way of exercising E-authority but of undermining it. Democracy makes it less likely that the group will be guided by the truth.

Another possibility, if the expert's E-authority is generally acknowledged within the group, is that each votes in accordance with the expert's assertion instead of on the basis of his own assessment of the evidence. Such a vote would not deprive the group of the benefits of the expert's expertise, but neither would it add anything to simply deferring to her *ab initio*. That is, a vote, regarded as a mechanism by which the members of a group can reach a decision about which of a competing set of judgments to accept, is redundant when each votes in accordance with the assertions of someone acknowledged as an expert—although it might have some value as a public demonstration that a given individual has this status for all.[42]

These points focus on the voting aspect of democracy, but introducing the deliberative aspect does not alter the situation. To be sure, collective deliberation might improve the exercise of a given individual's E-authority by bringing to her attention pieces of evidence of which she was not previously aware. But as long as the members of the group have good reason to acknowledge her as an E-authority on the matter at issue, they will usually do better to accept the assertions that she finally makes after hearing all the evidence than to combine her vote about what the evidence supports with theirs. Similarly, shared deliberation might improve the competence of the nonexperts over time and eventually create a situation in which all in the group had the same level of expertise; but prior to the attainment of this state of affairs, the nonexperts

---

[42] Actually, this is not quite correct. Estlund (forthcoming) argues that in some circumstances, the epistemic advantages of voting revealed by the Condorcet jury theorem can be grafted onto an individual's expertise with the result that voting on whether to accept her assertion improves the group's chance of being right.

would usually do better to defer to the expert's judgment than to let their beliefs be determined by a vote.

Where there is legitimate E-authority, then, there is little place for democratic decision making. This point applies as well when someone has practical E-authority that is expressed in directives. The rationale for accepting these directives is still that one better complies with the reasons that apply to one by doing so. This includes the case in which C-authority is based on expertise in identifying solutions to coordination problems. In all of these cases, democracy will usually either dilute the benefits of expertise or provide a redundant echo of them. These points are not new, having first been made by Plato. In *The Republic*, he describes an ideal society in which certain people hold political authority by virtue of their superior knowledge of the good, and he argues that democracy is as inappropriate when such people are available as it would be on a ship in which some people possessed expertise in navigation.[43]

This stark result is softened somewhat, however, if we add to the picture the possibility of disagreement among experts. People who are experts, in the sense that they are more likely to make correct judgments about certain matters than the average member of the population, can still disagree with each other. Such disagreement tends to undermine E-authority by providing a reason for not deferring to the judgment of any one of the putative experts. When this happens, the members of the population at large must decide the question at issue themselves. And when it is a question about what they should do as a group, democratic procedures will be appropriate for deciding it.

To be sure, in such cases, the deliberative stage of democratic decision making will have a somewhat different character than it does when all are equally expert and deliberation is merely a way of benefiting from the fact that on any given occasion, any member of the group might have a better idea. The disagreeing experts will tend to dominate discussion, since the rest will want to hear what they have to say before making up their minds. Indeed, debates among the experts might be the best form for democratic deliberation to take in such a case. But a vote by the group as a whole will still be necessary to decide the issue, and the justification for it will be that proceeding in this way best serves the values of fairness and welfare maximization.

In cases of the latter sort, we cannot really speak of a democratic way of exercising E-authority since by hypothesis, no one individ-

[43] Plato (1945), 488a.

ual, or group sharing a method, has the social status of an E-authority (in the sense that everyone in the group is prepared to defer to her judgment). What we have instead is a democratic way of benefiting from differences in expertise. Indeed, there is a continuum of possibilities here. Ordinary democracy, at least where votes express rationally revisable judgments, is justified in part by the fact that it enables the group to benefit from the possibility that on any given occasion, one of its members may have a better idea. If some members have a better "batting average" than others, but there is still disagreement within this subgroup, the situation is transformed into the one that we have just been considering. There will be individuals whose views the rest of the group will always want to hear before making up their minds, or who the rest will want to see debate each other. And if one individual demonstrates superior competence so often that there seems to be good reason for the others to abandon any efforts to assess the evidence themselves and simply defer to her, the situation becomes one in which E-authority is established, and democracy is usually inappropriate or redundant.

So far we have been considering what role democracy might play in a group's acceptance of the communications of individuals possessing greater expertise. A related question concerns the role of democracy in a decision regarding whom to install in an office when expertise is relevant to the successful exercise of the de facto authority associated with the office. Among the more important cases of this sort are those in which some have expertise in identifying coordination problems and solutions to them. As we have seen, in these cases E-authority merges into C-authority. In other cases, experts in some technical field may be given the authority to direct cooperative efforts to achieve certain preestablished ends by technical means. It would, for example, be plausible to make a civil engineer director of a dam-building project.

If everyone in the subject population accepted the superior competence of the same individual, her democratic appointment to an office for which her competence was a qualification would not be necessary to insure the legitimate exercise of the de facto authority associated with it. Someone who simply seized the office, or who was appointed without consulting the subordinates by an individual or group possessing a conventionally established power of appointment, could still be acknowledged by the subordinates as having the sort of record of success that would justify deferring to her judgments. Similarly, the decision regarding who has the expertise to occupy a given office might be one that it takes a certain sort of expertise to make. Thus, other experts, rather than the subordinates, might be best qualified to decide who had the technical expertise to lead a group of people engaged in building a dam. Again, if the person chosen enabled the subordinates to perform better, they would have a good reason for complying with her directives, despite the fact they had not elected her.

When the case is not this ideal one, however—when there is disagreement in the subject population about who possesses the expertise needed to fill an office—the values of fairness and welfare maximization require that the occupants of offices be chosen democratically by their future subordinates.

Representative Democracy

These points are relevant to the justification of representative democracy. In representative democracy, democratic decision making takes place in two parts. First, there is democratic election of representatives, with the three stages of proposal, deliberation, and voting being engaged in by those choosing a representative. Then, the representatives decide, using the same three stages, what directives will guide the group. Before we examine how differences in expertise might play a role in justifying representative democracy, however, it is useful to consider what can be said for this form of democracy when all are equally expert.

Some political theorists have suggested that representative democracy is not really a method by which a people rules itself. Rather, it is a method by which a people chooses a government to rule it. Various members of the elite compete with each other for political office, and the people choose some of them.[44] On this view, the virtues of democracy are purely protective. Power corrupts, but democracy—understood as the choosing of governors by election—gives the members of the population in general a means of replacing one ruler, or set of rulers, by another before the corruption advances too far.

This picture is plausible as long as the candidates for office are members of elite groups. But if we make the assumption, admittedly counterfactual in the current circumstances, that all have an equal opportunity to run for office, a people can be regarded as ruling itself under representative democracy no less than under direct democracy. At least this is so if candidates for office reveal to the

[44] See Schumpeter (1950), pp. 269–73.

electorate a consistent value system, and if they can be relied upon to put it into effect once they take office. Then, to choose someone to occupy an office is simply to choose the principles that will be used to decide questions that arise in that office, and this is, in effect, to decide these questions oneself. To be sure, the individual chosen as a representative may not have exactly the value system as any of the electors. She is chosen as the most acceptable of all the candidates. Thus, even those who vote for her will probably not find her decisions optimal. But this is usually true in direct democracy as well. The winning proposal may not be regarded by anyone in the majority as optimal.

If the account of representative democracy just provided is acceptable, it would seem to be as fair and welfare maximizing a way of deciding what directives will guide a group's actions as direct democracy.[45] Of course, direct democracy is preferable if participation in political activities is regarded as intrinsically valuable, but only some members of the population will hold such a view. From the standpoint of those who have the opposite view—who would like to have as little to do with the political process as possible, consistent its production of fair and welfare maximizing outcomes—representative democracy will be preferable.[46]

A further consideration, however, supports representative over direct democracy. Representative democracy is more efficient. Decision making is time consuming, and there are limits to the amount of time that a group can rationally devote to it. These limits derive from the fact that the enterprise of generating directives has a point only on the assumption that they will be put into effect. But a group will have only a finite number of person-hours at its disposal, which must be divided between decision and execution, and the more time is devoted to decision making, the less there will be for execution. Direct democracy, however, can be very time consuming, the more so the larger the group. Thus, a group may find it appropriate to opt for representative democracy.[47] To put it another way, in deciding what to do, a group must restrict itself to alternatives that can be implemented in the time remaining after the decision is made. The group may, however, find it appropriate to limit the resources it

[45] I set aside the question of whether proportional representation is preferable on grounds of fairness and welfare maximization to representation of districts.

[46] Cf. the distinction that Rawls (1988, sec. 7) makes between civic humanism and classical republicanism.

[47] For a statement of a case for centralized decision making based on the desirability of economizing on the transmission of information, see Arrow (1974), p. 68.

devotes to decision making so as to make available a wider range of alternatives, in which case representative democracy will be a more suitable choice than direct democracy.

These considerations are similar to those encountered earlier when we saw that authority is preferable to norm formation as a device for facilitating cooperation when decisions must be made quickly. Likewise, within the sphere of democratically exercised authority, representative democracy is preferable to direct democracy when decisions have to be made quickly. And when they have to be made very quickly, electoral dictatorship may be preferable to representative democracy.

Now that we have looked at the choice between representative and direct democracy on the assumption that no one has the status of an expert, let us reintroduce this element. It is common in discussions of representative democracy to pose the question whether representatives should be understood as simply carrying out the instructions of those who have elected them or as having been elected to use their judgment. The exercise of judgment could have as its object what would be best for a given representative's constituents, or what would be best for the group as a whole, or what the group as a whole ought to do, which would sometimes involve sacrificing its interests for the sake of people outside the group. Let us call these two views of representation the agency view and the trustee view, since in the former case representatives have the status of agents who have a duty to act under the direction of those who elect them, while in the latter case they have only a duty to assess responsibly the reasons applicable to some group.

Expertise could be relevant to the choice of representatives of either sort. Some might have technical expertise that would make them better agents. For example, they might be better than most at building coalitions to achieve the objectives their constituents wanted; or they might be more skilled at making emotional appeals that would move other legislators, or more likely, those for whom these legislators were serving as agents. Alternatively, some might be regarded by their constituents as having expertise that qualified them to judge what policies the society as a whole should adopt. This latter possibility modifies somewhat the social role of debates among disagreeing experts. When such debates take place in a legislative assembly, the whole society can be educated by them, but the decision about who has formulated the best case is made by the legislators alone. This could be advantageous from the standpoint of the larger group if the greater expertise of the legislators made them better than the average person at determining who had won a debate.

Conclusion

We should emphasize the important role that expertise plays in all forms of democratic decision making when the matters to be decided appear to be susceptible to rational assessment. Even when no one in a group employing democratic procedures has the status of an expert on the matters being decided, democratic deliberation is essentially a way of harnessing the fact that on any given occasion, some member of the group may have a better idea than others or be in possession of facts that others do not possess. Similarly, if some have the sort of superior competence that justifies routinely consulting them, democracy is essentially a way of harnessing this fact for the benefit of the group. The group may make collective decisions only after hearing what they have to say, or elect them to offices where they will have de facto authority over the group, either individually or as part of a representative body. These are important points to bear in mind in light of the egalitarian image of democracy. Democracy is egalitarian in the sense that in the end each voter has an equal say in the question of where the expertise lies or of what judgments or arguments are superior on a given occasion. But at bottom democratic deliberation is a competitive process that seeks to identify the best argument. It is a way of exploiting unequal competence for the benefit of the group.[48]

Finally, this discussion of democracy has concerned itself with its relation to C-authority and E-authority. Nothing has been said about the democratic exercise of P-authority, but the reasons are clear. Whether morality requires that those who promise to obey someone participate in the decision-making process that determines what directives will guide their actions depends on the content of the promise. If one promises to obey conditional on one's having equal input, one's promissory obligation will only require complying with democratically generated directives. But if one does not make such a promise, there is no presumption that P-authority should be democratically exercised.

[48] Thus Mill's notorious proposal that the better educated get more votes is approximated in the actual operation of democratic procedures that give each one vote. Those who are better judges convince people other than themselves in the course of democratic deliberation, and this has the same practical effect as giving them more votes. See Mill (1958), chap 8. For related discussion, see Sugden (1993).

PART II

MANAGERIAL AUTHORITY

CHAPTER SIX

MANAGEMENT AND MORALITY

Now that we have considered authority and democracy in general and in government, we can turn to the managerial case. As I mentioned in Chapter One, the principal focus of my argument is the question of whether nongovernmental organizations should be democratically managed by their employees. There I proposed that the question of democracy in the managerial sphere be approached as it is in the governmental sphere, not by considering whether it is called for by certain conceptions of the good life, which may not be widely shared, but rather by considering whether it is required if managerial authority is to be appropriately exercised.

The case with which I am primarily concerned is that of large corporations and other large organizations. I argue that managerial authority is better viewed as C-authority than P-authority, and I explore the implications of this for the appropriateness of managerial democracy. As we have seen, the values of fairness and welfare maximization create a presumption that C-authority should be democratically exercised, but in the managerial case, there may be other considerations capable of rebutting this presumption.

The Moral Dimension of Management

Before we can proceed, we must address some preliminary questions. The first of these concerns the nature of the directive-independent reasons that apply to employees. As we have seen, in an authority relation, the subordinate allows authoritative directives to preempt his judgment of what the applicable directive-independent reasons require, and an adequate justification of authority must justify this preemption. Whether preemption is justified in a given case will depend, however, on what the applicable directive-independent reasons are. What can justify the preemption of some reasons may not be able to justify the preemption of others.

As I have indicated, I am assuming that what a given subordinate has moral reason to do, independently of the directives he confronts, is what the reasons comprised within his conception of the moral good support, all things considered. Of course this will differ from person to person, but for people who have been raised in the same culture, the differences are more likely to take the form of disagreements about the relative weight of considerations generally acknowledged to have moral force than about what considerations have this force. I assume, then, that conceptions of the moral good are built up out of the considerations identified in Chapter Three as components of commonsense morality: deontological constraints and other requirements of fair treatment, morally important social values, and positive permissions to decline to promote these values when the sacrifice involved would be too great. As I said in Chapter One, I believe that to comply with managerial directives is often to contribute to a moral or political agenda that one does not share. This means that an adequate justification of authority must explain how managerial directives can preempt moral reasons for declining to comply.

The claim that for employees to comply with managerial directives can be for them to contribute to a moral or political agenda that they do not share involves two subclaims: (1) moral considerations are often relevant to the decisions by which managers establish policies for an organization or its parts, and (2) there is disagreement among the members of an organization about whether the policies that managers adopt are in fact morally appropriate. In this chapter I concentrate on defending the first subclaim; I address briefly the second subclaim at the end of the chapter.

It should be emphasized at the outset that in considering whether moral considerations are relevant to managerial decisions we are looking at the matter from the standpoint of the employees. Managers may in fact be guided solely by narrow economic goals such as increasing profits, market share, or stock price, or they may regard moral norms merely as features of the environment in which they operate to which lip service must be paid if corporate goals are to be achieved. But this is irrelevant for our purposes. To justify managerial authority is to justify it from the standpoint of the employees, and thus what matters is whether the moral considerations that they acknowledge—or ought to—bear on the choices that managers make.

The claim that some managerial decisions have moral significance would probably be accepted by most people. A decision to lobby against family-leave legislation would be an example. But I believe that a stronger claim is defensible. I believe that virtually all decisions of top managers have a moral dimension, in the sense that commonly acknowledged moral considerations are relevant to them and will be seen by those sensitive to these considerations to support some of the alternatives under consideration over others. I believe that virtually all decisions of middle-level managers have a moral dimension in this sense as well.

It may be useful to note at the beginning of this discussion that the way one contributes to a moral or political agenda by complying with managerial directives can differ from the way one contributes by obeying the law. James Coleman distinguishes between authority that is proscriptive, in the sense that authoritative directives prohibit certain actions, and authority that is prescriptive, in the sense that authoritative directives enjoin certain actions; and he also distinguishs between authority that is broad, that entails a right to direct a relatively comprehensive range of behaviors, and authority that is narrow.[1] The authority of governments is typically broad and proscriptive, with some prescriptive elements, most notably the requirement to pay taxes. Managerial authority, on the other hand, is typically narrow and prescriptive.

Fairness

Let us begin with the requirements of fairness. Earlier, I said that the fact that managers are concerned solely with the attainment of narrowly economic objectives such as the maximization of profit, market share, or stock price does not establish that these are the only goals relevant to the moral assessment of organizational performance. Indeed, they may not be relevant at all. But even if morality allowed managers to be concerned only with such goals, it would not follow that managerial decision making lacked a moral dimension. For considerations of fairness, in the microlevel sense of treating people fairly in the course of pursuing one's ends, would still have application. As I indicated in Chapter Three, the conventionally acknowledged deontological constraints can be regarded as identifying salient kinds of unfair treatment. But there may also be unfair treatment that is not associated with any one act type often enough to warrant the incorporation into conventional morality of a principle identifying it, and this, too, is to be avoided.

Claims of unfair treatment by managers pursuing their goals for an organization can arise from a number of quarters. Employees, consumers, and the neighbors of productive facilities could potentially have such claims. If, as some managerial theorists have ar-

---

[1] James Coleman (1990), pp. 83–84.

gued, the goals of managers can depart from what would be in the best interests of the shareholders, shareholders, too, can potentially claim unfair treatment by managers.[2] Examples of claims by members of these groups that could be regarded as claims to fair treatment include the claim of employees to a safe workplace, the claim of neighbors not to be showered with pollution, the claim of consumers not to be saddled with defective products, and the claim of investors to a reasonable return on their investment. In all of these cases, we can speak of potential unfairness since by violating these claims managers would gain (in the sense of more fully achieving their goals for the organization) inappropriately at the expense of other people.

My claim that employees, investors, consumers, and neighbors ought not to be treated unfairly in the course of the efforts of managers to achieve their goals for an organization must be distinguished from claims that can be made by using the "stakeholder" model that businesspeople sometimes employ to describe the moral terrain in which managers operate. This model attempts to extend to other groups a certain view of the responsibility of managers to shareholders.

On one way of looking at this responsibility, which I am inclined to favor, shareholders are regarded as investors whose money managers use to attain their (the managers') goals. Thus, the responsibility of managers to shareholders is a responsibility of microlevel fairness not to advance managerial goals inappropriately at their expense. But the responsibility of managers to shareholders can also be viewed in another way, as a fiduciary obligation to advance the interests of the shareholders. While as we have seen, managers are not technically agents of the shareholders, this way of looking at them treats them as, in effect, trustees for the shareholders. The stakeholder model attempts to extend this idea that managers are trustees charged with promoting the interests of shareholders to other groups as well.

The theoretical basis of the stakeholder model is, however, unclear. A plausible story can be told about why managers should advance the interests of shareholders. It can be said that the shareholders are the owners of the productive property associated with the firm, and this gives them a moral right to stipulate that it be used in a way that confers benefits on them. This moral idea finds expression in the law of corporations as the provision that the board of

---

[2] For a discussion of the evidence bearing on whether the goals of managers depart from those of shareholders, see Munzer (1990), pp. 320–46.

directors, which is the locus of managerial authority, be elected by the shareholders. As I have indicated, I do not think that the moral relations of managers to other groups can simply be read off from their legal relations. And the account that I have just provided of the claims of shareholders as claims to fair treatment reflects my conviction that they are better regarded as suppliers of a certain kind, namely, suppliers of capital. Nevertheless, the idea that managers have a fiduciary *moral* obligation to advance the interests of shareholders that mirrors their legal obligations is not silly. But no comparable rationale can be provided for the suggestion that managers should advance the interests of the other commonly identified "stakeholders." In general, commonsense morality does not regard the mere fact that one has an opportunity to benefit somebody as creating an obligation to benefit him (to some extent), that is, common sense does not regard each as a trustee for all. Something more is required before an individual can be said to have a claim that one promote his interests.[3]

Considerations of interactive fairness can provide the missing element. That is, one way of distinguishing the interests that have a claim to our attention from those that do not is to say that interests that will be *unfairly* damaged by our actions in pursuit of our goals have such a claim. Similarly, considerations of fairness can be regarded as constraining what managers may do, or order done, in the course of promoting their goals for an organization. Moreover, many of the people who can make claims to fair treatment by managers are members of the groups identified as stakeholders by the stakeholder model. But the basis of their claims is not that managers have a fiduciary obligation to promote their interests, analogous to the obligation of a trustee. The basis of their claims is rather a general requirement that falls on all moral agents not to treat others unfairly in the course of advancing morally permissible ends.

Replacing the view that managers should consider the interests of various "stakeholders" with the view that they should avoid treating people unfairly would, I think, help to clarify the moral dimension of management. The stakeholder view provides no way of judging the relative importance of affected interests and leads to a strategy of trying to give everyone something. The concept of fairness, by contrast, enables us to judge some of the members of af-

---

[3] Utilitarianism requires that all the people whose interests could be affected for good or ill by a decision be given equal consideration in making it. But if this is the idea behind the stakeholder model, clarity would be promoted by simply replacing this model with the claim that managerial decision making should be guided by the principle of utility.

fected groups as having no valid claim to consideration, and others as having very strong claims. And when claims clash, the concept of fairness provides a basis other than the intensity of the associated desires for deciding which are more important.

Earlier, I noted that there is more to treating people fairly than respecting the deontological constraints. These constraints identify certain act types the instantiation of which usually brings unfairness into the world. Even when none of the acts being considered violate these constraints, however, the concept of fairness may still have application. An example that illustrates this is the firing of an employee just before he would qualify for pension benefits, solely to spare the company the expense of paying them. This seems unfair, but it does not appear possible to capture the unfairness with any of the conventionally acknowledged deontological principles. Employers do not typically promise to refrain from such actions, and they could absolve themselves of any charge of having intentionally induced employees to rely on continued employment by simply reminding all employees at appropriate intervals that the terms of their employment allow their dismissal at any time. Thus, we must accommodate the possibility that some managerial actions can be judged unfair even if they do not violate any of the commonly acknowledged deontological constraints. Of course, it is to be expected that reasonable people will disagree about these questions.

Morally Important Social Values

Social Values and Organizations

Microlevel fairness is a moral concept that applies to agents in so far as they are trying to achieve certain purposes. It regulates how the people affected by an individual's actions in pursuit of her purposes—those used and those who are bystanders—may be treated. We have just seen how the requirement to refrain from unfair treatment of individuals might constrain the efforts of managers to pursue nonmoral goals such as maximizing profits, market share, or stock price. But morality does not just constrain action in pursuit of certain goals; it also sets goals. This fact expands the moral dimension of management and creates a further respect in which complying with managerial directives may involve contributing to a moral or political agenda that one does not share.

The main way that morality presents organizations with demands to promote certain ends is in the form of what I have called morally important social values. As we saw in Chapter Three, some of these are social states of affairs the maintenance of which or promotion of which contributes to the *welfare* of individuals. Examples include the maintenance of an effective national defense, the preservation of the environment, the advancement of knowledge, the development of culture, the fostering of community, the promotion of prosperity, and the advancement of public health. Moreover, as we have also seen, the value of *fairness* is capable of application not only at the microlevel but also at the macrolevel, where it finds expression as another morally important social value, that of distributive justice. Some conceptions of the moral good will call for the promotion of the welfare-based values only in ways that are compatible with distributive justice—in ways that make fair shares larger—while others may employ the aggregation interpretation of the value of welfare maximization, which can conflict with the requirements of justice and fairness.

How is the claim that the activities of organizations are appropriately assessed on the basis of their impact on the morally important social values to be understood? One possibility is that there is a social division of labor that assigns to each kind of organization the task of promoting one of the morally important social values.[4] To insure that the total social effort to promote the moral good—the whole set of valid moral considerations taken together—is effective, something must be done to coordinate the efforts of the different organizations. This is the role of government. It makes decisions about the relative importance of the components of the moral good for which each organization is responsible; it makes judgments about what justice requires in the distribution of these goods; and it issues directives—in the form of legislation or administrative regulations—designed to advance the conception of the moral good it has adopted for the society as a whole. In a democracy, the conception of the moral good that guides the government's decisions is determined in part by voting.

If we adopt this view of how organizations contribute to the morally important social values, there is still room for conflict between organizational goals and considerations of fairness. The most effective way for an organization to promote the morally important social value for which it is partly responsible might involve treating some people unfairly. Although the resolution of some of these conflicts may be anticipated by governmental regulations, organizations will usually have enough discretion that their managers must consider these issues as well.

---

[4] I consider another possibility later.

It will be useful to have a clearer picture of what is involved in conflicts between fairness and the morally important social values. An organizational action or policy, that is, plan of action, that can be justified as promoting a morally important social value will effect some incremental gain in its realization. The overall social attainment of this value will remain at a certain level in the absence of the contemplated action, or it will rise or fall due to other factors, and the contemplated action will add something to the degree of realization the value would otherwise have had. The larger the incremental change, the stronger the reason for the contemplated organizational action. And the stronger the reason for the action, the more likely that it will prevail in conflicts with fairness. Similar reasoning covers the case in which the damage that would be done to a morally important social value creates a reason against an action.

These points apply to the actions of individuals as well, but there is an important difference. Individuals acting outside of organizational contexts can usually make only small changes in the degree of realization of morally important social values. Thus, it will seldom be the case that individuals find themselves in a situation in which unfair treatment of others could be justified by the incremental improvement in the degree of realization of some morally important social value that would result. The actions of large organizations can have a much bigger impact, for good or ill, on these values. So managers must pay more attention to these values than individuals must. This is one respect in which the moral climate of organizational decision making differs from that of private life.

If the moral climate of organizational decision making is in these respects more demanding, in another respect it may be more permissive. Precisely because organizations can do much more to advance the morally important social values than private individuals, managers may sometimes be justified in adopting policies that treat people unfairly. A pertinent example would be layoffs due to bad economic conditions. In many such cases, an organization could avoid layoffs by reducing everyone's pay. It can, moreover, be argued that if an organization does not do this, those who are retained will gain at the expense of those who are let go, which could be unfair. But layoffs may nevertheless be justified all things considered because they will enable the organization better to promote, in the long run, the morally important social value to which it is supposed to contribute. My intention is not to argue for a particular view of such cases. Here, too, people may disagree. It would not, however, be implausible for someone to regard such layoffs both as unfair and as justified by their effect on the promotion of some morally important social values.

This latter possibility introduces a Machiavellian dimension into the management of large organizations. Machiavelli is notorious for having claimed that reasons of state may sometimes justify rulers in treating people in morally impermissible ways.[5] To be sure, he often seems to speak as if the personal interest of established rulers in retaining power constitutes a valid reason of state. But his view can be made more respectable if it is understood as a view about the relation of morally important social values to fairness. Sometimes governments may find it necessary, in order to avoid important social losses, to treat people unfairly, for example, to lie to the populace about treaty negotiations. A similar point can be made about the managers of nongovernmental organizations, to the extent that their actions have a large impact on the overall level of attainment of morally important social values in a society.[6]

Two caveats are in order here. First, it is only the promotion of morally important social values that can justify unfair treatment of people. The promotion of nonmoral goals never can. These remarks, then, provide no justification for managers to treat people unfairly in the course of promoting narrow economic goals such as the maximization of profits, market share, or share price, unless promoting these goals can be seen as a means of promoting morally important social values. Second, while the beneficial effects that large corporations and other large organizations can have on the morally important social values typically far exceed what private individuals can accomplish, their capacity for unfairness usually far exceeds that of private individuals as well. Large organizations can unfairly impose serious losses on many people, and this may nullify any extra justificatory force the morally important social values might lend to certain of their actions.

In concluding this section, it may be worth emphasizing again that my aim here—as in the earlier discussion of fairness—is not to establish what managers may or may not do, but to show that the moral dimension of management is extensive. Given that disagreement about the moral appropriateness of managerial policies is likely, it follows that there are many respects in which employees may regard themselves as contributing in their work to a moral or political agenda that they do not share.

[5] Machiavelli (1977), esp. chaps. 15–18.
[6] I discuss the Machiavellian aspect of management in detail in McMahon (1981).

The Value of Social Prosperity

The idea that organizations participate in a division of moral labor that associates each with a morally important social value it is charged with promoting seems plausible in the case of nonprofit organizations. Hospitals promote public health, schools promote the advancement of knowledge, museums promote the development of culture, and so on. But questions might arise about whether this analysis can be extended to profit-seeking firms. They seem to be constituted to promote private ends that have no moral character. In fact, however, profit-seeking firms can be regarded as promoting a morally important social value, too. They can be regarded as promoting the value of social prosperity through the market mechanism.

This is the core idea behind the doctrine of the invisible hand. Adam Smith famously claims that individuals aiming at private gain in a market are led as if by an invisible hand to promote the good of society.[7] To say this is to say that a market in which producers seek private gain is a useful instrument for promoting the well-being of society, and by extension, that the profit-seeking activities of firms in a market have instrumental value as well.

We must be clear about the import of the doctrine of the invisible hand, however. It is not the absurd doctrine that if everyone single-mindedly pursues self-interest, everything will be for the best. The general, unconstrained pursuit of self-interest is a Hobbesian state of nature, which Hobbes describes as follows.

> In such condition, there is no place for Industry; because the fruit thereof is uncertain: and consequently no Culture of the Earth; no Navigation, nor use of the commodities that may be imported by Sea; no commodious Building; no Instruments of moving, and removing such things as require much force; no Knowledge of the face of the Earth; no account of Time; no Arts; no Letters; no Society; and which is worst of all, continuall feare, and danger of violent death; And the life of man, solitary, poore, nasty, brutish, and short.[8]

Hobbes arrives at this characterization of the economic consequences of the unfettered pursuit of self-interest with the help of certain controversial assumptions about what motivates people, but the general idea is sound. The unfettered pursuit of self-interest by

---

[7] Smith (1985), book 4, chap. 2, para. 9.
[8] Hobbes (1968), chap. 13, para. 9.

all would be bad for everyone. The doctrine of the invisible hand must, then, be interpreted as the thesis that if people pursue self-interest subject to certain constraints, the moral good will be advanced in one important respect: there will be greater prosperity. The constraints are usually said to be constraints on force or fraud, but the determination of precisely what sorts of behavior are conducive to, or detrimental to, the promotion of prosperity through the market mechanism is a task for economists.[9]

In contemporary economic theory, the doctrine of the invisible hand finds expression as the fundamental theorem of welfare economics. This is a theorem about the effects of perfect competition. It states that a perfectly competitive general equilibrium is a Paretian optimum. A distribution of goods or services is Pareto optimal if no one can be made better off without making someone else worse off. Pareto optimality is a desirable property for a state of affairs to have from the standpoint of the aggregation interpretation of the value of welfare maximization that is associated with utilitarianism. It constitutes a way of regarding aggregate welfare as maximized that does not require interpersonal comparisons of well-being. But because Pareto optimality is blind to distributive considerations—which have derivative importance for utilitarianism since equality is conducive to the maximization of aggregate welfare—it cannot be assumed that a Pareto-optimal state of affairs will count as optimal from the standpoint of the principle of utility.[10]

The conditions of perfect competition rarely obtain in the real world, and thus we cannot explain how firms promote social prosperity simply by invoking the fundamental theorem of welfare economics. The explanation must take a different route. We may begin by noting that social prosperity is meant to be one morally important social value among many. *Welfare economics* treats the maximization of aggregate welfare, understood as the attainment of a Pareto-optimal distribution of the social product, as the sole reference point for judging the performance of institutions. On the view that I am advancing, however, *morality* is regarded as distinguishing, with

---

[9] In McMahon (1981), I call the constraints that must be respected if markets are to promote social prosperity "the implicit morality of the market." On the view I take there, questions of business ethics are to be decided by first determining whether the activity at issue contributes to the promotion of social prosperity through the market mechanism—which is to say, whether it is in accordance with the implicit morality of the market—and then considering whether other moral considerations are weightier than prosperity in the case at hand. This approach has the consequence that the first question in any inquiry in business ethics is a question for economists.

[10] For discussion of the feasibility of regarding Pareto optimality as an approximation of the utilitarian standard see Buchanan (1985), pp. 8–11.

different morally important social values, different aspects of the social promotion of welfare. How, then, is the aspect identified by the value of prosperity to be understood?

We may begin by noting that welfare economics recognizes that markets can fail to achieve a Pareto-optimal distribution of goods and services. Among the most important reasons for this is the presence of positive and negative externalities of production. These are found where the actions of a producer have effects on individuals who do not participate in the market transactions in which the producer's activities are embedded. Sometimes the effects are detrimental, as when a production process generates pollution that imposes a cost on those other than the purchasers of the product. These are negative externalities. Sometimes the effects are beneficial. This happens when the product of some productive activity is a public good, a good that cannot be provided for some of the members of a group without being provided for all. These are positive externalities.

Profit-seeking firms behave rationally, given that their goal is to maximize profit, when they produce to the point where the marginal cost of an additional unit produced equals the marginal gain to them, which is to say, when it equals the market price of a unit. Under conditions of perfect competition, this behavior results in an optimal allocation of resources to productive activities, in the sense that the distribution that results when the products are sold at the market price is Pareto optimal. But when there are externalities, this mechanism breaks down. When there are positive externalities resulting from the production of public goods, profit-maximizing firms will not produce enough of these goods, because some of the ways that production would benefit people will not be communicated to the firm as increased demand. When there are negative externalities, profit-maximizing firms will overproduce goods, because there will be social costs that do not find expression in the firm's cost of production. Thus, when it produces at the point at which the marginal cost to it equals the marginal benefit, the cost to society will exceed the benefit.

If welfare is to be maximized where there are externalities, then, a society cannot rely on competitive markets alone. It must take positive steps to produce public goods and curb negative externalities. But the welfare-based morally important social values (other than prosperity) can be regarded as identifying important positive and negative externalities of profit-seeking activity. In establishing nonprofit organizations, some of which may be governmental agencies, to promote morally important social values, a society takes steps to insure the adequate production of public goods that the market will not supply in sufficient quantity. And when it enacts regulations to promote other morally important social values, it often takes steps to eliminate negative externalities.

Many of the welfare-based morally important social values can, then, be linked with important positive and negative externalities of production. But how is the value of social prosperity to be understood? Basically, this value identifies the beneficial effects on welfare that markets can have when they are functioning well. But social prosperity has been presented as one morally important social value among many. So given the account just provided of the other welfare-based morally important social values, if we are to provide an adequate account of the value of prosperity, we must get clearer about how the well-functioning of markets is to be understood when there are externalities.

We can begin by considering how social prosperity can be understood as a value over and above the fairness-based value of distributive justice, which is not associated with positive or negative externalities. Even when externalities are absent, the operation of markets will often be objectionable from the moral point of view. Depending on the initial distribution of resources, the results markets produce may be open to criticism from the standpoint of justice. A distribution in which a few have most of the goods produced and everyone else has virtually nothing could be Pareto optimal. This has led some to claim that the important theoretical result concerning markets is not the fundamental theorem of welfare economics, but its "converse."[11] This shows that any given Pareto-optimal distribution—and thus any such distribution that satisfies the best theory of distributive justice—can be produced by a market. We can, then, see markets as working in tandem with an extramarket distributive mechanism that creates certain initial holdings to yield a distribution of the social product that is both just and Pareto optimal. I have noted several times that the value of welfare maximization admits of two interpretations. It can be given an aggregation interpretation that may conflict with fairness or it can be regarded as subordinate to fairness, calling for the maximization of fair shares. The converse of the fundamental theorem of welfare economics shows how markets will achieve maximally large fair shares when the initial distribution is appropriate.[12]

[11] See Sen (1985), esp. pp. 9–14. Sen notes that applying the converse result presents difficult practical problems, but here we are concerned only with elucidating the concept of social prosperity.

[12] In general, the promotion of the fairness-based morally important social value

We may offer the following provisional definition of the value of social prosperity as one morally important social value among others. It is the good that consists in the maximization of fair shares of what the market distributes. So understood, prosperity can be regarded as one morally important social value among others. Consider first the case in which resources have been allocated to the production of public goods, regulations have been designed to curb negative externalities of production, and the market-oriented activities that remain are generating fair shares of what is distributed by the market. We can still raise the question of whether there is another fair distribution that is Pareto superior to the actual one.[13] And if there is such a distribution, the value of social prosperity will support bringing it about.

On this way of viewing it, the value of social prosperity is the value of the maximization of fair shares of what the market distributes after measures to insure an appropriate posture toward the welfare-based morally important social values associated with positive and negative externalities have been taken. But we need not regard the value of prosperity as playing a role only after a prior decision about the importance of the other values has been made. We can also provide an account of trade-offs between this value and others. They are trade-offs between the respects in which our lives are made better when our fair share of what we get through interacting in markets is larger and the respects in which our lives are made better when public goods are produced and negative externalities curtailed. Some might judge goods of the first sort important enough to justify sacrificing some goods of the second sort, and some might have the opposite opinion.[14]

---

of distributive justice is not something about which the managers of corporations and other organizations need be concerned. Comprehensive social measures of the sort that only the government can effect, such as tax and welfare policies, are usually necessary for this. Compensation policy might seem to be an area where something could be done, but except in the case of senior executives, market pressures determine what firms must pay. And in all cases, excessive compensation can be easily corrected at the societal level by the appropriate tax policies.

[13] Distribution A is Pareto superior to distribution B if and only if at least one person is better off in A than in B and no one is worse off. Presumably, however, if a distribution that is Pareto superior to a fair distribution is itself to be fair, everyone must be made better off.

[14] Here I am making the simplifying assumption that responding appropriately to externalities benefits everyone equally and thus does not present issues of distributive justice. One could understand social prosperity as capable of conflicting with the requirements of distributive justice, as well as the other morally important social values, by evaluating the performance of markets in distributing goods by reference to the aggregation interpretation of the value of welfare maximization alone. If it is thought that there are moral objections to exchanging goods of certain sorts—for

It may help to appreciate the force of this view of the market as an instrument for promoting the moral value of social prosperity to contrast it with the justification for markets that would be offered by libertarians. Libertarians claim that each person has certain rights that create an area within which she may do whatever she wants, and that morality requires only that these rights be respected. Markets will be the likely result, given that market exchanges make both parties better off and do not violate any rights. The difference between this way of viewing the moral significance of markets and the way I am employing here can be illustrated by comparing market transactions with marriage. No one would think of defending a policy of allowing people to marry whomever they want by arguing that with perfect information and no transaction costs, the result would be a Pareto-optimal distribution of spouses. The justification would refer entirely to people's rights. But this means that to justify markets by some variant of the doctrine of the invisible hand is to introduce a new moral consideration different from rights, a morally important social value. The justification for markets that results thus has a consequentialist structure; markets are viewed as instruments for promoting prosperity.

Earlier, I said that the narrow economic goals typically pursued by the managers of profit-seeking firms—maximizing profits, market share, or stock price, for example—have no moral significance unless these activities can be regarded as conducive to the promotion of a morally important social value. But seeking profit in reasonably competitive markets is conducive to the moral value of social prosperity. This provides some support for the pursuit by managers of traditional managerial goals. It should be noted that this license comes at a price. Technical disagreements about how best to achieve the goal of maximizing profit become moral disagreements, which means that a justification for complying with even technical directives that one believes mistaken must be capable of justifying the preemption of moral judgments.

---

example, sex—in markets, the definition of social prosperity can be modified to accommodate this. What I have offered is an account of how a *system* of profit-seeking firms can be regarded as promoting social prosperity, understood as an aspect of welfare maximization. The question might arise how each firm is to assess the importance of its contributions to prosperity. This is a task for economists, but it seems plausible that gross revenues might be as important an indicator as profits. I shall not consider how the value of social prosperity is to be understood in societies that do not employ markets, but I take it that the notion could still be given application, perhaps as the (fair) maximization of the satisfactions obtainable from consuming private goods.

The Limits of Specialization

So far we have been exploring a view of the status of organizations that posits a division of moral labor. Each kind of organization is associated with a particular morally important social value that it is constituted to promote, and government coordinates their actions. This means that only the decisions of the government give expression to a full conception of the moral good. This may not, however, be the best way to understand the moral dimension of management in large corporations and other large organizations. While a given organization may be constituted as a means of promoting an end which can in turn be correlated with a particular morally important social value, it does not follow that the other morally important social values are irrelevant to the assessment of its actions and thus to the decisions that its managers make.

There are several reasons for this. First, even if there is one morally important social value that we can regard an organization as constituted to promote, the relevant question in assessing its performance is not, "What is it aiming at?" but "What is it doing?" An organization that aims to promote one goal may nevertheless perform actions that foster or impinge on other morally significant values. This is true of both nonprofit organizations and profit-seeking firms. While all profit-seeking firms can be regarded as promoting the value of social prosperity through the mechanism of the invisible hand, their activities can be assessed from the standpoint of other values as well.

This is clear in the case of those values that identify negative externalities of production, which are to be avoided. The managers of profit-seeking firms may have to decide, for example, whether a particular activity can be justified as promoting social prosperity or must rather be avoided as damaging the environment. But profit-seeking activities will often produce public goods as well. Companies with research and development departments, for example, contribute to the advancement of knowledge as well as to prosperity, and so do newspapers and broadcasting companies. Similarly, drug companies, profit-seeking hospitals, and insurance companies contribute to the moral value of public health as well as to prosperity, as measured by market criteria. In general, then, the managers of profit-seeking firms will have to decide whether maximizing profits is the best course of action, taking all the morally important social values into account.

It might be argued that these are not questions for managers or their employees to be concerned about. The adjustment of the activities of organizations so that they best promote the moral good as a whole is the task of governments, acting through regulatory agencies. Governments decide whether the moral costs of a given moral benefit are too great, and the role of organizations is simply to promote the particular value with which they are associated as effectively as they can within the framework of the regulations that give expression to the government's judgments.

Of course, actual managerial practice gives the lie to this claim. Managers constantly try to influence regulation of their industries, and usually with an eye to what will be most conducive to the realization of narrow organizational goals. But more important, it is undesirable to place responsibility for all of the moral questions that arise in the course of running a nongovernmental organization in the hands of governmental agencies. So many decisions would have to be transferred that the benefits of decentralization would be lost.

We can, then, formulate the following principle of the inverse relation of governmental regulation and moral decision making by managers. As governmental regulation of nongovernmental organizations declines, the moral dimension of managerial decision making becomes more pronounced. For when regulation is less than complete, the managers of organizations will have to make the same sorts of decisions that governmental officials would have to make in regulating them. They will have to bring to bear a full conception of the moral good to decide what course of action to take. This is important for our purposes since the larger the set of moral considerations that managers must take into account, the more likely it is that reasonable people will disagree about whether the decisions they make are correct, and thus the more likely it is that employees will find themselves contributing in their work to a moral or political agenda that they do not share. The only way this result can be avoided is by increasing governmental regulation.

Employer Rights

We have been discussing the moral considerations that are relevant to the assessment of managerial decisions. But it might be claimed that we have overlooked the rights of employers. Employers may have rights to act in certain ways, and this may affect what they are morally required to do, which in turn affects what employees can judge that *they* are required or permitted to do by the applicable directive-independent reasons.

The case of natural persons (human beings) will illustrate what is at issue here. Natural persons have negative rights which give them the moral power to make others refrain from certain courses of action. These rights can be regarded as correlates of the deontological constraints, or more broadly, of requirements not to treat others unfairly. People have the moral power to decline to be affected in certain ways on the ground that affecting them in those ways would be unfair. This power protects each of us against certain actions that others might take in pursuit of either their personal projects or consequentialist moral considerations.

This line of thought can be extended. If the pursuit of personal projects is to be protected, we need more than the moral power to resist attempts by others to use us in certain ways. We also need protection from consequentialist demands that we may acknowledge ourselves. That is, even when we have a right to decline to be used by others to promote consequentialist considerations, we may still be forced to conclude that these considerations require us to make the sacrifices that others would impose on us. Someone whose death could plausibly be thought to be justified on consequentialist grounds—say he is the only possible organ donor for a Nobel Peace Prize winner whose efforts on behalf of humanity must be fostered in every way possible—needs protection not only from the efforts of others to kill him but also from the implication that he should commit suicide. As we saw in Chapter Three, this has led some writers to propose incorporating into the set of valid moral considerations positive permissions to decline to make all the sacrifices that consequentialist considerations could potentially require.[15] Permissions and rights usually work together. The permission licenses the act of exercising the right which in turn blocks interference by others.

Given these rights and permissions, employers who are natural persons will have a moral license to behave in certain ways that others, including their employees, may deem suboptimal. For example, it is plausible that people have a moral right (within limits) to determine how their children will be raised, and this would be a consideration that a baby-sitter would have to take into account in deciding whether to implement the instructions given to him by his employer.

Corporations and other organizations, however, do not have personal lives. Commitments to personal projects do not figure in the good of an organization. Moreover, even if they did, the thesis of

[15] Such a permission can be regarded as grounded in the value of fairness if it is seen as what might be called an "internal right," that is, a right that the part of a person that undertakes commitments to personal projects has against the part that feels the pull of consequentialist considerations.

moral individualism implies that the benefits that organizations received by pursuing their projects would have no moral significance. From the standpoint of this thesis, corporations and other organizations are merely instruments. They have moral importance only to the extent that they serve the morally legitimate purposes of individuals. Thus, corporations cannot claim that being made to promote a particular moral end would place an undue burden on them. There is no such thing as treating a corporation or other organization, as opposed to the individuals who are its members, unfairly. Similarly, there is no basis for ascribing to corporations or other organizations permissions to decline to make the sacrifices that consequentialist moral considerations could potentially require of them. The individuals who are their members may have such permissions, but the organizations themselves do not.[16]

These points have the effect of simplifying the moral decisions that managers must make. They must decide which morally important social values would be affected by the various alternatives available to them in the circumstances, and what the whole set of these values supports all things considered. They must also decide whether the means that would best promote these values as a whole would involve treating some individuals, employees or others, unfairly. That is, they must insure that they choose an alternative that properly respects the claims of fairness as well as of the applicable consequentialist considerations. But there is no place for any judgments that assert that doing what would best promote the applicable morally important social values would place too great a burden on the organization. The only way a less than optimal effort could be justified is by consequentialist reasoning—that is, as a conclusion to the effect that the organization could promote the moral good most effectively in the long run if it declined an opportunity to promote it now.

---

[16] A similar point has been made by Dan-Cohen (1986), chap. 4. He distinguishes between autonomy rights and utility rights. Autonomy rights are rights that protect agents in the pursuit of the projects that give their lives meaning. Utility rights, by contrast, are merely acknowledgments of the fact that an action open to an agent would have a positive effect on total aggregate welfare. In Dan-Cohen's view, organizations can have utility rights but not autonomy rights.

The permissions of employees have limited significance for my argument. It might be thought that the threat of dismissal for failure to comply with managerial directives would justify an employee in ignoring any components of her conception of the moral good that might provide a reason for disregarding a directive. But here we are considering what justification there is for according managers the power to make this threat, and thus we must suppose them to lack it and see what employees would then have reason to do. In general, permissions will play a role only when an employee's using her job to promote her own conception of the moral good would entail sacrifices *exclusive of dismissal* significantly greater than those involved in complying with managerial directives.

Do Managers Exercise Authority?

Let us consider some other objections that might be made to my suggestion that complying with managerial directives often means contributing to a moral or political agenda that one does not share.

Do Managers Issue Directives?

First, it might be claimed that talk about employees complying with directives is misleading. Managers do not issue directives, and thus the whole premise of this book, that managers are in positions of authority over employees, is mistaken.

It does indeed appear that managers rarely make utterances that have the grammatical form of imperatives. In the case of managerial employees—middle-level managers, for example—subordinates are expected to be adept at reading the wishes of their bosses and putting them into effect without being told in so many words to do so.[17] And when managers explicitly say what they want, they often only state the objective that they want achieved, leaving the decision about how to achieve it up to the subordinate. The case of lower-level employees is similar. Although managers are more specific about the actions that they want lower-level employees to perform, they rarely indicate this with utterances in the imperative mood. Rather, managerial communications are likely to take the form of questions such as: "Would you mind doing X after lunch?" or "If you get a chance this afternoon, could you do Y?"

The last observation, however, is a red herring. What is important is not the grammatical form of the communications that managers address to employees, but their illocutionary force—what speech act is performed.[18] It is perfectly clear that questions of this sort, when asked by a manager of an employee, have the force of orders, and moreover, orders that are expected to preempt the employee's own judgment about what she ought to be doing with her time. Employees who do not do what is "asked" of them will be reprimanded or fired. The case of managerial employees is similar. Although they may not be explicitly told what to do, they are usually able to infer what their boss wants them to do, and the basis of these inferences is controlled by the boss. That is, bosses are aware of the inferences that employees will make in a given situation, and they control the situation to insure that the inferences are correct. Em-

---

[17] See Jackall (1988), p. 135.
[18] For an account of illocutionary forces, see Austin (1962), esp. Lecture 8.

ployees who cannot read these clues will suffer. In doing this, however, managers give what they do and say the force of relatively specific orders.

There is another kind of sociological observation that might seem to suggest that managers do not exercise authority in the sense of issuing preemptive directives to their employees. This is that the structure of most modern organizations departs in many respects from Weberian ideal bureaucracy.[19]

The Weberian ideal assimilates organizations to the model of agency; the employees of the organization are regarded as agents acting under the direction of some principal, which may be either an individual or the organization viewed as a distinct entity. As I noted in Chapter Three, an organization can be regarded as issuing directives if its constitution is such that certain acts of its members count as its acts. Weberian bureaucracy expands the scope of agency by introducing a number of intermediate positions or offices, each of which carries with it the right to direct the activities of occupants of the offices defined as subordinate to it. Only the natural person or corporate actor at the top of the hierarchy is an undirected source of directives. The organization is thus a tool or instrument by means of which this person can achieve his, her, or its goals. The activities of employees are governed by the fundamental norm of agency, namely, that the actions of the agent, in her capacity as agent, are to be guided by the interests of the principal rather than her own interests. Subordinates are thus expected to bracket their own goals when they act in their official capacities. They may promote their own goals only off the job, using the compensation that they receive for their services.[20]

Many modern organizations fail to conform to this model in one way or another, but it is a mistake to suppose that if they do not, their employees are not parties to authority relations marked by preemption. It has been suggested that in many organizations, policies are generated by a complex social processes of bargaining and negotiation within the organization, and thus cannot be regarded as expressing the will of any one individual, or group of individuals.[21] Even if this is so, however, we still need a reason why employees who disagree with company policy should comply with the direc-

---

[19] Even if contemporary organizations are not pure Weberian bureaucracies, there has been a clear movement in the twentieth century toward more bureaucratic structures in the workplace. For an account, see Edwards (1979).

[20] In this account of the Weberian ideal, I am following James Coleman (1990), pp. 422–23.

[21] See Cyert and March (1963), chap. 3.

tives that they confront in the workplace. That is, for the question of whether the relations within an organization are authority relations, the important point is that employees comply with directives that they believe to be mistaken on the merits, not how these directives are generated.

Similarly, in many organizations, there has been a movement away from the Weberian assumption that employees leave their interests at home. Rather, employees are regarded as bringing their interests to work with them, and the role of management is to structure the incentives that operate at each position in the organization so that employees pursuing their interests will contribute to corporate goals.[22] This, too, does not eliminate managerial authority as I have defined it. In taking these steps, managers clearly exercise directive power. They do not rest content with whatever level of performance the incentives elicit from employees; instead, employees from whom the incentives do not elicit what management regards as sufficient efforts will be fired. All that really happens in such a system is that the policing mechanism is shifted a bit to the carrot end of the carrot-stick continuum; and it is used not merely to insure compliance with managerial directives but also to communicate them, that is, to impart information about what management wants. Where managers exercise directive power, however, we must consider whether they are functioning as legitimate authorities.

Finally, there is a general movement toward participatory management or management by consensus in many organizations, and this is often described as an erosion of hierarchical relations.[23] To the extent that this phenomenon is taken to mean that contemporary organizations are moving toward a condition in which no authority is exercised in the workplace, however, it is being misinterpreted.

First, employees within each participatory unit may still find themselves contributing to projects that they regard as morally inappropriate if the decision is made by a vote or the consensus reached is weak. Second, even when consensus is achieved and thus hierarchy is eliminated within the group, the organization as a whole still remains hierarchical. The trend toward participatory management is essentially a trend toward making each node in the

[22] As James Coleman puts it, "The modern corporation can increasingly be seen not as a machine with parts but as a system of action comparable to an unconstrained market, a system whose organizational structure lies not in defining expectations and obligations and exercising authority, but in structuring reward systems and providing resources" (1990, p. 436).

[23] It is sometimes claimed that the management style of women is especially likely to conform to this model.

organizational hierarchy—each unit of manager and associated subordinates—democratic. When a manager is charged with implementing a directive, the decision about how it will be put into effect by the group that she supervises is made collectively by all of them, rather than unilaterally by her. Similarly, the directive she brings to the group may have been made collectively by a group in which she had the position of a subordinate. But decision making at each level is limited by what was decided at the levels above. Thus, even if the question of why one should comply with a democratically enacted decision is thought to need no answer—and we have seen that this is not so—the problem of managerial authority remains as the question: Why operate within the framework of the decisions made at higher levels?

Although modern organizations may depart somewhat from Weberian ideal bureaucracies, then, employees still have the status of subordinates who find themselves confronting directives that are supposed to preempt their own judgments about what to do in the circumstances. To justify such an arrangement is to justify authority.

Do Employees Disagree with Management?

I have argued that commonly acknowledged moral considerations apply to virtually all managerial decisions. But it might be claimed that if the problem of justifying authority is justifying it from the standpoint of the subordinates, what matters is not whether morality applies to managerial decisions but whether the employees think it applies—and if they do, whether they in fact disagree with the decisions their bosses make. There are at least three possible objections here: (1) employees do not care much about morality at all, (2) although employees care about morality, they believe that moral concepts do not apply to managerial decisions, and (3) although employees care about morality and believe that moral concepts apply to managerial decisions, they think that it is inappropriate for them, as opposed to managers, to be concerned with such questions.

The first two of these objections are easily dealt with. People who lack moral concerns are not fully developed as human beings, and thus a system of authority that can be justified only on the assumption that the subordinates are such people cannot claim a legitimate place in a human society. As for the second objection, if sound arguments show that moral concepts and principles accepted by employees in other contexts apply to a wide range of managerial decisions, employees who think otherwise are simply making a mistake about what the reasons that they accept require. They are failing to judge like cases alike. It is, however, no recommendation of a particular way of justifying managerial authority that it is feasible only if subordinates are mistaken about what is required by the reasons that they acknowledge. It should be emphasized that to establish this latter point we need only show that commonly accepted moral concepts apply to managerial decisions, not that there is agreement about what they require when they are weighed against each other.

The third possibility, however, goes to the heart of our project. Here, employees think that only their managers should consider what is required by the applicable moral considerations. As one manager cited by Robert Jackall puts it, "What is right in the corporation is what the guy above you wants from you. That is what morality is in the corporation."[24]

But to the extent that employees take this view, they accord de facto authority to their bosses; and as we have seen, while the existence of de facto authority makes coercion unnecessary, it does not eliminate the need for justification. De facto authority exists when the people in some group comply with directives because they believe that there are good reasons for doing so. But authority is legitimate only if there really are good reasons for the subordination associated with it. Such reasons must justify authority to the subordinates, that is, from the standpoint of the reasons that apply to them. In the case at hand, this means that an arrangement in which managers make moral decisions for their subordinates will be justified only if there are good reasons for the subordinates to allow managerial directives to preempt the judgments they would otherwise make about what the applicable directive-independent moral reasons require. This is so even if the habit of deference is so ingrained that no subordinate seeks such a justification.[25]

It is worth noting an aspect of the phenomenon of de facto authority that is especially important in the managerial sphere. Powerful forces of socialization are at work in organizations, and these can lead to the internalization of certain organizational values or a certain "corporate culture." These values will typically call for adherence to organizational norms and compliance with the directives of

[24] Jackall (1988), p. 109.

[25] This is similar to the approach that political philosophy takes to the legitimacy of government. Legitimate, as opposed to de facto, authority is not guaranteed by the fact that deference is so ingrained that no one in the subject population thinks to object to what the government is doing. It is determined by what the reasons that apply to the subjects really support.

one's superiors. As we have just seen, the fact that such values are internalized does not mean that authority is not being exercised. To the extent that employees are positively disposed to comply with directives and be good team players, they accord de facto authority to their bosses. Thus, the internalization of these attitudes reduces the need for managers to make coercive threats to secure compliance with their directives. But as before, whether compliance with managerial directives is justified must be determined by an independent argument that establishes what the subordinates would have sufficient reason to do in the absence of this form of directive power, that is, if the socializing forces were not present.

MANAGERIAL AUTHORITY
AS P-AUTHORITY

In complying with managerial directives, employees often contribute to a moral or political agenda that they do not share. In Chapter Six, I argued that a wide variety of commonly acknowledged moral considerations are relevant to the decisions that managers make in issuing directives, and I think it will be readily conceded that there is usually disagreement among those who accept these considerations about their relative importance in a given case. From these two observations we can conclude that there will often be disagreement about whether a given manager is acting as morality requires (or permits) in issuing a particular directive.

By itself, this does not establish my claim that to comply with managerial directives can be to contribute to a moral or political agenda that one does not share, for it has not yet been shown that complying with a directive involves promoting (in a significant way) the conception of the moral good implicit in the decision to issue it. Only if this is so will employees have good directive-independent reasons, grounded in their own conceptions of the moral good, for declining to comply. Thus, only if this is so will there be a need for a demonstration that there are good reasons for employees to allow managerial directives to preempt their judgments of what the applicable directive-independent reasons require, that is, for a justification of managerial authority. Showing how complying with managerial directives involves promoting in a significant way the boss's conception of the moral good is one of the principal tasks of this chapter.

The other task will be to begin our investigation of what kind of authority managers should be understood as having. Employment contexts are various, but the context of principal concern here is that of an organization. Typically, organizations have the legal structure of corporations. This legal structure creates what might be called the organization's constitution. It defines a number of offices to which legal powers are attached, chief among which is the power to exercise legal property rights in the productive resources associated with the organization. As we have seen, given the conditions of human life, control of productive property carries with it directive power. Those who control such property can get people, in particular, the members of the organization who occupy subordinate positions, to do what they are told by threatening to exclude them from the organization. Thus, the constitution of a nongovernmental organization allocates directive power.[1]

Given the thesis of the priority of right or authority to directive power, however, the de facto powers associated with the legal constitution of an organization cannot simply be accepted as they stand. It must be shown that those on whom the constitution confers directive power have the right to exercise this power, and in the sort of case with which we are primarily concerned, this means showing that they are legitimate authorities. The directive power conferred on managers by an organization's constitution must not exceed the authority that managers can legitimately claim.

This project of evaluating constitutions by reference to the thesis of the priority of right or authority to directive power is not peculiar to the investigation of managerial authority. A similar project is central to the investigation of the authority of governments. The constitution of a state is a legal structure that confers directive power on certain individuals. This power is coercive in that certain legally established penalties will usually be imposed on those who do not comply with directives issued in ways the constitution provides for (that is, with duly enacted laws). If the legitimacy of the constitution is generally accepted, the directive power of governments will also take the form of de facto authority, which is a feature of the managerial case as well. Before we can endorse any such structure, however, we must establish that the directive power it creates does not exceed the boundaries of legitimate authority.

An investigation of managerial authority might try to show that managers cannot claim legitimate authority at all unless their authority is understood in just one way, but I do not pursue this strategy. I believe that managers could claim legitimacy for their authority on any of several grounds. As we have seen, however, the different grounds on which legitimacy might be claimed have different implications for the robustness and reach of authority. The ultimate goal

---

[1] For an economic account of the directive power of employers see Bowles and Gintis (1992). Their view has interesting affinities with the account of organizational slack in Cyert and March (1963). See n. 24 below.

of our investigation, then, is to determine (1) whether, from the standpoint of the employees, there are reasons to prefer managerial authority to have more rather than less robustness and reach, and (2) what the consequences of the answer are for the sorts of legal constitutions nongovernmental organizations should have. Of particular interest will be whether the directive power that the law as it presently is confers on managers can be vindicated from the standpoint of the employees.

I begin with the possibility of viewing managerial authority as P-authority. It is natural to begin here since legally, employees are understood as agents of their employers, which means that they are understood as having contracted to act on behalf of and under the direction of their employers. Thus, if the moral structure of managerial authority mirrors its legal structure, managerial authority will be P-authority. I argue that given the assumptions we have made about the moral context in which managerial decision making is carried out, when managerial authority is understood as P-authority, its robustness and reach is reduced to a point where it cannot underwrite all of the directive power that the legal constitutions of nongovernmental organizations currently confer on managers. It should be noted that this argument presupposes that managers are not appropriately regarded by their employees as experts on what morality requires. That is, it presupposes that there is no reason for employees to subordinate their judgments of what the moral good requires to that of their bosses.

Preliminary Objections

Before we consider how much directive power can be underwritten by promissory obligations on the part of employees, we must look at some arguments that seem to show that managers cannot be P-authorities at all. The first points to the prominent place of the doctrine of employment at will in the law's understanding of the employment relation.[2] The law may be moving away from this doctrine as it applies to employers, but it raises a question about any view that regards managerial authority as P-authority. The doctrine of employment at will holds that either party in an employment relation may terminate it at any time. The fact that employees can quit at any time is not completely incompatible with the idea that they are agents. An employment agreement might still be understood to provide

---

[2] For a discussion of the doctrine of employment at will, see Werhane (1985), chap 4.

that the employee is not to act contrary to the employer's interests and that the employee's actions count as the employer's. But the element of agency that consists in agreeing to act under the principal's direction seems to have been whittled down to nothing, since employees do not have a promissory obligation to perform whatever action, within some range, they are ordered to perform.

This forces us to rethink the promise that employees can be regarded as making when they accept employment. It is not typically a promise to obey for a given period of time.[3] This remains the case even if we broaden the notion of promising to include any intentional induction of reliance. Employees cannot induce employers to rely on their remaining on the job for a certain period of time when the law provides that they may quit whenever they choose.[4] But if employees do not promise, as a part of the agreement under which they are employed, to comply with whatever managerial directives they may receive, what do they promise to do? The most plausible answer is that they promise to comply with directives *in return for pay*. That is, employees promise not to receive what the employment agreement calls on the employer to provide while failing to provide in return what the agreement calls on them to provide—compliance with directives.

We should, then, understand the question of whether a promise can justify managerial authority in this light. The question is not whether a promise to obey managerial directives provides a sufficient reason to stay when one would rather quit. The question is whether a promise not to accept pay while disobeying managerial directives provides a sufficient reason for so acting, that is, for quitting if one is not going to comply. I mentioned a case in which it seems not to in Chapter One. Presumably any employees of the German State Railroad during World War II who had been ordered to facilitate the conveying of detainees to concentration camps would have been justified in retaining their jobs and continuing to accept pay while allowing the detainees to escape, even if in accept-

[3] The freedom of employees to quit at any time seems to be a central feature of the modern idea of a labor market. During and after the Civil War, attempts were made to get the recently emancipated slaves to go back to work on the plantations under one-year labor contracts that prohibited them from leaving unless the employer allowed this. These contracts were immediately criticized as incompatible with free institutions. See Foner (1988), pp. 55, 165.

[4] There is a social convention to the effect that employees must give employers adequate notice of their intention to leave, and this can be explained as reflecting the fact that employees have induced the reliance of their employers. Advance notice gives employers a chance to avoid losses resulting from the disappointment of reliance. But this is not the same as inducing the employer to rely on compliance with managerial directives over a period of time specified in advance.

ing employment they had implicitly promised not to accept pay without complying with managerial directives. One of the principal objectives of this chapter is to determine how often employees could find themselves in such a situation. This determines what the robustness and reach of managerial authority as P-authority is.

Of course, the police powers of employers will usually eliminate the option of continuing to accept pay while disobeying managerial directives. But as I have said, we are interested in the moral basis of this police power, and in particular whether it can be justified as forcing employees to do what they have, independently of this power, good reason to do. To pose our question clearly, then, we must imagine the employer to have no police power and consider what employees would then have good reason to do.

Another objection to regarding managerial authority as P-authority derives from the claim that employment, or employment on the terms the employer offers, is coerced because those who do not own productive resources must have access to them through employment if they are to live decent lives. Since coerced promises are generally void, the truth of this claim would imply that managerial authority could not derive from a promise by employees to obey.

It seems doubtful that this line of argument could establish that managerial authority cannot be P-authority. It is quite plausible that the directive power of employers is in part coercive. To coerce is to secure compliance with one's directives by threatening harm, and dismissing a long-term employee usually harms him.[5] Thus, the threat of dismissal for noncompliance can be regarded as coercive. Our main task here is to determine whether a promissory obligation to comply with managerial directives can underwrite this directive power. Managers, however, acquire the ability to harm employees in this way only when they have been on the job for a certain period of time. So this line of argument cannot establish that declining to hire someone in the first place harms him; what we have here is the denial of a benefit. If the hiring transaction itself is to be coercive, it must be because employers coerce potential employees by simply threatening to deny them the benefit of employment. But it is controversial whether *offers* of employment can be coercive; and if they cannot, we cannot regard any promise to obey that may be part of an employment agreement as void because coerced.[6]

[5] Here I am supposing that the baseline level of well-being by reference to which it is determined whether an individual has been harmed (by being moved below this baseline) or simply denied the continuation of a benefit (by being returned to the baseline) changes after his life has formed itself around a job.

[6] For a discussion of these matters, see D. Zimmerman (1981). Zimmerman argues

It is worth noting, however, that inducing someone to make a promise out of weakness of will may also render the promise void. Weakness of will is displayed when one intentionally acts contrary to what one judges, all things considered, one ought to do in the situation.[7] It is possible because the considerations that an agent accepts as relevant can have a causal force in determining action that is out of proportion to their rational force in determining judgment. Inducing weakness of will is relevantly similar to coercion in that in both cases, one compromises someone's autonomy; the other party is made to act on motives with which he cannot identify.[8] The situation of some prospective employees, however, may be such that they would agree out of weakness of will to accept employment with an organization that they regarded as pursuing morally impermissible policies. So if the employer can be regarded as inducing this weakness of will, any promise the employee might make in accepting employment will be void for the same reason a coerced promise is void.

A more important objection to the hypothesis that managerial authority is P-authority comes from the thesis of moral individualism. According to this thesis, only individuals have a claim to moral consideration, and it seems to follow that only individuals can have promissory rights. But if so, only employers who are individuals can have P-authority over their employees; employers that are organizations cannot.

We should be clear about what is being claimed here. As we have seen, large corporations and other large organizations can be regarded as issuing directives if their constitutions are such that certain actions of some of their members count as their actions. Given such a constitution, it is possible for all of the members of a corporation to be agents of it; those who issue orders can be regarded as agents who have the status of lieutenants to whom the corporation's powers as principal have been delegated. Moreover, there is no

---

that exploitation may render a promise void even in the absence of coercion. In general, exploitation is a matter of taking advantage of someone's vulnerability in some respect, and it is morally objectionable when one morally ought instead to aid the vulnerable person. Thus, offering to throw a life ring to drowning man if he promises to give one everything in his wallet upon reaching shore involves morally impermissible exploitation because morality requires one to throw the life ring in any case. If Zimmerman is right, such a promise is void (see pp. 134–35.) But it may be doubted whether employers exploit potential employees in this sense, since it is unclear what assistance employers are morally required to provide to those not yet employed—especially if a welfare system is in place.

[7] For an account of weakness of will, see Davidson (1969).

[8] See the discussion in Chapter Two.

barrier to the idea that one can legally bind oneself by a contract with an organization. The legal conventions in force in a given society may provide that organizations can have contractual rights. Our concern, however, is with the moral domain, and there seems to be a problem with regarding employers that are organizations as having promissory rights to compliance by their employees with managerial directives. Organizations, understood as entities distinct from their members, cannot have moral rights. There as no such thing as treating them, as opposed to the individuals associated with them, unfairly.

This does not mean that organizations cannot have authority over individuals. As we saw earlier, while to have authority is to have a right to direct the actions of another, this right need not be a personal right. It is enough for something to have such a right that complying with its directives is the *right thing* for certain people to do, and complying with the directives of an organization could be the right thing for its employees to do. The problem that we are now discussing arises when we move on to the question of what can justify this authority—the question of why compliance with the organization's directives is right. It does not appear that the explanation can be that the employees have a promissory obligation to obey, for organizations, understood as distinct entities, cannot hold promissory rights.

To be sure, this is not the only way that managerial authority could be justified as P-authority. The subordinates might have promised someone else to obey managerial directives. In particular, the promise to obey might be made to some or all of the other individuals who are members of the organization. If the promise to comply with managerial directives is regarded as made to all of the members of the organization, we get a picture according to which each member stands in the relation of agent to a principal consisting of all of the members of the organization considered collectively, with the organization, understood as a distinct entity capable of issuing directives, serving as a lieutenant exercising the powers of this collective principal on its behalf. This resembles some interpretations of contractarian political theory that regard the promise that creates a political society as made not to the government but to the other members of the society.

It is not clear how successfully this line can be pursued in the managerial case, however. The holder of the promissory right is not plausibly regarded as the individual who actually hired a given employee. And it if we say that in accepting employment, each employee induces all of the rest of the employees to rely on her complying with managerial directives, we depart significantly from the picture that it seems natural to associate with the idea that managerial authority is P-authority, namely, that employees are agents, not principals who collectively vest their right to direct in the organization. The remaining possibilities are that in accepting employment, each employee induces senior management (the board of directors) or the whole set of shareholders to rely on her complying with managerial directives. The latter alternative, however, is dubious since it can plausibly be maintained that shareholders are not principals in an agency relation but rather suppliers of a certain kind. The former has the consequence, which is also a problem for all the others, that membership in the board changes, so the induction of reliance by employees will have to be understood not only as having taken place at the time of employment but as constantly updated.

This objection that managerial authority in large organizations cannot be P-authority because organizations cannot hold promissory rights may be decisive. Still, I do not want to rest my argument on it. For the purposes of the present chapter, then, I assume that organizations can be the holders of promissory obligations. More generally, I assume, contrary to the dictates of moral individualism, that organizations can be treated unfairly.

A final general objection to the hypothesis that managerial authority is P-authority was adumbrated in Chapter Four. If virtually all managerial decisions in large organizations have a moral dimension, virtually all disagreement with managerial decisions will be moral disagreement. But as we saw in Chapter Four, promissory obligations cannot usually be regarded as preempting an individual's judgment of what the applicable directive-independent reasons require when these reasons are moral. Rather, they must be balanced against any competing moral considerations. Thus one of the defining features of authority, that authoritative directives are preemptive reasons for action, is not satisfied in the case that we are most concerned with, the case of managers of large organizations.

These points are technically correct, but as was noted earlier, they may be without practical significance. Even if promissory obligations cannot preempt competing moral considerations, they can outweigh them; and when a promissory obligation to comply with someone's directives does outweigh the competing considerations, the result will be the same. The recipient of a directive will have sufficient reason to comply with it. In considering the robustness and reach of managerial authority underwritten by a promise to obey, then, we must allow for the possibility that even if the promise that employees make to comply in return for pay does not preempt the competing moral considerations, it will often prevail against them.

The Limits of P-Authority: Fairness

Initial Considerations

I take it that no matter what moral mechanism underlies the creation of moral reasons for action by promising, certain conditions must be met.[9] For our purposes, the most important of these concern promising to do something morally impermissible. In general, a promise to do something explicitly characterized as morally impermissible is void. To be sure, as we saw in Chapter Four, a promise to do something that turns out to be the wrong thing to do in the circumstances may not be void. In such a case, there may be innocent reliance in the sense that the promisee has relied to his detriment on the performance of the promised act not knowing that, absent this reliance, there would have been sufficient moral reason not to perform it. However, even when innocent reliance is taken into account, unforeseen circumstances may justify breaking a promise.

As we saw in Chapter Four, the relevance of these points to the possibility of regarding a promise to comply with someone's directives as creating a reason to do so lies mainly in the fact that in the case of such a promise, one can foresee much less clearly than usual what the situation will be at the time (that is, the times) performance is due. This is the whole of an indefinite future, and the situation one faces at any point in it depends not just on the external circumstances but also on which of many possible actions one is told to perform. Thus the likelihood that one will find oneself confronting countervailing considerations that are strong enough to outweigh one's promise to obey is greater than in the case of a simple promise.[10]

It should be emphasized that the weighing of competing considerations is done from the promisor's point of view. The promisor makes a decision whether to keep the promise by assessing the relative force of all the moral considerations that she regards as applicable. It may be that the promisee wants the promisor's contribution to a project that he, the promisee, regards as morally important. But a promise to obey someone's directives is not a promise to be guided by his perception of whether the promise is outweighed by competing considerations. No autonomous moral agent could

[9] For one list of these conditions, see Grice (1967), pp. 52–53.
[10] For related discussion see Greenawalt (1990), esp. pp. 283–91.

agree to this. From the promisor's point of view, then, the moral judgments of the promisee are just so many preferences. They have a bearing on her decision about whether to keep her promise only in the sense that they introduce a hedonic consideration—the frustration the promisee will experience as a result of the nonachievement of his moral aims—that must be considered in calculating the moral costs of breaking the promise.

The Strength of a Promise to Obey

In Chapter Six, we saw that there are two main kinds of moral considerations that bear on whether the actions of employers are morally permissible and thus on whether employees would, absent legitimate authority, be doing right in complying with managerial directives. These are considerations of fairness governing the choice of the means by which organizational goals are to be achieved and morally important social values that may underwrite these goals. Let us begin by examining how considerations of fairness could affect whether an employee is justified, all things considered, in keeping a promise to comply with managerial directives.

The reason to keep a promise to comply with a managerial directive—namely, that one has promised not to accept pay without complying—can be regarded as a reason of fairness. To accept pay without doing what one has led the employer to expect in return is, presumptively, to treat the employer unfairly. Considerations of fairness could, however, also count as reasons for breaking such a promise, typically because one believes that one has been directed to treat other people unfairly. I assume that the directed act is not explicitly characterized as unfair treatment by the employer. Rather, the employee is directed to do something that she believes constitutes unfair treatment of certain people, but the employer does not. This is a situation that might be faced by any employee directed to promote organizational goals by acting on people—either other employees or nonemployees—in certain ways.

To pose our question clearly, we must imagine that employers have no police power, for we are considering what could justify the use of such power. The only relevant question is thus what the applicable moral considerations require of employees. Let us, then, consider a case in which an employer would have little police power, that of an employee who is a middle-level manager in charge of a remote facility the activities of which are reported to headquarters only by her. Suppose she receives an order the implementation of which she believes would involve unfair treatment of some people by her company, that is, it would involve her company's gaining inappropriately at their expense. Let us say she is ordered to cut the delivery of electric power to local inhabitants from a company-owned plant, despite the fact that an earlier agreement calls for it to be provided, in order to put pressure on them to permit mining operations that would be disadvantageous to them. Suppose further that, (1) her employer will not rescind the order if told about her reservations, (2) if she quits, she will be replaced by someone who will fully implement the order, and (3) by the time disobedience on her part is discovered, it will be too late for the company to pursue its plan, and she will be safely ensconced in another job. What should she do?

The short answer is that she should weigh the unfairness of the actions she is ordered to perform against the unfairness to her employer of remaining in her job while disregarding the order. For our purposes, however, we need to know in more detail what the latter sort of unfairness consists in. It may be resolved, I think, into at least four components.

If our employee ignores the order she may, first of all, disappoint (innocent) reliance induced by some of her past actions. Quite apart from any pay she receives, the company is committing resources in the expectation that she is doing what she has been told to do, and this means that it may suffer losses as a result of her behavior.[11] Second, she will deceive her employer if she falsely reports that she is doing what she is not doing. Third, she will violate her employer's property rights by using company property in a way that the employer has indicated it is not to be used. And fourth, by continuing to accept pay, she will violate the promise we are supposing her to have made not to accept pay if she is not going to do what she is told. It might also be possible to regard this latter sort of unfairness as fraud or theft.

Are there any circumstances in which an employee might be justified in doing these things? We often think that disappointing reliance is justified when it conflicts with another moral requirement. One would be justified in missing a party at which one was expected, for example, if one encountered an accident and had the only vehicle capable of conveying the victims to a hospital. Of course, in our case, the employer will lose a lot more by having reliance disappointed than the party-goers would, but the unfairness that the employee could prevent might be substantial, too.

---

[11] Recall that for the sake of argument, I am assuming that organizations can be treated unfairly.

Similarly, we think that deception can sometimes be justified. Most people, for example, would agree that one may deceive a criminal to prevent a crime. While our employee may not regard her employer as having criminal intent, but rather as simply mistaken about what is morally permissible, it is conceivable that a reasonable person could regard deception as justified in such a case as well.

The third respect in which our employee treats her employer unfairly is by violating its property rights. In our discussion so far, we have been interested in property rights mainly as the source of the considerable directive power that employers have. Given that nonowners of productive resources must have access to these resources, at least in the form of employment, in order to live well, the threat of firing recalcitrant employees, which is an exercise of legal property rights, usually enables owners to secure compliance with their directives. Our case has been described so that the employer lacks this directive power. But, this does not mean that property rights play no role. If the employer's ownership of its productive property is consistent with distributive justice, its property rights will carry moral weight in the sense that anyone who uses its property in a way that contravenes its known wishes will treat it unfairly. As we have seen, a property right is not a right to direct labor, but property rights do allow one to bar others from using the items one owns in ways that one does not want.

Still, moral property rights are not absolute. There are cases in which we regard people as justified in using the property of others in ways that they have not permitted. An example is the famous scene in the film *Dr. Strangelove* in which a phone call that promises to prevent a nuclear war is temporarily delayed because the money to make it can only be obtained by robbing a Coke machine.[12] The humor of the situation derives from fact that the moral considerations in favor of making the call obviously outweigh the property rights of the Coca-Cola company. And this would be true even if the company had been contacted and had explicitly refused the request.

The reasons that have been identified so far as reasons for quitting rather than ignoring a managerial directive would also apply to people working for organizations as unpaid volunteers. But the fact that one is being paid to comply seems to introduce a powerful new consideration in favor of quitting if one is not willing to do what one's employer, or an individual to whom the employer's authority has been delegated, tells one to do. The unfairness to the employer

[12] Kubrick, George, and Southern (1963).

of taking the money without performing as directed seems great.[13] Nevertheless, there might be circumstances in which even with this element thrown in, ignoring the order would be morally preferable to quitting. The case of the German railway workers is one. Another would be the case of a law enforcement officer sent to infiltrate a corporation suspected of illegal activities. He must accept pay to remain in a position to gather evidence, and he is justified in ignoring managerial directives to the extent that he can. But it seems plausible that an individual who was not an agent of the government might sometimes be morally justified in doing this as well, for example, to prevent what she regards as a morally disastrous corporate policy from being implemented.

The moral permissibility of continuing to accept pay while ignoring managerial directives must not be misunderstood. One is justified in doing this only as a means to the accomplishment of a moral purpose. One accepts pay to avoid suspicion, and one may also have to accept it to support oneself while doing what one regards morality as requiring. It would be impermissible, however, to retain any money in excess of what is needed to do this. If finding some way to return it surreptitiously to the organization would not subvert one's moral purpose, one must do so. Otherwise, it must be given to some worthy cause. Even if one uses one's pay for personal gratification, however, it does not follow that one has sufficient moral reason to comply with managerial directives. One is merely doing something wrong while rightly preventing a morally unacceptable policy from being implemented.

It appears, then, that none of the respects in which our employee would be treating the employer unfairly by ignoring the directive in question can be regarded as decisive against her doing so. Still, it must be conceded that the unfairness she could prevent by disobeying the directives she receives would have to be substantial to outweigh the combined effect of all of these considerations. Normally, only if she is ordered to do something that would constitute seriously unfair treatment of a large number of people will an employee who could get away with it be justified in retaining her job and using it to promote her own conception of the moral good, as opposed to quitting. This means that a promissory obligation can usually underwrite the authority of employers whose directives rarely call for

---

[13] Recall that we are assuming that the employer has no police power, so that compliance depends only on what an employee judges she has good moral reason to do.

actions that affect large numbers of people—individuals employing domestic help, for instance.[14]

The Limits of P-Authority: Morally Important Social Values

We have just explored how considerations of fairness might justify breaking a promise to obey managerial directives. But the morally important social values can also provide directive-independent reasons for declining to comply with managerial directives. And they might be able to tip the balance in favor of keeping one's job (continuing to accept pay) while disobeying one's boss even when all considerations of fairness taken together dictate quitting. Under what circumstances this is so is the subject of this section.

Before proceeding, however, we should note that introducing morally important social values may strengthen the considerations of fairness that support compliance with directives. Strictly speaking, organizations cannot be treated unfairly, but the morally important social value of distributive justice—or laws and conventions endorsed by this value—may underwrite the claims of a variety of different *individuals* to the revenues of an organization. Thus, it may be possible to argue that retaining one's job while disobeying managerial directives emanating from an organization is straightforwardly unfair because it deflects some of the revenue to which these people have a legitimate claim. Any reasons that favored retaining one's job while disobeying would then have to outweigh these unproblematic considerations of fairness.

Collective Wrongdoing

Considering how morally important social values can provide directive-independent reasons to decline to comply with managerial directives—and whether these reasons are strong enough to justify an employee in remaining in her job while using it to promote her own conception of the moral good—requires us to examine the phenomenon of collective wrongdoing. As I have said, I regard an action of an organization as an event that is collectively produced by some of its members. Most organizational actions are produced not

---

[14] In cases of the latter sort, the assumption that managerial authority is grounded in a promise is unproblematic because the employer is a human being and not an organization.

by the whole set of members but by some subgroup.[15] Still, an organizational action that seems questionable in light of a morally important social value is almost always an event—or state of affairs in the case of an organizational omission—that is collectively produced.

It might seem that no morally important social value could provide a reason for ignoring managerial directives strong enough to justify an employee in retaining her job while disregarding such a directive. As we have seen, the strength of the reason for action provided by an opportunity to realize some morally important social value more fully, or to prevent a reduction in its realization, is a function of the incremental gain that would be achieved or loss that would be prevented. It is initially plausible to argue, however, that even when an action of an organization has a substantial negative impact on the degree of realization of some morally important social value, the contribution that any one employee makes to this result by complying with the directives addressed to her—and thus the moral improvement she could effect by declining to comply—is minuscule. And if the wrong done by each employee in complying is slight, a promise to comply if she is going to remain in her job might be decisive. For the unfairness to the employer, or to the individuals who have a claim to the organization's revenue, involved in accepting pay without complying would normally be more significant from the moral point of view than the good the employee could accomplish by doing this. But then the only acceptable course for an employee who finds herself ordered to contribute to what seems, because of its impact on the morally important social values, to be an organizational misdeed will be to quit.

To assess this contention, we must examine in detail how the rational force of the particular value in light of which an organizational action counts as a misdeed from a given employee's point of view gets translated into a reason for her to act, or refrain from acting, in certain ways. This is the problem of how collective wrongdoing gets distributed to the members of the group producing it.

I mean to distinguish the topic of collective wrongdoing from the topic of collective responsibility. Most discussions of moral responsibility identify two necessary conditions. The agent must be aware of the moral nature of her act (its intrinsic wrongness or its harmful effects), and she must have been able to do otherwise, or at least her

---

15. In Chapter Three, I suggested that it may be possible to regard all of the members of an organization as contributing to each of its acts because all help to maintain the constitution that makes them possible. But I do not want to rely on this assumption here.

performance must fall below some standard which is achieved by most agents in similar circumstances.[16] When moral responsibility is characterized in this way, to hold an individual responsible is essentially to say that she performed the action voluntarily in the Aristotelian sense of being informed about the particulars and not being compelled to act.[17] Aristotle's account of voluntariness is meant to elucidate when praise or blame is appropriate.

Moral responsibility must be distinguished from legal responsibility, understood as liability to be punished or to pay damages. Strictly speaking, legal responsibility is a sociological fact, and thus of no relevance to a normative inquiry. But it is appropriate for a normative inquiry to consider the moral boundaries of legal responsibility, that is, the circumstances under which morality endorses holding individuals legally liable for damages or applying legal punishment to them. An initially plausible position is that holding someone legally responsible for an act or an omission is justifiable only if she is morally responsible for it. As Joel Feinberg has shown in some detail, however, this view is too narrow.[18] There may be good moral reasons for the institution of strict liability, that is, liability without contributory fault, in some cases. One especially important subspecies of this is vicarious liability, the liability of a principal for even unauthorized actions taken by her agents in their capacity as agents, or more generally, of someone in a position of authority for even unauthorized actions taken by her subordinates in their capacity as subordinates.

It is common for writers on collective responsibility to argue that those who occupy positions of authority have greater responsibility for organizational misdeeds than their subordinates because they are better informed about what the organization is doing and freer to do otherwise. But the question of who is responsible for a group's misdeed does not even arise unless the group has done something wrong. And when we move to the level of wrongdoing, there is less basis for distinguishing between superiors and subordinates. The actions of groups are events that are collectively produced, and everyone who contributes to the collective production of a morally unwelcome event has, presumptively, done something wrong— irrespective of whether he knows this and thus can be held responsible. It is the phenomenon of collective wrongdoing that is of importance for our investigation of whether employees morally ought

[16] For discussion of this last point see Cooper (1968).
[17] Aristotle (1985), 1109b30–1111a25. Aristotle's considered position appears to be that coerced action is voluntary. Most modern writers, however, would not agree.
[18] Feinberg (1970).

to disregard the directives of managerial P-authorities. What we wish to know is whether the wrong an employee would actually do in complying with a given managerial directive is greater than the wrong he would do by breaking the promise. In what follows, I examine how collective wrongdoing is to be understood and how it gets distributed to the members of groups that do wrong.[19]

I understand doing (presumptive) wrong as doing what there is a good moral reason for not doing. That is, the fact that a certain action is wrong is a reason to refrain or desist from it. The question of how a group's wrongdoing gets distributed to the members of the group is, then, the question of the extent to which an individual member of the group has a good reason to refrain from contributing to a certain collective action when the group as a whole has a good reason to refrain from performing this action. Because the idea of groups as opposed to individuals having reasons for action is problematic, however, the question is better posed as a question about how much of the force of the reason an individual has for wanting a group of which he is a member not to do something—that is, for wanting a certain event not to occur—translates into a reason for him to do or refrain from doing something.[20] The latter reading is also useful in providing an account of the distribution of collective wrongdoing to individuals when there is disagreement within the group about whether what is being done is wrong. Of particular interest for our purposes is the question of whether the reason that a group member has to refrain is *as strong as* the reason he regards the group as a whole as having to refrain—or the reason he has for wanting the group to refrain.[21]

For the time being, I focus on the case where a single morally important social value underlies the judgment that a group is doing wrong—either because it is bringing about a reduction in the overall level of realization of this value, or because it is foregoing an opportunity to raise its overall level of realization. That is, the group's misdeed is the collective production of an event or state of affairs

[19] Discussions of collective responsibility that touch on some of the issues that I shall address under the heading of collective wrongdoing include: Held (1970), Bates (1971), Benjamin (1976), Schedler (1983); M. Zimmerman (1985), May (1987, 1990), Sverdlik (1987), and Mellema (1988).

[20] The strength of a reason for wanting a group not to do something is the strength of the reason that one would have for preventing it if one could do this by one's actions alone, for example, if one were a dictator.

[21] Since the complex of moral reasons facing a group may be different from those facing an individual, we cannot in general say that when a group acts wrongly, all things considered, that is, in light of all the reasons that apply to the group, each of its members acts wrongly, all things considered, in light of the reasons that apply to him. See Copp (1979), p. 185.

that has these features. It is worth noting, however, that questions of collective wrongdoing are not restricted to cases in which a group fails to act optimally in light of a morally important social value. Unfair treatment of individuals can also be collectively produced.

Reasons and Wrongdoing

I believe that the best way to approach the question of how the force of a reason that militates against a group's action gets distributed to the individual members of the group is by means of the principles of collective and individual rationality. As we have seen, collective rationality is not the rationality of a group understood as a distinct entity. Rather, it is an aspect of the rational behavior of individuals. The distinction between collective and individual rationality marks the fact that what constitutes rational action for individuals is affected by whether other rational agents are present. In considering to what extent individuals can be regarded as doing wrong when the groups of which they are members do wrong, we must consider both violations of the principle of individual rationality and violations of the principle of collective rationality.[22]

Let us begin with cases in which the principle of individual rationality explains how individuals do wrong when a group of which they are members does wrong. These are cases in which the contribution of each member of a group is necessary for the group's misdeed. Here the defection of any of the members of the group would prevent the group from doing wrong, and thus the principle of individual rationality justifies regarding each of the group members as having acted wrongly when the group does, that is, it justifies regarding each as having acted in a way that he or she had good moral reason not to act. Moreover, as Derek Parfit has shown, the wrongness of the group's actions is not to be divided among the group's members. That is, the "share of the total" view is false. Instead, the whole of the wrong is to be attributed to each individual; for each could have prevented all of it.[23]

This is not to say that the decision whether to defect from the group is straightforward if one is in such a situation. The nonparticipation of any group member removes the reason the others have to refrain or desist from the acts that would have constituted their contributions. Thus, if nonparticipation or withdrawal involves costs, each may delay hoping that someone else will bear these

---

[22] For these principles, see Chapter Four.
[23] See Parfit (1984), pp. 67–70.

costs. The situation thus has the structure of a game of chicken. But if no one desists, the whole of the group's misdeed is appropriately attributed to each, for each could have prevented it alone.

The case of the misdeed of a perfectly designed organization would be of this sort. In such an organization, the actions of each employee directed to contribute to a particular organizational deed would be necessary for its production. In all actual organizations, however, there is organizational slack that allows the organization as a whole to achieve its objectives even when some of its members have ceased to perform their functions.[24] The cases of concern to us, then, will usually not be of the sort we have just been considering. Rather, they will be cases in which there is overdetermination, either in the sense that more people are contributing to a misdeed than are necessary to produce it, or in the sense that some group misdeed—though not exactly the same one—will result even if one group member declines to contribute or withdraws from the group. In such cases, the principle of individual rationality will not suffice to establish wrongdoing because individual defection will not prevent the group's misdeed.

It is useful to provide some examples.[25] Group wrongs displaying overdetermination can have either a "step" or an "incremental" structure.[26] An example of a group misdeed of commission having a step structure would be gang of hoodlums, but larger than necessary, pushing a parked car over a cliff. An example of a misdeed of omission having a step structure would be a community's failure to protect itself from a flood by repairing a break in a levee with sandbags. An example of a misdeed of commission having an incremental structure would be a group's polluting a river by dumping waste into it. An example of a misdeed of omission having an incremental structure would be a community's failure to make contributions to a fund for the purchase of various public goods, such as park land, from a more or less open-ended list.

In the cases involving misdeeds of commission, it is tempting to invoke the concept of causation to account for the distribution of the group's misdeed to the members. Each acts against a good moral

---

[24] I take the term "organizational slack" from Cyert and March (1963), pp. 36–38. Their use of this concept is broader than my use here.

[25] Since they do not play an important role in organizational contexts, I do not discuss cases of overdetermination in which two or more independently performed (and appropriately timed) actions are both sufficient to bring about a given result. An example would be a case in which two people each shoot someone in a way that would have been fatal all by itself. For a discussion of such cases, see Parfit (1984), pp. 70–73.

[26] See the discussion in Chapter Four.

reason because the action of each is a cause of a result that can be seen as morally undesirable.[27] This is not the place for an extended discussion of causation, but J. L. Mackie's account can provide us with enough to proceed.[28] The centerpiece of Mackie's account of causation is the concept of an "INUS-condition." An INUS-condition for an event is a condition that is an *insufficient* but *necessary* part of a further, complex condition that is *unnecessary* but *sufficient* for the event. Mackie's example is a short circuit that is said to have caused a fire. The short circuit by itself would not have produced the fire—it had to take place in the presence of flammable materials—but the flammable materials would not have produced the fire alone either. The complex condition that consists in the occurrence of the short-circuit in the presence of flammable materials is sufficient but not necessary for the fire since it could also have resulted from, say, smoking in bed.

When the production of a step bad involves causal overdetermination, we can use the concept of an INUS-condition to establish that the actions of all the people who contributed were causes of the result. Consider the case in which the hoodlums push the car over the cliff. The set of all the pushing actions can be divided into a number of subsets each of which would be just large enough to do the job, that is, sufficient to do it. Each action in such a minimally sufficient subset is necessary if all of the actions in it taken together are to be sufficient, but no subset itself is necessary since any of the other subsets could also have produced the same result. Thus, each action of each group member is an insufficient but necessary part of a condition that is itself sufficient but unnecessary. The only difference between cases that involve causal overdetermination and cases that do not is that in cases of overdetermination, some of the other complex conditions that are also sufficient to produce the result in question are actually realized in the situation instead of being mere counterfactual possibilities.

The case of incremental bads is simpler. Strictly speaking, there is no overdetermination in such cases since all of the actions performed are necessary to produce the actual degree of badness displayed by the result. Each makes a small contribution, and the nonproduction of any of them would have slightly reduced the badness of the overall result. Thus, they are all straightforwardly causes of

---

[27] We do not usually regard omissions as causing results unless they constitute departures from an expected or required pattern. In general, the nonoccurrence of an event is said to cause effects only when it is unusual. Thus, a drought (the nonoccurrence of normal rain) may be said to cause the deaths of plants and animals.

[28] Mackie (1975).

the actual (degree of badness of) the result. The absence of over-determination can also be made clear by noting that each action is the sole cause, in its setting, of an increment of the bad result. There is, however, still a sense in which talk of overdetermination is appropriate, since more actions are performed than would be necessary to produce some, substantially similar, bad result.

We can, then, regard each action that contributes to a group misdeed of commission as a cause of the bad result associated with it. But it is unclear how strong a reason the fact that his action would count as a cause of such a result gives each group member to refrain from it. When there is overdetermination in the production of a step bad, it may be that the reason that the fact that his action would be a cause of the bad result gives each to refrain is not as strong as the reason he has for wanting the group as a whole to refrain.[29] Similarly, in the case of an incremental bad, it seems plausible to regard the strength of the reason each agent has to refrain that derives from the fact that his action would be a cause of the bad result as a function only of the incremental change refraining would produce.

Collective Wrongdoing as Collective Failure to Desist

Let us relate these results to complying with a directive. On the causal-contribution approach to the distribution of collective wrongdoing, it seems that an individual directed to contribute to the production of what she regards as a group misdeed may not have a reason for rejecting the directive that is as strong as the reason she has for wanting the group as a whole to refrain. This means that her reason for declining to comply may not be strong enough to justify her using her job to do what she thinks right rather than quitting; it may not be strong enough, that is, to outweigh the reasons of fairness that militate against ignoring managerial directives while accepting pay. A different approach, however, allows more definite conclusions about the strength of the reason for refraining that an employee in such a situation would have. This approach reduces our four cases to two. As I said earlier, the reason for action provided by the fact that something is wrong is a reason to refrain or desist from it. But a reason to refrain or desist from an action is a reason to create a state of affairs in which the action is not performed. Thus, the misdeeds of commission are relevantly similar to the misdeeds

---

[29] One important question here concerns whether we can regard some of the causes of an event as more important than others in the sense of making a greater causal contribution. I shall not consider this issue.

of omission; they, too, involve a failure to create an outcome that there is good reason to create.

In the cases involving omission, the group's misdeed takes the form of failing to produce a good—either one having a step structure, as in the case of repairing the levee, or one having an incremental structure, as in the case of providing public amenities. In the cases involving commission, the group also fails to produce a good, the good that consists in the *nonoccurrence* of a certain bad event or the *nonexistence* of a certain bad state of affairs. Again, the cases are of two kinds. Where the bad has a step structure (a certain threshold number of contributions are required to produce it), the good that consists in the nonexistence of this bad also has a step structure (a certain threshold number of contributions are required to produce *it*—where the contributions take the form of refraining from producing the bad). For example, a certain threshold number of hoodlums must refrain to prevent the car from being pushed over the cliff. Similarly, where the bad has an incremental structure, the good that consists in its nonexistence also has an incremental structure. Thus, if the bad is polluting a river, the incremental good of reducing pollution is produced when members of the group decline to pollute, that is, they dispose of their waste in some other way. The more who do this, the greater the good.

In Chapter Four, we saw how a group facing the problem of producing a good having one of these structures can solve it. The production of a step good typically presents a battle of the sexes problem, perhaps with elements of a chicken game playing a role at various places; and individual rationality has the resources to solve such problems, although collective rationality may be of assistance in enabling a group to avoid chicken games. The production of an incremental good typically presents a generalized prisoner's dilemma problem, which collective rationality has the resources to solve.

A member of a group that is ordered to produce an event or state of affairs that she regards as morally undesirable may, then, have a reason under the principles of collective or individual rationality to produce the contrary event or state of affairs that consists in the nonexistence (or mitigation) of the ordered event or state of affairs. The strength of the reason that she has to ignore the directive she receives will depend on how much of the reason she has for wanting this contrary event or state of affairs to be produced translates into a reason for her to contribute to its production by declining to do what she is told. But on the procedure for deriving reasons for individuals to act from reasons for groups to act that we are now considering—

one that invokes rational cooperation justified by the principles of collective or individual rationality—this will turn out to depend on how many others in the group cooperate with her in securing the result she wants. In these cases, the strength of the reason one has for refraining from contributing to an organizational misdeed is given by the strength of the reason one has to participate in the *collective* production of the contrary event or state of affairs (the nonoccurrence of this misdeed).

The bad consequences of organizational misdeeds are typically much worse than those of the misdeeds of individuals. Thus, if each employee directed to contribute to what she regards as an organizational misdeed has a reason to decline that is as strong as the reason she has to want the group as a whole to refrain—that is, to produce collectively the good of refraining—it is plausible that each will be justified in remaining on the job while ignoring the directive. For preventing the organizational misdeed can only be done by remaining while ignoring the directive, and on the present hypothesis, the reason each has to do this will be very strong (and thus often strong enough to outweigh the considerations of fairness to the employer that support quitting if she is not going to comply). But if the reason that each has to decline is not as strong as the reason she has for wanting the group to refrain, a promise not to accept pay if she is not going to comply with managerial directives may prevail, in which case the employee should either comply or quit.[30]

Producing an Alternative Incremental Good

Let us begin with a case in which the good that a group produces by refraining from some course of action is a public good (within this group) with an incremental structure. This need not imply that all in the group have the same preferences or value system. It is enough that by his own lights, each regards general cooperation to produce the good as preferable to general noncooperation. And let us assume that the assurance problem is solved. This means that each has good reason to believe that his contribution will be supplemented by those of the other group members. This might be the case if the members of the group had employed some internal decision-making procedure to generate a directive calling for all to refrain.

In this case, the reason each group member has for refraining will

---

[30] Again, we are assuming that employers lack police power. To make this vivid, we might suppose that they have issued orders but have no way of telling whether they are being carried out.

be as strong as the reason he regards the group as having for refraining, or the reason he has for wanting the group to refrain. This is a consequence of the way the principle of collective rationality works. The principle of individual rationality directs each contributor to measure the cost to him of contributing against the incremental increase in the value of the good that his contribution will produce, and to contribute only if the contribution will yield a net gain. But the principle of collective rationality directs each to imagine his contribution as producing the whole of the good (that is, the whole value to him of the public good that all the contributions produce), and to contribute if *this* exceeds the cost to him of doing so.

This can be seen by reflecting on the fact that even in the case of an incremental public good, there is a threshold. No one has a reason, under the principle of collective rationality, to contribute to the production of such a good unless enough others contribute so that the value to each of the good that all the contributors produce together exceeds the cost to each of his contribution. The threshold case is that in which enough others have contributed so that what one's contribution adds will make the good just large enough to justify contributing. But this means that in the threshold case, each weighs the cost to him of contributing against the whole value to him of the good all the contributors produce together. And if the principle of collective rationality works in this way in the threshold case, it should work this way in other cases too. That is, the strength of the reason each has to contribute should be given by the amount of good he regards all the contributors as accomplishing together.

These results can be extended, with appropriate modifications, to the case where by refraining from contributing to a group's misdeed, a subgroup can effect a significant reduction in the bad result that the larger group is producing.[31] If the assurance problem within this subgroup is solved—perhaps because the members met and decided to refrain—then each member will have a reason to refrain that is as strong as the reason the subgroup as a whole has to produce the reduction it can produce.[32]

The implications of these results for compliance with managerial directives are as follows. Suppose (1) that a group of employees is directed to produce an organizational action that some or all of them think will have a morally undesirable result with an incremental

[31] Here I am assuming that this subgroup is large enough to cross the threshold at which contribution becomes rational under the principle of collective rationality.

[32] Recall that the strength of the reason for action provided by a morally important social value is determined by the size of the incremental change in its level of realization that the action in question can produce or prevent.

structure; (2) that by refraining together, those who regard the ordered action as having this undesirable result could effect a reduction in its badness large enough to justify, under the principle of collective rationality, each in refraining; and (3) that the assurance problem is solved within this group. Then, each has a reason to decline to comply with the directives facilitating this organizational misdeed that is as strong as the reason he regards the group as a whole as having to refrain, that is, the reason he has for wanting the group as a whole to refrain.

Now let us suppose that the good that consists in the group's (or subgroup's) refraining or desisting from a misdeed has the status for all within it of a public good of sufficient size, but the assurance problem is not solved. In this case, we cannot say that if the group fails to prevent or mitigate the misdeed each group member fails to do what he has good reason to do; collective rationality dictates contributing only if enough others will contribute as well. But this is not the end of the matter, since it may be relatively easy for the members of the group (or subgroup) to solve the assurance problem. By hypothesis, they all have the required motivation, so all that is necessary is to make this fact common knowledge among them.[33] Presumably this could be easily done at a meeting of all of them. But then the group will do wrong if it fails to hold this meeting, that is, the members will fail to do what they have good reason to do. In general, where there would be good reason, under the principle of collective rationality for the members of a group to do something if the assurance problem were solved, there is good reason to solve the assurance problem.

How strong is the reason each acts against if the group could solve the assurance problem and fails to do so? If, as will often be the case, each member could solve the assurance problem by himself—say, by providing assurances to all that he had spoken to everyone and each had agreed to participate if the others did[34]—the principle of individual rationality would justify charging each with the whole cost of the problem's not being solved, which is the cost of the group's failure to do what it has, under the principle of collective

---

[33] They all have the required motivation because each accepts the principle of collective rationality and thus none wants to be a free rider. A fact is common knowledge within a group when each knows it, each knows that each knows it, each knows that each knows that each knows it, and so on.

[34] Strictly speaking, common knowledge of a willingness to contribute if the others do—each knowing that others know, and so on—is required. But I shall ignore these complications; assurance problems do in fact get solved.

rationality, good reason to do. To put it another way, each, individually, acts against a reason as strong as the reason he would have if the assurance problem were solved. As we have seen, this is a reason as strong as the reason each has for wanting the group to perform the act in question.[35]

Now let us consider the case in which a member of a group regards what the group is doing as seriously wrong, but not enough others share this view to allow the formation of a subgroup large enough to make refraining rational under the principle of collective rationality, that is, a subgroup of at least threshold size, in the sense that the reduction it can produce (as judged by each member) in the bad effects of the larger group's action exceeds the cost to him of his contribution. Here, efforts to solve the assurance problem will be of no avail; others simply do not have the requisite motivation. Thus, whether it is in accordance with reason for such an individual to refrain will be determined solely by the principle of individual rationality. The incremental change that he could produce by refraining must be large enough to outweigh any considerations that might count in favor of contributing.

Now let us bring a promise to comply with directives (if one is going to accept pay) back into the picture. Do the members of a group directed to produce some organizational action that they feel ought not to be produced have a reason for ignoring the order that is strong enough to justify their remaining on the job, continuing to accept pay, so that they can prevent the misdeed? Or, must they quit if they are not willing to comply? When the whole force of the reason that each employee regards the group as having to prevent an organizational misdeed devolves on each, it is likely that remaining in the job while ignoring the order will be justified all things considered. That is, each employee will be justified in acting with the others to thwart the organizational misdeed. For organizational misdeeds have large effects on the morally important social values, and the prevention of these effects could be important enough to outweigh the unfairness to the organization or its dependents of accepting pay while not complying. By contrast, when an individual may appropriately consider only the incremental change he can effect, a promissory obligation to comply with managerial directives if he is going to accept pay will have a better chance to prevail. For the

[35] If the assurance problem must rather be solved by collective action—say a subgroup must take on this task—then the situation has the structure of a battle of the sexes problem. Such cases will be discussed shortly.

219

unfairness entailed by accepting pay while rejecting the directive may be enough to outweigh the incremental moral gain refusal would produce. If this is the case, the employee morally ought to quit if he does not want to comply.

Intermediate cases in which subgroups of the organization refrain, mitigating but not eliminating the misdeed, could go either way depending on the details. The reason that each member of such a subgroup will have to want it to perform the action of refraining from contributing to the organizational misdeed will not be as strong as the reason he has to want the organization as a whole to refrain (because this subgroup's refraining will not completely prevent the organizational misdeed), but it may still be strong enough to outweigh a promissory obligation to comply with managerial directives if one is going to accept pay. If some members of an organization are directed to engage in activities that would pollute a river, for example, the members of a subgroup within this group may be justified in thinking that the reduction in the pollution the organization causes that they could bring about by declining to participate warrants their retaining their jobs while ignoring the managerial directives.

Which of these possibilities is realized in a given case will depend on how much agreement there is among the members of the relevant group about what there is adequate moral reason to do and how effectively they could organize if they tried to. It is one of the premises of this book that moral disagreement is a basic fact of social life. Still, it seems plausible that cases in which there is so much disagreement that each should consider only the incremental change that he can produce alone will be less common than cases in which each can find enough others who agree with him to form a group of at least threshold size, with the result that each will have the stronger reason to desist that collective rationality provides. Further, while there will usually be costs involved in determining whether enough have similar views to make collective action rational, they will not be great in the case of relatively small subgroups. It may be appropriate to repeat that we are assuming that mangers lack police power. Thus, what employees do depends solely on what they think morality requires.

Of course, these are "iffy" conclusions. But they are sufficient for our purposes because they establish that there will be much room for doubt about whether a promissory obligation to comply with managerial directives in return for pay is strong enough to prevail over the competing considerations in a given case, and such doubts affect the robustness and reach of managerial authority as P-authority.

Producing an Alternative Step Good

Now let us consider the case of step goods. Here, the undesirable result of an organization's misdeed has a step structure—a threshold number of contributions are required to produce it—and thus the corresponding good of the organization's not performing this action also has a step structure. When enough of those ordered to produce the organizational action refrain, it is impossible for the rest to produce it.

This case parallels the incremental case. If all of the members of some group within the organization regard this group as having an opportunity to produce a good (preventing an organizational misdeed) that has a step structure, they face a battle of the sexes problem. They must select a set of producers, or to be more precise, they must make it common knowledge within the group that one has been selected. Since a battle of the sexes problem is a coordination problem, to make the selection of a set of producers common knowledge within the group is to make salient one of the possible coordination equilibria. Once this is done, individual rationality gives each designated producer a reason to contribute, for individual rationality suffices to solve coordination problems if one of the coordination equilibria is made salient. As was noted in Chapter Four, this requirement that one of the equilibria be made salient is an analogue of the assurance problem associated with multiperson prisoner's dilemmas. To relate these observations to the prevention of collective wrongdoing, suppose that in our case of the hoodlums and the car, a number of them larger than that necessary to prevent the misdeed by declining to participate would like the group to desist, but declining carries costs and each would prefer that others bear them.

The strength of the reason that each designated producer has to contribute to the effort to prevent the organizational misdeed is determined by the value that she places (from her point of view) on the realization of the coordination equilibrium that has been made salient—which is to say, on everyone's doing what they must do to realize it. This means that the reason that each regards herself as having is as strong as the reason that she has to want the group to behave in this way. Conversely, if one of the coordination equilibria has been made salient and yet the designated producers do not produce the good, each of them fails to act on a reason as strong as the reason she regards the group as a whole as having.[36]

[36] If there is some slack, a game of chicken may arise within the designated set of producers to determine a smaller set of producers. We saw in Chapter Four how this complication is to be handled.

Collective wrongdoing that takes the form of failing to produce a step good—in the present case, failure to prevent an organizational misdeed having a step structure—is more likely, however, to involve failing to make one of the coordination equilibria salient. Here, the situation is like that of a group that fails to produce an incremental good because, although all have the required motivation, they fail to solve the assurance problem. Given that all have the preferences that engender several different coordination equilibria, it should be relatively easy to make one of the equilibria salient. The group could, say, hold a meeting at which a lottery was conducted. If each could organize such a meeting, and yet no one does, the principle of individual rationality yields the conclusion that each has acted against a reason as strong as the reason she regards the group as a whole as having to produce the step good in question. In the normal case, this good would be produced once a set of producers had been designated.[37]

As in the case of an incremental good, disagreement, among those ordered to create a particular organizational action, about whether it is wrong need not deprive those who think it is wrong of a good reason to desist. They need only identify a sufficiently large number of like-minded people to create the step good in question: blocking the organizational misdeed. Moreover, the number required to do this may not be large. Although there is usually organizational slack, there will not be an enormous amount of it in efficient organizations. Thus, it will often be possible for relatively small groups to block, by nonparticipation, organizational actions that they regard as wrong. Even smaller groups may be able to block an organizational misdeed if the strategies available are broadened to include not just desisting but also sabotage. Of course, employees would need a stronger reason to justify destroying their employer's property than to justify simply declining to comply with directives while continuing to accept pay. But reasons of the required strength may sometimes be available.

As we have seen, an individual who regards a group as having an opportunity to produce an incremental good by collectively ignoring a managerial directive may have a reason (albeit a weak one) to ignore the directive herself even when no others share her view of the situation. This is also true for an individual who regards a group as having an opportunity to produce a step good, if the good takes

---

[37] If organizing a meeting requires the collective action of a subgroup, so that the group faces a preliminary battle of the sexes problem in organizing it, the same reasoning applies.

the form of refraining from the production of a bad with a step structure, for example, refraining from pushing a car over a cliff. As we have seen, in such a case the actions of anyone who contributes can be regarded as a cause of the result the group produces, and this is enough to create some reason—although it is unclear how strong—to refrain.

The implications of these points for our question of whether those who have been directed by their bosses to produce what seems to them to be an organizational misdeed have a reason for disobeying that is strong enough to outweigh a promissory obligation to obey (if they are going to retain their jobs and continue to accept pay) are as before. Sometimes each employee's reason for disobeying will be as strong as the reason she has for wanting the organization as a whole to refrain, and sometimes this reason will be weaker than the reason she has for wanting the organization as a whole as to refrain. Once again, the result is that the robustness and reach of P-authority will vary greatly depending on the circumstances; and it will be something about which reasonable people can disagree.

This account of collective resistance to managerial directives supported by a promise to obey can be generalized to other kinds of collective action for moral purposes. Thus, acting effectively to achieve political objectives *within* the constitution of a state or other organization often involves forming political parties or interest groups; whether people have good reason to take such actions, and how strong these reasons are, can be determined as above.

Unions and Preventing Wrongdoing by Others

We have found that those members of an organization who are directed to contribute to the production of an organizational action that they regard as wrong will sometimes have a moral reason to ignore the directive that is strong enough to outweigh a promissory obligation to comply if they are going to accept pay. By not complying they can eliminate or mitigate an organizational misdeed, and doing this may be more important than avoiding the unfairness involved in retaining their jobs while ignoring the directive. But the principles of individual and collective rationality may also provide others within the organization with a reason to intervene to prevent organizational misdeeds.

Commonsense morality makes a distinction between what one does and what one allows; it regards the reason that one has to prevent harm as weaker than the reason one has not to do harm. It thus combines a strong requirement of nonmaleficence with a weaker requirement of mutual aid, which is usually formulated as a requirement to help others when one can do so without serious cost to oneself.

The principle of mutual aid is not restricted to cases where one could prevent accidental harm without serious cost to oneself. It also applies to cases where one could prevent wrongdoing by others without serious cost to oneself. And, of course, this holds for preventing wrongdoing by groups as well as by individuals. Thus, a reporter on the scene of a collective crime who could prevent it without serious cost to himself clearly acts contrary to the principle of mutual aid if he does not. Moreover, groups as well as individuals can do wrong by failing to prevent wrongdoing, for sometimes a group can prevent harm if each member performs an action that does not involve serious cost to himself.

This latter possibility is of special importance for our project because the number of people who can be regarded as producing a given organizational action will usually be substantially less than the whole population of employees. Thus, only a relatively small group of employees will be in a position to prevent an organizational misdeed by refraining from obeying an order to produce it. The other employees may, however, still do wrong if, by acting collectively, they could intervene to prevent an organizational misdeed.

The responsibility of groups for failing to prevent misdeeds has been discussed by Virginia Held.[38] She describes a case in which an unorganized group can be regarded as doing wrong through failing to prevent a misdeed. One of the people in a subway car starts to assault another of the people in the car, and while none of the remaining members could stop the assault alone, several different subsets of this group could. In this case, Held argues that the group of bystanders can be regarded as doing wrong, in a way that distributes to each individual, if none intervene.

We can explain why the individual members of the group do wrong when the group fails to prevent the attack in the same way that we explained collective wrongdoing earlier. Basically, the situation is one in which the group fails to produce the step good of effective intervention. Held's case is meant to be one in which it is clear to all what ought to be done: A sufficient number of them must act together to prevent the assault. This can be regarded as establishing that the knowledge condition for collective *responsibility* can be met even in an unorganized group. But it is also germane to whether each member does *wrong*—that is, acts against a good moral

[38] See Held (1970).

224

reason—in failing to intervene. For if there is to be a reason for them to prevent the attack, the assurance problem must be solved. And if it is common knowledge within the group what ought to be done, the situation is such that the assurance problem is at least partly solved. Indeed, it is completely solved if its being common knowledge what ought to be done can be taken to imply that each knows that all are motivated to do what they think ought to be done. Otherwise, we must make this additional assumption.

Given that the assurance problem is solved, however, collective action can be easily secured. It will be enough if one member of the group says, "Let's stop this," or perhaps simply moves to intervene. But then, as we have seen, if no one does anything, all will be acting contrary to a reason as strong as the reason the group has to prevent the attack—which is to say, a reason as strong as the reason an individual who could have prevented the attack by himself would have had.[39]

Held provides further support for this analysis when she argues that when there is no shared understanding of what is to be done, the members of a group do not do wrong by failing to prevent harm. She considers a case in which three people must act together to move a beam that is crushing someone, but each thinks a different plan is best, and consequently nothing is done. If each would be willing to cooperate to implement any of the three plans even though he regards his as optimal, the case presents a simple battle of the sexes problem in which the group must choose one of the available coordination equilibria.

Held says that the group's failure in this case does not distribute to the individuals, and we can account for this by supposing that nothing in the situation makes one of the coordination equilibria salient, so that the members of the group have no reason to realize any of them. But Held argues that this is not the end of the matter because the members of the group may be responsible for not establishing a decision procedure that would enable them to reach an agreement on what to do—which is to say, to make one of the equilibria salient. As we saw earlier, when the members of a group in fact have the motivation required to cooperate, it is usually relatively easy to provide the common knowledge necessary to make cooperation

[39] Here I am interpreting the assumption that it is common knowledge within the bystanders that all are motivated to intervene as equivalent to the assumption that it is common knowledge within this group that all have the status of designated producers of this good. Thus, the elements of a battle of the sexes problem that might be presented by the fact that not all need to intervene are absent. The case might, however, have elements of a chicken game.

rational, and in failing to do so the members of the group act wrongly.[40]

Drawing all these points together, we get the result that when the members of a group regard some other individual or group as doing wrong, and by acting collectively they could prevent this wrongdoing without serious cost to any of them, each does wrong—acts contrary to a good moral reason—if he does not join such an endeavor, given that the assurance problem is solved, or join in solving it if it is not. The results established earlier about how strong this reason is are applicable to this case as well.

Held's case involves an unorganized group, and its interest lies partly in the fact that it shows that organization, in the sense of possession of an internal decision-making procedure, is not necessary for a group's wrongdoing to distribute to the members, that is, for the members to fail as individuals to act as reason requires. Her results need not be limited to unorganized groups, however. An individual who could without serious cost to himself prevent wrongdoing by an organization of which he was a member—by leaking information to the press, for example—does wrong if he does not do this. The same can be said of dissenting groups within the organization. It may be that by organizing *in another way*, the members of such groups could prevent an organizational misdeed. So if organizing in such a way was relatively easy, they would be acting contrary to a good moral reason by not doing so. Indeed, the point also applies to outsiders. They, too, could organize to prevent misdeeds by corporations and other organizations. But our purpose here is to consider the limits of managerial authority, and managers have no authority over outsiders. So I shall focus on the case in which the members of an organization could organize to prevent what they regard as organizational misdeeds directed by management.

Of the groups that could play this role, the group of all the employees considered together is of special interest. Let us call an independent organization established by all the employees of some corporation or other organization to prevent managerially directed wrongdoing by it a "union". I have chosen this term because of the similarity such an organization would have to the trade unions that are familiar in contemporary society. But we should not allow the

---

[40] Although Held (1970) does not discuss it, this point applies not only to cases in which there is disagreement about the best means to a shared end but also to cases where there is disagreement about ends. For in such cases, there might be enough common ground that it would be relatively easy to find a basis on which all could cooperate.

terminology to blind us to some important differences. Trade unions are primarily collective bargaining agents. Their goal is to promote the interests of their members by evening out the disparities in bargaining power that would otherwise exist between individual employees and their employers. As I am viewing them here, however, unions are formed for the purpose of preventing organizational misdeeds. These may include unfair treatment of workers, but need not be limited to this. Further, they are not organized along craft lines, but are rather "company unions" that represent all the employees of an organization, regardless of the jobs they perform. All but the highest ranking managers—those on whose ultimate authority managerial directives are issued—would have a good reason to join. For all but these people could find themselves considering whether they should try to prevent the implementation of a managerial directive.

In order to play the role of preventing organizational misdeeds, unions must have a decision-making structure. Presumably the members of a company union would often disagree about whether an organizational action constituted a misdeed or how best to prevent it, and they would need some way of resolving these disagreements. Thus, the question of legitimacy would arise with respect to the authority exercised within the union. But there would be no question of basing this authority on a promise. Rather, the authority of the union's leaders would be C-authority, authority justified as making possible mutually beneficial cooperation.

To avoid the collective misdeed of failing to prevent the implementation of managerial directives that are morally mistaken, the members of corporations and other organizations whose managers are regarded as P-authorities should form unions (which they can do without serious cost to themselves) and contribute to the efforts of these unions to check morally mistaken policies (to the extent that these contributions can be made without serious cost to themselves).[41] This means that employees will have a good moral reason to ignore any managerial directives that are incompatible with their joining a union and participating in its activities. Unions might decide that their members should leave their work stations to prevent

[41] It might be suggested that since all of the members of an organization contribute to the maintenance of the constitution that makes possible the ascription of actions to it, the distinction between preventing misdeeds by others in one's organization and refraining from wrongdoing oneself is untenable. If this is right, the reason that the members of organizations have to prevent misdeeds anywhere in the organization is the strong one associated with refraining from wrongdoing oneself, not the weaker one associated by preventing wrongdoing by others. See the discussion of collective responsibility as the violation of a negative duty in Pogge (1989), pp. 31–33.

some organizational misdeed, which would involve ignoring managerial directives. And even in the case of actions that could be performed without ignoring routine managerial directives, such as picketing in their spare time to put pressure on their corporation to stop what it was doing, union members might be confronted with directives to desist. In either case, employees would then have to decide whether their promissory obligation to obey (if they were going to retain their jobs) was stronger than the reasons that supported engaging in these activities.

Of course in the real world, company unions of the sort that I have described would have little power to act effectively on their decisions—if indeed they could be formed at all—since management controls the property associated with the organization and can threaten to fire employees who engage in union activity. But as I have repeatedly emphasized, our concern here is with what justifies the use of these police powers, and in particular with whether their use exceeds the legitimate authority a firm's managers can be regarded as having. The important question, then, is what the employees would have good reason to do in the absence of these powers. To make this vivid, we might suppose that the collective actions employees are contemplating are actions that can be undertaken in secret, or for some other reason with impunity.

Similar points apply to the case in which a union regards the wrong it could prevent as so great that a strike seems appropriate. For the union to strike is for it collectively to prevent an organizational misdeed by collectively preventing all organizational actions (with the exception of those that senior management can produce alone). Most often this will happen because the union regards the organization as wronging not outsiders or society as a whole but its members. The reason for the strike will then be self-defense—a reason that can justify bearing burdens heavier than those the principal of mutual aid can justify bearing. In such cases, too, employers might order the members of the union to desist and return to work. Actual managements could bring to bear considerable directive power in support of such an order, namely, the threat of replacing those who did not comply. But again, our concern here is with what can justify such exercises of directive power, so we must imagine managers to lack it.[42]

---

[42] Here I am assuming that by striking, the employees would make it impossible for the organization to pay them, and thus that the loss of pay consequent on striking would not be an exercise of managerial power. For a discussion of what workers may legitimately do to counter the directive power of corporate authorities, and some important differences between collective resistance to such authorities and civil disobedience of the laws of a state, see Walzer (1970).

Conclusion

In the present chapter, we have been viewing managerial authority as P-authority. As we have seen, the robustness and reach of P-authority depend on the strength of the competing moral reasons. But as we have also seen, when individuals cooperate to produce outcomes that they could not have produced alone, the reason on which each acts can be much stronger than the reasons he or she would usually have as an isolated individual. This means that when a number of employees believe that by cooperating they could prevent a misdeed by their employer, each will have a reason to ignore managerial directives that may be strong enough to outweigh the reasons of fairness that militate against remaining in one's job and continuing to accept pay while disregarding managerial directives. When we admit the possibility of collective resistance by employees, then, the robustness and reach of managerial P-authority are diminished. Moreover, this can happen not only when employees are called on to contribute actively to the production of what they regard as an organizational misdeed but also when by organizing without serious cost to themselves they could prevent wrongdoing in other parts of the organization. The upshot is that a promise to comply with managerial directives in return for pay cannot justify the routine exercise of managerial authority.[43]

These results were established for the most part by considering how objections to an organization's actions deriving from a single morally important social value are translated into moral reasons to ignore managerial directives, but they are only strengthened when we bring full conceptions of the moral good into the picture. For this will increase the chance that an employee will find a given organizational action morally objectionable.

It might be thought that the problems associated with basing authority on a promise to obey could be avoided if it was stipulated that the organization's constitution was just. This would seem to entail that no competing considerations strong enough to outweigh

---

[43] In this chapter I have argued that the moral reason an employee has to combine with like-minded others to promote common ends can be stronger than her promissory obligation to obey her employer. It might be objected that if collective action magnifies the strength of the reasons employees have to disregard managerial directives, it also magnifies the strength of the reasons they have not to. But in the first place, employees promise individually, not collectively, to comply with directives in return for pay. And second, while they may collectively perpetrate unfairness of some other kind, this will often be outweighed by the good they can do. This is especially likely if only unfairness to humans beings—for example, those who have financial claims against the organization—need be considered. A small loss to each of a large number of people may not be very important from the standpoint of fairness.

the promise were present. It would be an analogue of the rider that John Rawls attaches to his principle of fairness to the effect that voluntary acceptance of the benefits of a beneficial practice binds us only if the practice is just.[44]

Whether this will work depends on what is meant by saying that a practice is just. If to say that a practice is just is to say that taking all the components of the moral good into account, there are no serious moral objections to doing what one has promised to do—that is, the action is permissible all promise-independent things considered—then the promise will provide a decisive reason for compliance. But this is to stipulate that the problems we have been discussing do not arise. It does not provide a solution to these problems when they arise.

More important, however, this latter construal of the term "just" is not what would normally be meant by saying that a practice or institution was just. We think of justice as a relatively abiding property of practices, having something to do with the fact that competing claims are appropriately reconciled within them. But if these are moral claims, to say that the constitution of an organization is just is to say that it provides an appropriate framework within which people with competing moral views can work together. It is plausible, however, that any institution satisfying this condition must at least organize cooperation in a mutually beneficial way. And if an institution organizes cooperation in a mutually beneficial way, the authorities that guide it can be regarded as C-authorities. So if we take this line, we are saying that consent having the force of a promise can justify complying with the directives emanating from some source only if this source can be regarded as possessing legitimate C-authority. But then, invoking P-authority is redundant.[45] The possibility of viewing managerial authority as C-authority is the focus of Chapter Eight.

[44] See Rawls (1971), pp. 111–12.

[45] Thus, the traditional contract theories, all of which present political authority as making mutually beneficial cooperation possible, could have dispensed with a promise to obey. Raz (1986), pp. 88–94, argues that instrumental consent to political authority (given to facilitate the attainment of ends one had prior to consenting) creates a valid reason to obey only when political authority is already justified by the normal justification thesis, but that noninstrumental consent (that expresses identification with one's community) can provide a reason to obey any just government, which he regards as a weaker condition than satisfying the normal justification thesis. But if a just government makes mutually beneficial cooperation possible, it will count as a C-authority; and as we have seen, legitimate C-authorities can be regarded as satisfying the normal justification thesis.

MANAGERIAL AUTHORITY
AS C-AUTHORITY

If the results of the last chapter are correct, when the directive-independent reasons acknowledged by employees include moral reasons, a promissory obligation will be able to justify compliance with managerial directives only intermittently. But is this anything to worry about? To be sure, as property rights in productive resources are now defined, the power they confer on those who exercise them does not have the intermittent character of legitimate P-authority. But why not simply redefine property rights so that this power conforms to the boundaries of P-authority?[1] The managers of contemporary nongovernmental organizations would probably not welcome such a reduction in their power, but this is irrelevant for our purposes. The justification of authority is its justification from the standpoint of the subordinates. So if we are to show that there is something objectionable about the intermittent character of P-authority when employees have moral concerns, the argument must be made from their point of view. We must show that there is good reason for them to want managerial authority to have greater robustness and reach.

In this chapter I argue that employees often have such a reason since P-authority does not enable them, as individuals trying to advance their moral aims, to realize fully the benefits of cooperation. Only if managerial authority is understood as C-authority will this be possible. But C-authority is able to produce these benefits precisely because it has, for such individuals, greater robustness and reach than P-authority. So there is good reason for employees who have moral concerns to want managerial authority to be stronger than P-authority.

One consequence of this fact that there is good reason for employees with moral concerns to view managerial authority as C-

[1] For reasons that will become clear shortly, we need not tackle the difficult question of what such a redefinition would entail.

authority rather than P-authority is that managers can justifiably retain more of the power that the law now gives them. But the price of preserving managerial power by making this move is a striking change in the way we think about the role of managers. From the legal point of view, employees are agents of their employers, and managers exercise authority that is delegated to them by the principal in this agency relationship. If managerial authority is best understood as C-authority, however, managers must be regarded as serving not a principal distinct from the employees, but rather the employees themselves, considered as a group. The justification for managerial authority will be that it enables the employees more effectively to promote their conceptions of the moral good in their work.

Viewing managerial authority as C-authority also has another consequence. As we have seen, the values of fairness and welfare maximization create a presumption in favor of the democratic exercise of C-authority. If managerial authority is appropriately regarded as C-authority, then, there is a moral presumption that nongovernmental organizations should be managed democratically by their employees, or at least that their managers should be accountable to, and chosen by, the employees. The implications of this are the focus of Chapter Nine.

C-Authority and P-Authority

I have said that P-authority does not enable individuals who are trying to advance moral aims to realize fully the benefits of cooperation. Why is this so?

The idea that mutually beneficial cooperation can be facilitated by promising to comply with directives having the appropriate content is a familiar feature of classical social contract theories. These theories regard political authority as making possible cooperation to leave or avoid the state of nature, and they present the basis of this authority as a promise to obey, where the promise is made either to the putative authority or to the other members of the group that would benefit from cooperation. Thus John Locke holds that those who remain within the jurisdiction of a given political authority can be regarded as having tacitly consented to comply with its official directives—the laws it promulgates—where consent is understood as a mechanism by which promissory obligations are undertaken.[2]

On the surface, the suggestion that P-authority can facilitate mutu-

---

[2] Locke (1952), sec. 119.

ally beneficial cooperation seems unobjectionable. It is generally accepted that cooperation in prisoner's dilemma situations can be achieved if the parties acknowledge a moral reason to choose the cooperative strategy, and mutual promises to cooperate can often provide such a reason. Thus the principal criticism to which Locke's theory has been subjected is that few if any of the members of most political societies have performed an action that can be regarded as constituting a valid promise to obey.

If we assume, however, as I have in this book, that individuals are trying to advance their conceptions of the moral good, there is another, powerful objection to using P-authority to facilitate mutually beneficial cooperation. If the directives emanating from some source are to facilitate such cooperation, those to whom they are addressed must have a reason for complying with them that is strong enough to defeat the reasons they have for adopting a noncooperative strategy—for being free riders on whatever level of cooperation the others produce. But when those who could benefit by cooperating are trying to advance their various conceptions of the moral good, the reasons that they have to be free riders will be moral reasons. Each agent will be able to make the world better, as he understands this, by acting in this way. And a promise to obey will often not be able to prevail against this sort of reason for free riding. As we have seen, when the considerations that argue against compliance with a directive are moral, a promise to comply can prevail against them only if it is capable, together with any other considerations that justify compliance, of outweighing them. This will happen only intermittently, however, and thus people who have promised to obey an authority that directs mutually beneficial cooperation will sometimes have sufficient reason, despite their promise, to adopt a noncooperative strategy, which means that they will fail to realize fully the benefits of cooperation.

The results of the Chapter Seven complicate this line of argument, but leave it intact. There we saw that members of organizations will be especially likely to have reasons strong enough to outweigh a promise to comply with official directives when they can join with others to thwart or mitigate what they perceive as organizational misdeeds. But if every group that finds itself in this situation disregards official directives, all will usually judge the results worse, in light of their own conceptions of the moral good, than if they all complied. So in this case too, P-authority is not able to secure the full benefits of cooperation.

This argument develops the results of Chapter Seven in a new direction. There we saw how, by acting in concert, groups of employees within an organization can give themselves moral reasons for disregarding managerial directives strong enough to outweigh the unfairness involved in accepting pay while not complying. Here, however, we are making the further point that if all the members of an organization who have such reasons act on them, each will usually find the result worse, in light of his conception of the moral good, than general compliance. Thus, just because their situation is that described in Chapter Seven, organization members who have promised to obey official directives, and who have moral concerns, will need the services of an authority that can direct mutually beneficial cooperation (in order to avoid the collectively disadvantageous effects of generally intermittent compliance). Since, however, they will need these services precisely because a promise to obey cannot justify routine compliance with official directives, such a promise cannot underwrite the mutually beneficial cooperation that the situation calls for.

What is required if individuals seeking to advance their various conceptions of the moral good are to realize fully the benefits of cooperation is a reason for pursuing the cooperative strategy that is capable of preempting the moral case supporting noncooperative action. But when an authority directs mutually beneficial cooperation, the principle of collective rationality justifies regarding its directives as preempting even a moral case for noncompliance, regardless of whether a promise to comply has been made. For compliance is supported not by a reason (such as a promissory obligation) that opposes the directive-independent considerations that justify noncompliance but by these very considerations themselves, as they are reflected in the principle of collective rationality. Each regards the outcome in which all (or most) comply as preferable, in light of the directive-independent considerations that justify noncompliance, to the situation in which none comply and each does the best he can by his own lights, and this is the reason for complying.[3]

It should be emphasized that these points are general, applying to the governmental as well as the managerial case. On the picture usually associated with consent theories of political obligation, the people in a given territory promise each other to act collectively in certain ways and then establish a government—which serves the group as an agent or trustee—to manage their common affairs. The

[3] As we have seen, the principle of collective rationality can play a role in facilitating the production of step as well as incremental goods if the producing group wants to avoid chicken games. There will be a further dimension of preemption in both sorts of cases if expertise in identifying and solving coordination problems plays a role.

reciprocal promises that justify obeying the official directives of the government will, however, be able to prevail over countervailing moral considerations only intermittently.[4] A promissory obligation to obey the law will be especially likely to fail when by acting collectively a subgroup within a state can block or mitigate policies that it regards as mistaken. Thus, when the competing considerations that authoritative directives must displace are moral, theories of legitimate authority that invoke a promise to obey have serious limitations in both the governmental and the managerial spheres.

Why has this problem with grounding authority in consent having the force of a promise to obey not been noticed before? The main reason, I think, is that promises are perfectly adequate to justify authority when the directive-independent considerations that authoritative directives must preempt are self-interested, and the classical contract theories view the considerations that provide reasons for disobeying the law as self-interested. To be sure, these theories regard people as having moral reasons for action, but they see political authority and morality as working in close partnership to solve the problems created by the pursuit of self-interest. For Thomas Hobbes, action on the laws of nature is rational only when a government is in place, since these laws have a conditional structure calling for performance only if one has good reason to suppose that enough others will perform as well.[5] For John Locke, government helps eliminate certain problems that can arise when self-interested people try to judge questions of right in their own case. And Jean-Jacques Rousseau sometimes speaks as if to create a political society is actually to create morality. But when the considerations that argue against compliance with authoritative directives are moral, as they increasingly are in modern life, and especially when we take into account the possibility of collective action by subgroups within the state to realize competing moral ends, a promise to obey cannot justify routine compliance with the directives of political authorities.[6]

[4] Any justification of authority that presents it as realizing one particular substantive value among many—including noninstrumental justifications that see it as internally related to certain goods—will have this problem.

[5] See Kavka (1986), pp. 338–49.

[6] Pateman (1979) argues that only in participatory democracies, where the legislative function is performed collectively by the citizens rather than by representatives, can political authority be understood as grounded in voluntarily assumed obligations. But even if this is so, the problem described in the text remains. Political obligation will still be one moral consideration among others and will not always prevail against them. Pateman is aware of this. Although she takes the Rousseauian position that the moral standard that legislation must meet is itself created by the social contract, she allows for the possibility that those who prevail in a vote can be

Authority justified directly as facilitating mutually beneficial co-operation is not absolute. When the recipient of a directive judges that the noncooperative outcome would be preferable to the cooperative outcome—either in itself, or (more likely) because she believes that it will be followed by the establishment of a new authority, or the issuing of new directives that are more to her liking—she will have no reason, deriving from either the principles of collective or individual rationality, for complying with the directive. As I noted in Chapter Four, how often this happens will depend on how we understand the noncooperative outcome. If it is the outcome that would result if all the people addressed by a given source of directives rejected all of them—that is, if there were a complete breakdown of authority—the recipients of a given directive will rarely find the noncooperative outcome preferable to general compliance with it (and the other directives with which it is associated), and thus will almost always have a reason to comply. If, however, the noncooperative outcome is relativized to the particular project the authority is attempting to organize, so that general noncompliance means only the group's failure to carry out this project, group members will more often find the noncooperative outcome preferable to general compliance, and thus less often will they have a reason to comply.

Given that C-authority is not absolute, it, too, can be said to have an intermittent character. Cases in which it loses legitimacy for a given individual will, however, be rarer than cases in which P-authority does, even if we adopt the project-relative understanding of the noncooperative outcome. A promise to obey will sometimes fail to justify an individual in contributing even to a cooperative project the realization of which he judges preferable to its nonrealization—that is, it will sometimes allow free riding in such a case—while the principles that underlie C-authority will not. Of course, something must be said about how directive power can be shaped to conform to the kind of intermittence that C-authority displays.

Managerial Authority and Rational Cooperation

Authority that facilitates mutually beneficial cooperation among individuals with moral aims is not, then, best regarded as P-authority

---

mistaken about what the society's shared values require, and thus that disobedience may be justified (pp. 159–62). But if all who disagree with each governmental decision disobey, each will usually find the overall social state of affairs morally worse, as he or she understands this, than that which would be created by cooperation to implement what seems to be a suboptimal plan. So here, too, P-authority must give way to C-authority.

justified by a promise to obey but rather as C-authority justified by the principles of individual and (especially) collective rationality. Before we can conclude that *employees* should regard the *managers* who direct their work as C-authorities, however, we must establish that these managers can be understood as facilitating mutually beneficial cooperation among the employees they supervise.

Let us assume that an organization has the legal structure of a Weberian bureaucracy, understood as a structure of agency relations established to promote some principal's ends. In general, a principal in an agency relation makes two sorts of decisions. She decides what ends she wants to promote, and she decides what general means her agents are to employ in promoting these ends or what subordinate ends they are to achieve. A Weberian bureaucracy is essentially an instrument for greatly expanding the making and carrying out of decisions of the second sort. A hierarchy of relations of subordination among agents is established, with supervising agents at each level directing the actions of a set of subordinate agents, who may themselves be supervising agents at a lower level. The supervisors convert the directives they receive from the principal, or from superior supervisors, into further directives to the groups they supervise; and they use their own judgment about what actions by these groups would most effectively bring about the events or states of affairs they have been ordered to produce.

The authority delegated to the supervising agents who choose the means by which the tasks assigned to their groups are to be carried out is authority originally vested in the principal (through agency contracts) by the members of the organization. Ideally, the ultimate result is a set of actions performed at various points in the organization that together either constitute or create an event or state of affairs that the principal wants produced. As we have seen, in some organizations, it may be possible to view the principal as the organization itself. The organization's constitution determines which actions by the individuals within it count as its actions, including, importantly, its issuing of directives. In this case, all of the members of the organization have the status of agents. Even those who choose ends for the organization exercise authority that is delegated to them.[7]

The question that we have raised about the possibility of regarding the mangers of organizations as C-authorities can now be posed

[7] Here I am assuming that while it may be problematic to view an organization as holding a moral promissory right (because organizations deserve no moral consideration), it is not problematic to regard organizations as parties to legal contracts in general and agency contracts in particular. For the law is just a set of conventions of a certain kind and these conventions can provide for legal obligations to organizations.

as follows. A Weberian bureaucracy, understood as a legal structure, confers directive power on those who hold offices within it. This power stems in part from the legal right that officeholders have to manipulate positive and negative incentives, and in part from the status they may have for the other members of the organization as de facto authorities. By the thesis of the priority of right or authority to directive power, we must find a justification for the exercise of this power. Two alternatives are especially worthy of consideration. The power of managers may be justified by their status as legitimate P-authorities, in which case the legal structure of the organization will mirror its moral structure. Or, the power of managers may be justified by their status as legitimate C-authorities, in which case the legal structure of the organization will not mirror its moral structure.

Since, as we have seen, P-authority is not suitable for facilitating mutually beneficial cooperation among individuals with contrary moral aims, the latter alternative will be indicated if general compliance with the directives of the managers of a Weberian bureaucracy can be understood as constituting mutually beneficial cooperation of this kind. This is so even if employees have made a promise to obey. The reason they have to cooperate will endorse cooperating whenever a promise would and at other times as well. Thus, the promissory obligation will be redundant.

As has been noted, two sorts of decisions are made in a Weberian bureaucracy: decisions regarding the ends the organization will promote and decisions regarding the means that will be employed to achieve these ends. Thus, the question we face is whether managerial decisions of both these sorts can be understood as facilitating mutually beneficial cooperation among employees with contrary moral aims. To show this it will be enough to show that the managers of Weberian bureaucracies can be understood as facilitating mutually beneficial cooperation among people with contrary aims of any kind. Having demonstrated this, we can simply insert the fact that employees seek to promote their conceptions of the moral good in their work to get a result that is applicable to our case.

There seems to be no problem about regarding the choice of ends for the organization as an exercise of C-authority. All that is necessary is that the ends chosen be ones the attainment of which each member can regard as preferable to the noncooperative outcome, in which all pursue their own ends. And although the choice of ends that takes place in an organization with the legal structure of a Weberian bureaucracy may not be made with the satisfaction of this condition in mind, its satisfaction is nonetheless likely. We shall consider why in more detail in the next section.

It might be doubted, however, that the choice of means to organizational ends can be regarded as an exercise of C-authority. Given that the members of a group are promoting an end that has been established by what they regard as a legitimate authority, they will accept it as their end. This seems to imply that the choice of the means that they use to promote it cannot be regarded as facilitating beneficial cooperation among people with contrary aims.

In fact, however, the choice of the means to be employed by a group to promote an end all its members share can be regarded as an exercise of C-authority. Just as there can be disagreement about the ends a group should promote, so there can be disagreement about the means by which a given end may best be promoted. The members of a group that accepts the appropriateness of promoting a certain end—or implementing a certain directive—may find that if each does what is called for by the plan for achieving that end that he or she judges best, the result will be what each regards as a lower level of success than could be achieved if all accepted as a basis for action a single plan, even one that each found deficient in certain ways. But then an authority that provides such a plan will be a C-authority that makes possible mutually beneficial cooperation within a group of people with contrary (intermediate) aims. Of course, this presupposes that all accept the end that has been set for the group. Only on this assumption will disregarding managerial directives to employ certain means result in an outcome that all regard as worse.

This result is even clearer if it is assumed that employees have moral aims, for then the disagreements that arise about which means would be best often will have a moral dimension. Some parties to these disagreements will object to certain means because they regard them as treating at least some people unfairly. Even the disagreement of those who merely regard a given plan as unlikely to be effective will have a moral character insofar as organizational effectiveness is understood in terms of the promotion of morally important social values. The problems accompanying reliance on P-authority when subordinates have moral aims will, then, be found when managers choose means to preestablished ends as well as when they choose ends.

In sum, even if an organization has the legal structure of a Weberian bureaucracy built up out of contracts that establish agency relations, the managers who hold offices within it can be understood as exercising C-authority. And if they are understood in this way, the employees will often have a good preemptive reason to comply with managerial directives even when a promissory obligation to comply would not be sufficient to justify doing so.

Given the arguments of the earlier part of this book, however, we cannot stop here. The values of fairness and welfare maximization create a presumption in favor of the democratic exercise of C-authority. Thus, if all issuing of directives within an organization—both that which sets ends and that which chooses means to them—involves the exercise of C-authority, there is a presumption that these directives be democratically generated. Because we are viewing democracy as reflexive authority, the appropriate decision-making body in each case is the group whose actions are shaped by the decision. This result would not follow if managerial authority were understood as P-authority. There is no presumption in favor of the democratic exercise of P-authority.

Managerial democracy is the topic of Chapter Nine, but it will be useful to say a bit more about it here. Our argument that directing the use of certain means to given ends can be seen as an exercise of C-authority does not presuppose that the end-setting decision is itself an exercise of C-authority. It could be an exercise of P-authority. A principal could direct a group of agents to produce some event or state of affairs, leaving it up to them to organize themselves to accomplish this. But although the fact that all of the members of this group have promised to obey the principal establishes the end in question as one they all have reason to promote, they may disagree about how best to promote it, in which case they will need the services of a C-authority. Its role will be to facilitate mutually beneficial cooperation within this group. Let us call this sort of mutually beneficial cooperation "agent-cooperation."

Agent-cooperation is of interest in connection with issue of managerial democracy. Where there is C-authority, the values of fairness and welfare maximization create a presumption in favor of its democratic exercise. But if the ultimate reason to comply with directives is a promissory obligation to obey, with C-authority entering the picture only as a device for resolving disagreements among the holders of this promissory obligation about how they might best discharge it, there will be a place for democracy only at lower levels. This is the form taken by most employee democracy in contemporary capitalist firms. Employees decide democratically how to implement directives that are ultimately generated in a nondemocratic fashion by managers who are not accountable to them.

Let us call this form of democracy "agent-democracy." It may be desirable as a way of giving employees an opportunity to develop or exercise their rational capacities, but it inherits all of the problems of reduced robustness and reach that P-authority faces. If a group member regards the promise that underwrites the legitimacy of the

authority that sets the end as outweighed by other moral considerations, she will have no good reason to comply with the directives
that organize cooperation in this group even if they are democratically generated. Unless otherwise noted, when I speak of managerial democracy, I have in mind full managerial democracy, in which
the choice of *ultimate ends* for the organization is made democratically by the employees, or more realistically, by managers accountable to them.

Since this is a crucial juncture in my argument, it may be useful to
repeat the main points. The justification of authority is its justification from the standpoint of the subordinates, and is accomplished
by showing that there is good reason for them to comply with authoritative directives. When employees have moral concerns, a
promise to comply with managerial directives can justify doing so
only intermittently, since the employees will sometimes judge that
competing moral considerations outweigh it. This will be especially
likely when, by acting collectively with other like-minded people,
they can promote their conceptions of the moral good more effectively. But employees will also regard what happens when all of
them comply with managerial directives only intermittently as undesirable, since opportunities for mutually beneficial cooperation
will be missed. They will thus see their situation as one in which it
would be useful if managerial authority could be understood as
C-authority. Then, they would have stronger a reason to comply
with managerial directives facilitating mutually beneficial cooperation than that provided by a promise. And indeed, managerial authority can be understood in this way. In coming to view managerial
authority as C-authority, however, they come to view it as authority
that, presumptively, ought to be exercised democratically.

The Structure of Organizational Cooperation

Now that we have seen how mutually beneficial cooperation can be
regarded as taking place within organizations, both in the choice of
ends and in the choice of means to them, we must consider in more
detail what its game-theoretic structure is. This will enable us to be
more precise about the reason that employees have to comply with
managerial directives.

Our ultimate concern is the case in which employees are trying to
advance their conceptions of the moral good in their work. But
several of the issues that we have to consider can be more easily
addressed if we first develop an account of the game theoretic structure that organizational cooperation would have if each employee

was regarded as cooperating solely to achieve self-interested benefits.

In fleshing out this idea, it will again be useful to employ the Weberian model of bureaucracy. According to this model, the reason for subordinates to comply with the directives they receive is a promise to comply in return for pay. The actions that an employee performs in complying do not in themselves contribute to the promotion of any of her interests; rather, she receives an extrinsic reward for performing them. But we can still view the actions that take place within a Weberian bureaucracy as constituting mutually beneficial cooperation among self-interested employees if we suppose that their compliance with the directives they receive makes it possible for the organization to pay them, that is, that their compliance enables the organization to obtain revenues, some of which are passed on to them in the form of pay.

Not all Weberian bureaucracies can be viewed in this way. The funds dispensed as pay by governmental agencies are often generated entirely by taxation, and thus there need be no connection between what the employees of such agencies do and the ability of the agency to pay them. But the managers of economically independent Weberian bureaucracies can be viewed as making possible mutually beneficial cooperation among the employees, where the criterion of benefit is personal monetary gain, if the actions they direct the employees to perform contribute to the *economic viability* of the organization. And the possibility of viewing managers as facilitating mutually beneficial cooperation among self-interested employees is reinforced if it is supposed that when an organization becomes more profitable—or more generally, when its revenues come to exceed its costs by a greater amount, whether it is profit-seeking or not—some of the gain is passed on to the employees. To take this view of organizational cooperation, we need not suppose that a profit-sharing scheme is in place. It is enough that if profits go up, pay will increase, and if they go down, it will fall, at least in real terms over time.

Some recent work in the economics of organization views organizational cooperation in this way. Writers in this field distinguish markets and hierarchies as different ways of creating combinations of actions that can be evaluated on the basis of their contribution to economic efficiency. In markets, the combinations are the product of mutually beneficial bargains, while in hierarchies they are the product directives issued by people who have directive power of some sort. The general claim that these writers make is that hierarchy can sometimes create combinations that are more efficient by economic criteria, that is, they make more people better off.

At least two reasons have been offered for this. One is that hierarchy contributes to efficiency by enabling managers to prevent shirking when there are technological inseparabilities. When such inseparabilities exist, the tasks facing a group cannot be divided into component tasks each of which is performed by one individual. A simple example would be loading items that are so heavy that no single individual can pick one up. In such cases, the market can only reward the workers performing a task as a team. But then there will be free-rider problems that reduce efficiency, so it is desirable to have such activities directed by supervisors who can adjust rewards to perceived effort.[8] It has also been claimed that hierarchy enables groups involved in sequential productive processes to avoid the transaction costs that they would incur if these processes were organized by market exchanges. If they were so organized, each person in the sequence would have to negotiate the terms on which he received inputs from those earlier in the sequence, and the terms on which he provided outputs to those later in the sequence, and this would be costly of such resources as time. When the process is directed by a supervisor, however, these transaction costs can be avoided.[9]

The writers making these arguments conclude that efficiency will be improved if employees contract for governance, that is, contract to enter a situation in which they are governed. If the argument of this book is correct, however, an actual contract is not necessary to establish a reason for employees to comply with managerial directives in such situations. Managerial authority can be regarded as deriving legitimacy directly from its role in facilitating mutually beneficial cooperation, since preventing shirking and avoiding transaction costs benefits everyone if it results in higher pay.

If we view the directives of managers as making possible mutually beneficial cooperation among self-interested employees, what is its game-theoretic structure? When compliance with managerial directives is regarded as making it possible for all the members of the organization to achieve a greater monetary reward, the good produced by the resulting cooperation can be seen as having a structure with both step and incremental aspects. In our discussion of these two sorts of goods in Chapter Four, they were presented as public goods, goods that could not be provided for any of the members of a group without being provided for all. But improving the profitability of a firm or other organization can be regarded as a public good for the members of the firm if some formula for distributing part of the

---

[8] See Alchian and Demsetz (1972).
[9] See Williamson (1975), esp. chaps. 3 and 4; and (1985), esp. chaps. 9–12.

gain as wage or salary increases is presupposed. For then it will be impossible for acts that improve profitability to benefit any member without benefiting all. Of course, managers may seek to manipulate compensation so that only those who actually contribute to improved profitability are rewarded. In so doing they exercise directive power, however, and we need a justification for according them this power. The suggestion we are now considering is that such a justification can be found in the fact that if everyone acts as directed, all will be better off by their own lights. Thus, employees will have a good reason to comply with managerial directives that is independent of the application of sanctions by management.

Economic viability is a step good. Over the long term, an organization must generate revenues that at least cover its costs if it is to remain viable. Failure to do so does not result in incremental losses to the organization's members, but rather in a precipitous loss: that associated with the dissolution of the organization. This point is quite general. Profit-seeking organizations must maintain economic viability, and so must nonprofit organizations. Beyond the threshold of economic viability, however, cooperation to achieve monetary gains has an incremental structure. Cooperation increases the amount by which revenues exceed costs, and if some of the resulting gains are distributed as increased pay, each employee realizes an incremental gain from the self-interested point of view.

Given that managers can be regarded as facilitating the production of a good with this complex structure, we can use the results of Chapter Four to provide an account of the reason that employees have to comply with managerial directives. Individual rationality will provide a reason for complying with managerial directives whenever the gain from complying exceeds the cost, or where failure to comply will result in a loss to the employee that exceeds what he could gain from noncompliance. One dramatic case of the latter sort is that in which the organization is at the threshold of viability with respect to a given employee's actions, so that his noncompliance with a managerial directive would result in its ceasing to be economically viable. If the organization's performance places it beyond the threshold of viability, by contrast, individual rationality will often dictate noncompliance with directives. For the situation will be such that while a given employee's failure to comply with a directive that facilitates cooperation will result in a (slight) reduction in overall profits and thus in his compensation, the gain from noncompliance may exceed the cost. Here I am supposing that self-interest encompasses not only monetary goods, but also nonmonetary goods such as leisure, and that the gain in leisure from free riding offsets the slight incremental reduction in compensation over time that will result.

Taking these two points together, we can say that from the standpoint of individual rationality, organizational cooperation has the structure of a battle of the sexes problem with components of a chicken game. Cooperation creates a good that benefits everyone. If the organization is performing beyond the threshold of viability, the good to which each contributes by cooperating will have an incremental character, and individual rationality will dictate being a free rider. Each will gain more in leisure by letting others do the work than he will lose monetarily. But if organizational viability is to be maintained, some way must be found to designate a set of producers of this good. Given the phenomenon of organizational slack, there will usually be several distinct sets of employees whose actions could keep the organization above the threshold of viability, but as we saw in Chapter Four, individual rationality can accomplish the task of selecting one since the situation has the character of a chicken game. Initially everyone places himself in the set of nonproducers, but as the time approaches when action to maintain viability is required, this posture threatens to be disadvantageous from the standpoint of individual rationality, and those who are most risk-averse "chicken out" and join the set of producers.

Collective rationality, however, takes a different view of the situation the employees face. When the members of an organization cooperate only as necessary to maintain its economic viability, riding free otherwise, each does less well than he could if they cooperated fully to implement a single plan. Flourishing profitability is better for all than mere viability. Moreover, if the members of the group want the distribution of benefits and burdens realized within the group to be fair, following individual rationality has the further drawback that producers are selected in a way—through a chicken game—that subverts any fairness that full cooperation on the basis of a single plan might have possessed. If the members of the group accept the principle of collective rationality, however, they will be able to avoid these results. Again, it must be borne in mind that we are considering what reason there is to comply with managerial directives in the absence of policing by the employer, that is, the application of sanctions for noncompliance. We are seeking a justification for according managers the power to apply such sanctions.

Given that organizational cooperation has this game-theoretic structure, the role of managerial authority is clear. Even if there were no reason to do more than maintain viability, so that the situation had the structure of a battle of the sexes problem, a set of producers would have to be designated and a plan for maintaining viability would have to be made salient within it. De facto managerial authority could perform this task. Similar points can be made if the employees accept the principle of collective rationality and thus regard themselves as having reason to cooperate to achieve additional gains. They will need to have the assurance problem solved, and managerial authority can perform this task. Indeed, the two cases are more alike than may initially appear. Where a variety of different plans for full cooperation would be regarded as mutually beneficial by the employees, but each prefers a different one, those who accept the principle of collective rationality will actually face a battle of the sexes problem as well. It should also be noted that managerial authority can make it possible for collective rationality to prevent mutually disadvantageous chicken games from arising.[10]

Now that we have considered the hypothetical case in which the employees of organizations regard themselves as cooperating only to achieve self-interested benefits, let us bring moral considerations back into the picture. Let us make the assumption that employees regard themselves as contributing to the moral good in their work, and that they want to use their jobs to promote their own conceptions of the moral good as effectively as possible. This is not an assumption of unnatural saintliness. In taking this view of their employment, employees do not ignore the respects in which their jobs provide them with monetary benefits. Instead, they subsume this consideration under the morally important social value of distributive justice, which in turn finds a place in their various conceptions of the moral good. Although they are concerned with deriving self-interested benefits from their jobs, they see their efforts in this regard through the lens of distributive justice—as bringing them, or not bringing them, what they are entitled to by considerations of justice—and they place these efforts in the wider context of promotion of the moral good generally, depending on how they view the claims that justice allows them to make as related to other moral considerations.

For example, an employee who is in a position to do so might feel that she has a good reason to act so as to force her organization into

---

[10] We should be clear about how the role of managers in selecting coordination equilibria when employees accept only the principle of individual rationality differs from its role when employees accept collective rationality as well. In the former case, the battle of the sexes problem takes the form of choosing between equilibria that partition the employees into producers and nonproducers. In the latter case, the battle of the sexes problem takes the form of choosing between equilibria all of which involve productive activity by all employees. The problem arises because the employees differ about which plan for organizing full cooperation would be best.

compliance with safety or environmental regulations, even though she knows that the result will be increased costs for the organization and ultimately a reduction in the compensation she would otherwise have received, because she thinks that she could not justifiably claim more for herself at the expense of the values supported by these regulations. Again, we are abstracting from any police powers the employer might have and considering what the employee would regard herself as having good reason to do in their absence.

Prior to the introduction of considerations relating to the legitimacy of managerial authority, an employee who evaluates her work in an organization by reference to her conception of the moral good will regard her job as providing an opportunity to advance this conception. To put it another way, the directive-independent reasons that she acknowledges will be provided by this conception. There are two main ways in which a job in an organization may provide one with opportunities to advance one's conception of the moral good. One may use for this purpose either the physical resources or the social resources of the organization. The social resources of an organization are the behaviors that others engage in by virtue of their place in it.

Both of these ways of using an organization to advance one's own moral aims typically involve free riding. The organization's physical and social resources are available only because others have cooperated, as directed by managers, to create them. Thus, the general case for regarding managerial authority as a form of C-authority (that makes mutually beneficial cooperation possible) is as applicable when employees act to advance their conceptions of the moral good as when they act to achieve self-interested benefits alone. If each tries to exploit the efforts of others, all will do worse—in the sense of promoting their conceptions of the moral good less effectively—than they would if they cooperated to implement a single plan, even one that each regarded as morally suboptimal. There is, then, good reason for the members of organizations who want to use their jobs to advance their conceptions of the moral good to cooperate with each other to produce a particular action specified by management. Most will regard this outcome as morally suboptimal, but most will also regard it as preferable to the outcome that would be realized if each tried to be a free rider. As was noted earlier, this conclusion remains valid when free riding takes the form of collective action by subgroups trying to promote their different moral goals.

We must consider what the game-theoretic structure of this sort of cooperation is. Many of the morally important social values have in themselves, that is, in their overall realization, an incremental structure. Their level of realization in society can be altered by small amounts more or less indefinitely. But the step structure of the good of economic viability has the consequence that when a morally important social value that is "naturally" incremental is promoted by an economically independent organization that is responsible for its own viability, any efforts to use the organization to promote this value will have the aspect of the production of a step good. The use of the organization to promote the value will depend on its remaining economically viable, and thus the step structure of the good of economic viability will be imparted to the morally important social value, insofar as it is promoted by the organization. It will not be possible to use the organization to make a contribution to any morally important social value if it ceases to be economically viable. Beyond the threshold of viability, however, efforts to promote a given morally important social value through an organization will have the character of efforts to promote an incremental good.

Since organizational cooperation has the same game-theoretic structure when the cooperating agents are regarded as seeking to advance their particular conceptions of the moral good as when they are seeking to realize self-interested gains, the conclusions we reached earlier about how the principles of individual and collective rationality provide reasons for cooperating within an organization apply to this case as well. From the standpoint of individual rationality, cooperation presents a battle of the sexes problem in that each would prefer to use his job to promote his moral goals in the most effective way possible, but is prepared to cooperate on other terms rather than see the collapse of cooperation. The selection of a particular set of producers can be accomplished by a chicken game. But an outcome that each would regard as preferable from the standpoint of his conception of the moral good to acting as necessary to maintain the organization at the threshold of viability but otherwise going his own way (while others go theirs) could be realized if all cooperated fully with the others to produce one specified outcome. For each will regard what can be gained by cooperation above the threshold as greater than what he could accomplish by acting unilaterally in a context in which others are doing this as well.[11]

<hr>

[11] The picture of the good of organizational cooperation that I have sketched—according to which it is a step good that has an incremental character after the threshold is crossed—may be applicable to the political case as well. That is, cooperation to maintain a political society may be similar in that (starting from full compliance with the law) acts of disobedience result in incremental reductions in the goods promoted by political society up to a certain point, after which further disobedience results in a precipitous collapse. Klosko (1992), appendix 1, argues, using Parfit's categories, that cooperation to maintain a political society has the structure of a small-

Given that the justification for cooperation is the same as before, the justification for managerial authority is the same as well. De facto authority makes possible the solution of the assurance problem that confronts agents seeking to cooperate as reason requires; it also makes possible the efficient selection of coordination equilibria. We should remind ourselves again that de facto authority is not the only social device that can serve this purpose. Norms can solve the assurance problem too. But norm formation is a slow process, and what would constitute mutually beneficial cooperation in the context of an organization changes often. Thus, it will be desirable to have in place a social mechanism that can make decisions about what the new circumstances require and provide assurances that all will act accordingly. As we have seen, de facto authority is such a mechanism.

It is useful to relate these points to my claim that to comply with managerial directives is often to contribute to a moral or political agenda that one does not share. If managerial authority is viewed as C-authority, complying with managerial directives is justified on the ground that cooperation to produce even an outcome that each regards as morally suboptimal is often preferable to general noncooperation, either within the organization or with respect to particular project. Thus, there is good reason (within limits) to contribute to a moral or political agenda that one does not share. Management chooses goals for the organization guided by its conception of the moral good, and the employees contribute to them even though they would prefer different organizational goals.[12] This result allows us to preserve the intuition that remaining in one's job while disobeying is justified in extreme cases, such as that of our German railway workers. They could plausibly regard the collapse of the project to which they were directed to contribute—and indeed the organizational "state of nature," collapse of the system of rail transportation generally—as preferable to the implementation of the policies to which they were directed to contribute.

C-Authority and Unions

In Chapter Seven, we saw that when managerial authority is understood as P-authority, employees will often have a good reason to

---

effects, rather than a small-chances, case. But if the suggestion I have just made is sound, it has both.

[12] The contribution may be greater in the managerial case than the political case since managerial authority is prescriptive rather than proscriptive. Thus, a larger percentage of the efforts of those who are subject to authority are devoted to realizing the ends the authority seeks to achieve.

organize to prevent the implementation of what they regard as morally suboptimal directives. In doing so, they give application to considerations of rational cooperation; this is appropriate because when managerial authority is understood as P-authority, these considerations do not enter into its justification. Now that we have introduced the possibility that managerial authority is to be understood as C-authority, however, the question arises whether there is any longer a place for collective resistance to managerial directives. To say that managerial authority can be understood as C-authority is to say that insofar as it is legitimate, it already provides, internally, a structure in which rational cooperation among employees with moral aims can take place—that is, a structure that enables employees to take advantage of the possibility of advancing their aims by collective action. Should we conclude, then, that there is no role for company unions when managerial authority is understood as C-authority?

Before attempting to answer this question, we should consider why complying with the directives of a managerial C-authority might seem preferable to trying to form a union. The results of Chapter Seven concerning collective resistance and the formation of unions depended importantly on whether the assurance problem was solved, or, if not, on what the members of the group could do to solve it. Collective resistance, like other kinds of collective action, is rational only if those contemplating it can rely on others to do their parts, and the required assurance can be hard to provide. This means that collective resistance to the directives of an established authority will often not be able to tap fully the potential for rational collective action. As we have seen, however, the role of de facto authority in facilitating mutually beneficial cooperation consists precisely in the fact that it can easily solve the assurance problem, since each member of the relevant group will have a good reason to believe that the rest will comply with its directives. This seems to force us to conclude that compliance with the directives of an established authority—at least when their content is such that compliance with them would constitute mutually beneficial cooperation—will be the preferred form of collective action.

A similar argument establishes that accomplishing social purposes through governmental action is frequently preferable to relying on voluntary efforts by the populace. It is difficult for individuals outside organizations to cooperate effectively with each other to achieve social ends because they must solve the concomitant assurance problem. To be more precise, they can cooperate easily only when their actions can be coordinated in ways that do not require the solution of the assurance problem, such as by means of markets. More extensive cooperation than this is often desirable, however, and a government that has de facto authority can easily bring such cooperation about by publicly promulgating directives, that is, enacting the required legislation. The case of managerial C-authority is the same. It provides a ready-made means by which the assurance problem associated with collective action can be solved. If the members of organizations whose managers can be understood as legitimate C-authorities want to cooperate to achieve moral ends, then, it would seem that they will usually be able to do so more effectively by complying with managerial directives than by trying to organize an extraorganizational cooperative endeavor.

Why then bother to try to form a union? On the account of legitimate C-authority with which we have been working, C-authority ceases to be legitimate for an individual if he could do better using the resources the C-authority directs him to contribute in some way that would be available if the authority did not exist. Since this includes participating in alternative cooperative arrangements, it is thus theoretically possible that a union could supplant management as the legitimate C-authority governing an organization. But this could only happen if all employees found the union's policies preferable to management's, which is unlikely. In the more likely case in which there is disagreement about the best managerial policies to follow, management could often claim legitimacy on the ground that the directive power at its disposal enabled it to be more effective than a union in preventing the chaos and mutual thwarting of projects that would result if subgroups holding different moral views went their own way.

There is, however, another reason for forming a union. As we have seen, to count as a legitimate C-authority, a source of directives need not be democratic. But the moral values of fairness and welfare maximization create a presumption in favor of the democratic exercise of C-authority. So the employees of an organization whose managers are legitimate C-authorities, but not democratically accountable to the employees, might have good reason to organize a union precisely because it provided some scope for the democratic management of their cooperative activity. Even if a union cannot claim greater legitimacy as an organizational C-authority than management, it may be able to claim greater moral validity if its decision-making processes are democratic. Of course, this presupposes that the union is able to influence managerial decision making. This possibility is discussed in more detail in Chapter Nine.

C-Authority and Power

Now that we have seen how managerial authority can be understood as C-authority, let us consider what the possession of this sort of authority by managers implies about how much power they may permissibly exercise. Recall that the legal right to control productive resources confers power because many people need access to such resources in the form of employment if they are to live well. For the most part, however, the issues that must be addressed here are not peculiar to the managerial case. Similar questions arise about the use of power by a government regarded as possessing C-authority. In the latter case, the conventions that confer power are not laws establishing property rights in productive resources but laws enabling the governments to support their directives with various coercive sanctions. Since laws are conventions of a certain sort, the ultimate basis of the power they confer is the readiness of the population as a whole to support them. But the thesis of the priority of right or authority to directive power implies that whatever conventions confer power on officials must be shaped so that this power does not exceed the legitimate authority that governments can be regarded as having. Thus, governments may coerce only those who have a good independent reason to comply with their official directives.

Before we consider what in particular the thesis of the priority of right or authority to directive power implies in the case of C-authorities, however, there is a matter that we should clarify. C-authorities need power not only to provide those who cannot see that they have a good reason to accept authoritative directives with effective motivation to do so but also to help solve the assurance problem. This means that they need power to *create* the reason for compliance that underwrites their legitimacy, as well as to insure the compliance of those who cannot grasp this reason. What determines whether a given source of directives is a legitimate C-authority is whether those to whom its directives are addressed would benefit, in the sense of better satisfying the reasons that apply to them, by complying with these directives. Only if this is the case for a given individual does assurance that others will comply as well create a reason for her to comply, and only if she has a reason to comply could it be permissible to force her to comply. So both the deployment of directive power to solve the assurance problem and its deployment to make people do what they have good reason to do are guided by the same prior consideration.

Basically, there is only one limitation on the use of directive power by legitimate C-authorities. A source of directives will lack the status of a legitimate C-authority for anyone who would prefer the noncooperative outcome to cooperation on the basis of the directives issued. Any use of directive power to secure the compliance of such an individual would be illegitimate, and steps of some kind must be taken to guard against it. The obvious step is to design the laws conferring power on authorities so that those who find that they have no reason to comply are free to leave the group. In allowing their citizens to emigrate at will, then, political societies can be regarded as taking a step to insure that their governments retain the status of legitimate C-authorities. A similar point can be made about the managerial case. Although one can imagine institutional forms in which workers who find that they have no reason to comply with managerial directives lack the legal right to leave—slavery would be one—the legal conventions now governing employment in most societies provide that employees may quit at any time.

There is, however, more to the ability to leave a group when one has no reason to contribute to the cooperative efforts taking place within it than the absence of legal barriers to doing so. Leaving a group often involves costs, and these may be so high that leaving is effectively precluded. This point is familiar in political philosophy. Thus Hume ridicules Locke's view that remaining within the territory administered by a government constitutes tacit consent to obey its laws by comparing the situation of someone born into a state with that of a man who is carried aboard a ship while asleep and upon waking (when the ship is well out to sea) must choose between jumping overboard or living under the captain's regime.[13] Remaining on board in such a case cannot plausibly be regarded as consenting—in the normative sense that creates obligations—to obey the captain because the costs of leaving are so high that the act of remaining cannot be seen as voluntary. In Hume's view, the linguistic and cultural barriers to assimilation in a different society put most people contemplating emigration in the same situation. Although this is formulated as an objection to consent theories, it can also be interpreted as an objection to the claim that we can insure that directive power of governments does not exceed their legitimate C-authority by creating a legal right to exit.

It appears that a similar point could be made about the managerial case. The legal freedom of employees to leave any job may not translate into the de facto ability to do so because the costs of quitting can be high, for example, accepting unemployment or a very much less remunerative position. We must be careful how we make this

---

[13] Hume (1948), p. 363.

point, however. It might be argued that the choice faced by employees contemplating quitting is different from that faced by someone contemplating emigration. In the political case, an individual in the situation we are now considering has the following preference ranking. She prefers most the noncooperative outcome; next, cooperation with the individual or set of individuals issuing directives to the group; and least, leaving the group. The relative position of the first two items implies that the source of directives does not have for her the status of a legitimate authority, while the relative position of the last two items implies that given a choice between leaving and complying, she will comply. Merely leaving open the legal possibility of exit is not, then, sufficient to insure that power never exceeds legitimate authority.

It is plausible, however, that the preference ranking of an employee who was contemplating quitting would be different. She could not prefer the noncooperative outcome to leaving since both would involve being out of a job (with that organization). That is, she must be indifferent between these two outcomes. Thus, if she ranks the noncooperative outcome higher than the cooperative outcome, she must rank leaving higher too, which means that the power that managers derive from a given employee's reluctance to leave can never exceed legitimate C-authority; it can never be used to force her to contribute to a cooperative effort that she does not regard as beneficial to her (in light of whatever aims she has).

This argument, however, assumes that the relevant noncooperative outcome for assessing the legitimacy of a managerial C-authority is that in which there is a total breakdown of authority within the organization, while I have suggested that it may be possible to interpret the noncooperative outcome as the outcome that would be realized if the project the manager is attempting to organize collapses. And a member of a group to which directives are being issued might prefer the situation that would obtain if a particular project failed, but she remained a member of the organization, to leaving it. On this weaker, but possibly more plausible, interpretation of the noncooperative outcome, then, the reluctance of employees to exit may well give managers power that exceeds legitimate C-authority. Can anything be done to bring this sort of power into line with legitimate C-authority?

One conventional device that would insure that power does not exceed legitimate authority in such cases would be a right—established by law or informal social convention—of selective conscientious objection, that is, a right to exempt oneself from participating in any project when one could not regard doing so as rational cooperation. It is an interesting fact that few constitutions, political or organizational, provide such a right. Contemporary institutions seem to reflect the conviction that a group has done enough to insure that no one is forced to participate in a cooperative venture that she cannot endorse by providing a formal right to exit, and thus need not concern itself with the fact that some may find availing themselves of this right too costly.

One explanation for this social fact might be that allowing selective conscientious objection would be too disruptive of the group's efforts as a whole. If so, we can regard the failure to provide for selective conscientious objection as reflecting a decision by established authority that in the long run each member would benefit most from cooperation if no one was given this option. The reason would be as follows. Exercising a right of selective conscientious objection would be disruptive of cooperative projects others value, and each would more often be in the position of valuing cooperation than in the position of wanting to exercise the right. But then those who found that they did not benefit from participating in certain projects could view themselves as nevertheless having a reason for doing so—namely, that in doing so, they were contributing to a *more comprehensive* scheme of mutually beneficial cooperation. If this is right, the power to secure their cooperation deriving from the costliness of leaving the group would not exceed legitimate authority after all. We consider a similar issue, involving the democratic limitation of democracy, in Chapter Nine.

There is another problem about the boundaries of the group over which authority is exercised that we should consider, a problem that is peculiar to the managerial case. This is the problem of the legitimacy of authority that is employed to direct some members of a group to leave it, as when employees are laid off for economic reasons. Here, mangers exercise powers that derive from legally defined property rights, but it might be doubted whether the issuing of such directives can be understood as a legitimate use of C-authority. How can an authority justified as making mutually beneficial cooperation possible within a group legitimately order a member to cease to participate in the scheme of mutually beneficial cooperation in which the group is engaged? How can compliance with this directive be justified as making beneficial cooperation possible for that individual?

I am not aware of any satisfactory answer to this question when the benefits created by cooperation are understood solely as self-interested. But if we suppose that employees are motivated by morality, and that the layoffs are necessary for maintaining the economic viability of the organization, an answer can be provided. Presumably a moral agent would find the situation in which he loses his job but the firm survives (and others keep theirs) morally preferable to the situation in which all lose their jobs. But then the problem that the group faces in downsizing is a battle of the sexes problem. The group is to be divided into a set of producers and a set of nonproducers, and in this case, everyone wants to be one of the producers. The problem of choosing who is to leave may be difficult, but the designated nonproducers have a good reason to act as they are directed to because the division of the group into producers and nonproducers constitutes a coordination equilibrium. If anyone departs from it—and in particular if those who are designated as nonproducers remain and continue to draw pay (until the organization fails)—no one better achieves his moral aims.[14]

C-Authority and Property

We have been considering what measures must be adopted to insure that directive power does not exceed legitimate authority. In the case of governments, power derives ultimately from legal constitutions (understood as systems of legal conventions) that give governmental officials the legal right to support their directives with various coercive sanctions, while in nongovernmental organizations it derives from constitutions that provide for the exercise by managers of legal property rights. But legal property rights in productive resources can be exercised by different groups of individuals. To take the most important alternatives, those exercising such rights may be either nonemployee owners, managers formally accountable to nonemployee owners but in most cases actually accountable only to themselves, or the employees as a group. Does the thesis of the priority of right or authority to directive power, as applied to the case of C-authority, have any implications for the choice between these alternatives? To put it another way, are any of these alternative constitutions for nongovernmental organizations ruled out if those issuing directives are to be regarded as legitimate C-authorities?

It will be useful to remind ourselves of why managerial authority can be regarded as C-authority. The argument for this presupposed that nongovernmental organizations have the legal structure of Weberian bureaucracies, and it showed that mutually beneficial co-

---

[14] As was noted earlier, another response to such pressures is to retain all employees but reduce their compensation. Thus, the account I have presented presupposes that there are good moral reasons, from the standpoint of each, to keep the organization economically efficient.

operation can be regarded as taking place within them. The claim was that if the potential for benefiting from this cooperation was to be fully realized, the authority of managers could not be understood as P-authority mirroring the legal structure but rather had to be understood as C-authority. This result regarding Weberian bureaucracy has implications for the question that we are presently investigating. It means that the managers of organizations in which ultimate legal control, and thus directive power, does not lie with the employees considered as a group can still claim legitimacy as C-authorities. Thus, if we consider only the basic requirement for the legitimacy of C-authority in our case—that the employees find compliance with managerial directives to be preferable, from the standpoint of their various conceptions of the moral good, to the noncooperative outcome—the answer to our question is negative. There is no reason in principle why those deriving directive power from any of the constitutions we have distinguished could not satisfy this condition.

Our claim that managerial authority is best understood as C-authority does not, then, imply that the present legal structure of nongovernmental organizations, and the attendant property relations, must be altered. All that changes is our understanding of what justifies the directive power that managers operating within such a structure exercise. As we have seen, however, there is a presumption, deriving from the values of fairness and welfare maximization, that C-authority should be democratically exercised. Thus, even if democracy is not strictly required for the legitimacy of managerial C-authority, many employees may still judge the managerial regime under which they work to be defective from the standpoint of important moral values if managerial authority is not democratically exercised. That is, they may regard democracy as required if managerial authority is to have moral validity. This would seem to have implications for the choice between alternative constitutions for nongovernmental organizations, raising questions about the acceptability of arrangements in which directive power is held by nonemployee owners or self-selected managers. Whether this is in fact so, and what the implications are for property in productive resources, is the topic of Chapter Nine.

CHAPTER NINE

MANAGERIAL DEMOCRACY

The argument that the values of fairness and welfare maximization create a presumption in favor of the democratic exercise of C-authority was presented in Chapter Five, but it may be useful to repeat the main points here. It is often the case that a given C-authority could issue a variety of different directives in a situation without losing its legitimacy. The subjects would regard cooperation to implement any of them as preferable to the noncooperative outcome. But the subjects will usually have conflicting preferences regarding the directive to be issued. Some will find cooperation on the basis of one directive best from their point of view, while others regard cooperation on the basis of different directives as best.

In a situation of this sort, the values of fairness and welfare maximization support democracy, understood as the determination of the directive to be issued by a vote of the subjects. Fairness supports democracy as a device for insuring that over time, each will get what he deems best about equally often (at least when there are no entrenched minorities), while welfare maximization supports democracy as insuring that the directive issued is deemed best by more people than not. As we have seen, joining democracy with liberal rights is a way of satisfying both fairness and welfare maximization when there are entrenched minorities.

In this chapter, we shall mostly be concerned with whether countervailing moral considerations offset the moral presumption created by fairness and welfare maximization in favor of the democratic exercise of C-authority in managerial contexts. This is a possibility that must be taken seriously. The actual management of almost all contemporary nongovernmental organizations is not democratic; managers are not accountable to their subordinates. Where democratic decision making is found, it takes the form of agent-democracy. Employees who are understood to be agents decide democratically how to implement the directives they receive from an authority who is not accountable to them, and thus managerial decision making is ultimately dictatorial. It is common in radical politics to explain the prevalence of dictatorial forms of authority in nongovernmental organizations as a product of efforts by a ruling class to maintain its dominance. But the explanation may rather be that sound moral considerations support such arrangements.

In this chapter, I confine myself to arguing for the following two claims. First, the case for democracy in nongovernmental organizations is weaker than the case for democratic government. Second, constitutions for nongovernmental organizations that fail to provide the employees as a whole with some sort of role in formulating *ultimate* managerial policy are problematic.

Constitutional Accountability

Before investigating the managerial case, it will be useful to say a bit more about democratic accountability. As I have characterized legitimate authority, the justification that establishes the legitimacy of a given de facto authority is always justification from the standpoint of the subordinates. Authority is legitimate just in case there is good reason for the subordinates to comply with authoritative directives. This means that, in a sense, all legitimate forms of subordinating authority, even P-authority and nondemocratic forms of C-authority, involve accountability to those over whom authority is exercised. Their legitimacy depends on the existence of a good reason, independent of the application of directive power, for the subordinates to comply with authoritative directives.

One consequence of this is that the legitimacy of what might be called absolute authority is ruled out from the start. In our discussion of preemption in Chapter Two, we distinguished two judgments a subordinate might make: a judgment of what the applicable directive-independent reasons require (which is preempted) and a judgment that there is a good reason for him to allow preemption to take place (which is not preempted). We can, however, imagine the displacement of this latter judgment as well, in which case the subordinate would be a kind of automaton reacting without reflection to the instructions he received. The adherents of some religions may think of the authority of God in this way. As I am using the term, an absolute authority is one whose directives have this totally displacing character. None of the forms of legitimate authority that we have considered are absolute in this sense. In all of them, legitimacy depends on the possibility of justifying preemption from the standpoint of the subordinates.

There is, however, another sense of accountability in which a dictator is not accountable to those over whom authority is exercised. This the sense in which accountability involves the conventional right to choose or replace the individual or group exercising authority. Subordinates in all sorts of authority relations have the moral (or rational) right to reject—in the sense of exempt themselves from—authority when the associated directives do not constitute good preemptive reasons for action. If a large enough percentage of them feels this way, they will probably be able to effect a change by extraconstitutional means, that is, by revolution. But some constitutions give subjects the conventional right to replace an authority, even when it is legitimate in the sense that general compliance with its directives is better than general rejection, because a majority would prefer directives with a different content. In this chapter, when I speak of authorities as being accountable to those over whom they exercise authority, I mean conventional accountability.

It is important to bear in mind, however, that accountability to the subjects is not the only form that conventional accountability can take. When we speak of conventional accountability, we are speaking of constitutional rights to decide who will occupy positions of authority, but the constitution of a group need not give this right to the subjects. It might give established authorities the right to decide whether they will remain in office or be replaced by different individuals or groups, or it might give third parties this right. It might even take the decision out of human hands, calling for authorities to be chosen by a lottery or by hereditary succession.

Accountability in this sense—grounded in a legally established constitution—falls on the power side of the power-authority distinction. On the positivist view that I adopt for the purposes of this book, laws are just conventions of a certain sort. They give individuals power because their existence entails a readiness on the part of most members of the society to act as they direct and to assist in efforts to make the recalcitrant comply with them. Thus, the people who have the legal right to choose who will occupy certain positions of authority have the de facto power to do this. What determines which of the various arrangements that confer this power is appropriate for a particular group?

In our previous discussions, we have invoked the thesis of the priority of right or authority to directive power to decide questions of this sort. Here, however, we are presupposing, in accordance with the results of Chapter Eight, that managerial authority is best regarded as C-authority and that constitutional measures have already been adopted to insure, to the extent that this is possible, that the power that authorities have does not exceed legitimate

C-authority.[1] Our problem thus concerns the choice between constitutional arrangements that give different people the power to determine who will exercise C-authority. As was argued in Chapter Five, to make this choice we must invoke moral values. So our question is, Which power-conferring conventions are best supported by the applicable moral considerations?

We have already considered one argument of this sort, the argument of Chapter Five that the values of fairness and welfare maximization justify the democratic exercise of C-authority. The discussion there focused mainly on direct democracy, and when democracy is direct, the question of how those who exercise authority are to be chosen does not really arise, since it is exercised jointly by everyone in the relevant group. But representative democracy—which involves choosing people to exercise authority, to generate the directives that will guide the group—is also justified by the values of fairness and welfare maximization, in combination with considerations of efficiency. Thus, representative democracy provides one case in which moral considerations justify certain relations of accountability, certain conventional rights to choose who will exercise authority. It follows that if different conventions of accountability are appropriate, all things considered, this must be because they are supported by other, weightier moral values. Determining what values might be capable of prevailing over the values that justify democratic accountability is the principal task of this chapter.

In the case of nongovernmental organizations, constitutional relations of accountability are heavily influenced by laws establishing, and governing the exercise of, property rights. As we noted in Chapter One, ownership is a complex of different rights, one of which is the right to manage: the right to determine who will use an item and how they will use it. This may be interpreted to include the right to appoint and replace managers. Determining which relations of accountability in nongovernmental organizations are supported by various moral considerations is, then, in large part determining which assignment of a certain property right, the right to manage, is supported by these considerations.

This establishes a new respect in which property is of interest as a source of power. As we have seen, those who exercise property rights in productive resources have the de facto ability to coerce employees to comply with their directives by threatening them with unemployment. The incident of ownership that provides the basis

---

[1] As we saw in the last chapter, these measures consist mostly in guaranteeing a right to exit.

of this power is mainly the right to possess, the right to exclude others from an item. But those who hold, or exercise, the right to manage have the legal power to choose who will exercise the right to possess. Thus, the laws that determine who has the right to manage determine who has ultimate control of the directive power brought to bear in a nongovernmental organization. An important part of our task in insuring that power is appropriately exercised in such organizations is insuring that there is a sound moral justification for assigning this right to whoever has it.

It must be emphasized that we are here concerned only with property as a source of power and considering only what moral considerations justify different assignments of this power, on the understanding that whoever exercises it must have the status of a legitimate C-authority. There may be other moral reasons for assigning property rights in productive resources to certain people. We might, for example, create the possibility of private ownership of productive resources so that we can reward those who perform entrepreneurial tasks for the society with property rights in what they have built.[2] But if we want organizational C-authority to be exercised in a morally appropriate way, we must give these additional reasons for creating property rights force only within the framework of whatever institutions are required by the considerations that determine moral appropriateness. That is, we must reward those who perform entrepreneurial tasks for the society only with such property rights as can be given to them consistent with authority being exercised appropriately within organizations.

The Democratic Limitation of Democracy

In the previous section, I noted that while considerations of fairness and welfare maximization justify making the individuals or subgroups that exercise authority accountable to those over whom authority is exercised, other moral values might justify different relations of accountability. If other values are to have this effect, however, they must be capable of overcoming the presumption in favor of democracy that the values of fairness and welfare maximization create. Is this possible?

This question is most easily discussed by formulating it as the question whether a democracy can vote itself out of existence because it believes that certain moral values, which it regards as more important than the values of fairness and welfare maximization that

---

[2] For such a view see Becker (1977), pp. 48–56.

support democracy, could be most effectively promoted by dictatorial arrangements. Of course, this raises the further question of what is meant by a democracy's voting itself out of existence. Let us understand this as voting to establish a new constitution that provides for dictatorial decision making and that contains no constitutional provision by which democracy could be reestablished.[3] Of course, a democratic decision of this sort is sociologically possible, but our question is normative. That is, when we ask whether a democracy can vote itself out if existence, we want to know whether its members could ever have a good reason for doing this.

The following argument seems to show that a democratic C-authority could never have a good reason to vote itself out of existence. As we saw in Chapter Five, when democracy is justified as a fair and welfare-maximizing way of exercising C-authority, the values of fairness and welfare maximization are, in effect, separated from other moral considerations by the preemptiveness of the directives of a legitimate C-authority. These directives exclude and take the place of the subordinates' judgments of what the applicable directive-independent reasons require, while the values of fairness and welfare maximization, in this employment, play the role of justifying certain ways of generating directives. Thus, other considerations cannot prevail against the values of fairness and welfare maximization (employed to justify democracy) because they have already been preempted by the time these two values are used for this purpose. This means that for those who accept the justification of democracy that I have given, all *ultimate* C-authorities must be democratic. The most that a democracy that felt that there was good reason for establishing a dictatorship could justifiably do would be to vote to delegate its authority to an agent who would rule as a dictator, subject to review by the group as a whole in its role as collective principal.

It might be thought that this argument proves to much, since it implies that a direct democracy could never justifiably vote to establish a representative democracy for reasons of efficiency. But the considerations of efficiency that justify the creation of representative systems work in concert with the values of fairness and welfare maximization. They alter the way fairness and welfare maximization justify democracy; they do not compete with these values.

Even if this argument is sound, however, it does not settle the

---

[3] To be more precise, it contains no provision by which the subjects could act collectively within the constitution to reestablish democracy. The dictator could be given the constitutional right to re-establish a democratic constitution.

question whether values other than fairness and welfare maximization could justify dictatorial arrangements in nongovernmental organizations. Although the argument shows that the members of such organizations who value fairness and welfare maximization could never have a good reason to vote to replace a democratic constitution with a nondemocratic one, it does not show that a democratic government could not vote to do this for them. Nongovernmental organizations, after all, constitute subordinate loci of decision making in a larger social framework. Thus, we must allow for the possibility that the larger society, acting through a democratic government, could vote to limit democracy in some or all of the nongovernmental organizations it contains.

One aspect of such a limitation would be constraints, dictated by higher authority, on what the members of a democratically managed nongovernmental organization could decide to do. But higher authority might also simply dictate—or make legally permissible—nondemocratic constitutions for such organizations. The kinds of constitutions that nongovernmental organizations can have are determined by law, and the creation of laws is a task for the larger society, acting through its government. So if the democratic authority that guided the larger society decided that it would be desirable to make the managers of nongovernmental organizations accountable to individuals or groups other than the employees, the employees, in their capacity as members of the larger society, would have good reason to accept an organizational constitution that provided for this. They would have this reason because the directives of the superior social authority would preempt any judgment that they might make that the values of fairness and welfare maximization supported the democratic exercise of C-authority in their organizations. That is, while compliance with the government's decision might result in an exercise of authority within the organization that seemed to its members to be unfair or to fail to maximize preference satisfaction within their group, they would nevertheless regard instituting such an authority as appropriate. For they would also be members of the larger society, and they would regard the larger society's democratically generated directives as preempting the moral judgments they made in their capacity as members of a subordinate group.

In light of this result, we can reformulate the problem of whether morality requires the democratic management of nongovernmental organizations by their employees. It is not a problem about whether the utility of dictatorship in promoting some morally important social value could justify the members of such organizations in choosing dictatorship over democracy. If they value fairness and welfare maximization, they could not. It is a problem about whether the promotion of some other value *by the society as a whole* could be important enough to displace considerations of fairness and welfare maximization *as they apply to the workplace*. On the moral theory that I have presented, fairness and welfare maximization do not automatically override other considerations. They achieve such immunity as they have when employed to justifying democracy by being shielded from opposing considerations by the preemptiveness of C-authority. From the standpoint of a higher authority choosing constitutions for nongovernmental organizations, however, these values (as they apply to such organizations) lose this protected status. Thus, we must consider what weight they have in relation to the considerations that compete with them for the attention of the higher social authority.

In sum, because in the larger social context managerial authority is a subordinate form of C-authority, the case for democracy in nongovernmental organizations is weaker than the case for democracy in a government that exercises ultimate C-authority in a society. This is the first conclusion that I said I would argue for in this chapter.

Before proceeding, there are two points that should be made. First, the problem a society confronts in deciding which constitutions for nongovernmental organizations have the best justification is shaped in an important way by our conclusion in Chapter Eight that managerial authority is most appropriately regarded as C-authority. It is because managerial authority is C-authority that the values of fairness and welfare maximization create a presumption in favor of democracy. But the fact that there is such a presumption means that any considerations that seem to justify dictatorial arrangements in nongovernmental organizations must do more work to prevail. It is not sufficient to show that such arrangements have certain morally desirable results. It must be shown that these results are *desirable enough* to justify forcing the members of these organizations to accept a decision-making structure that is unfair (in the sense that it enables some in the group to advance their conceptions of the moral good more effectively than others) or that countenances avoidable losses in overall satisfaction in the group (where satisfaction is understood in terms of realization of conceptions of the moral good).

Second, we should remind ourselves that fairness supports democracy most fully when there are no entrenched minorities. When such minorities exist, fairness seems rather to support a lottery or the supplementation of democracy with political liberalism—that is, the creation of certain legal rights to pursue components of one's conception of the moral good free from majoritarian interference. It is likely, however, that societies will decide to suspend the provisions of political liberalism in nongovernmental organizations. Managerial decision making in organizations determines what conception of the moral good the organization's resources will be used to promote, so political liberalism in this context would presumably involve giving individuals certain rights to use organizational resources to pursue personal projects as well. But rights of this sort would impair the effectiveness of organizations in promoting morally important social values, and a society might well decide that it did not want to make this sacrifice.[4] This would be, in effect, a preliminary ruling that fairness in nongovernmental organizations—or at any rate, one way of giving expression to it—had less importance from the moral point of view than other considerations, even before the issue of democracy was raised. Since fairness supports combining democracy with political liberalism when there are entrenched minorities, however, the result of this preliminary ruling would be that when there were entrenched minorities within organizations, the case for managerial democracy would have to rest more on the value of welfare maximization, and would thus be weakened.

Now let us consider what reasons might justify a social decision to create nondemocratic constitutions for nongovernmental organizations, that is, constitutions that provide, through assignments of property rights or in some other way, for the accountability of managers to people other than the employees.

Investment

One decision that will have to be made at the social level concerns whether to create or maintain a market system. This will mainly be a decision about how the value of social prosperity can best be promoted under the particular conditions the society faces, but it will also take account of other moral values that might be affected by the choice between markets and planning.

For the time being, I focus on market systems, but we should be clear about the relation of the choice between markets and planning to the choice of constitutions for nongovernmental organizations. An organization's constitution might give the government the right

---

[4] Of course, the members of organizations would retain other rights. They have rights, derived from the requirement that they not be treated unfairly in the pursuit of organizational goals, to due process in any decisions affecting their welfare. And if organizations are democratic, they will have procedural rights to equal participation.

to appoint its managers, in which case there would be a sense in which it was publicly owned, since the government would hold one of the most important property rights, the right to manage. If the government does not have the legal right to appoint managers, by contrast, there will be an important sense in which the organization is privately owned. The choice between these two kinds of constitutions need not, however, coincide with the choice between a planned and a market system. Organizations that were privately owned in the above sense could be directed by legislation to contribute to a central plan, and organizations that were publicly owned in this sense could interact with each other in a market. Still, even if there is no necessary connection between the choice of relations of accountability and the choice between markets and planning, there is clearly a correlation. Markets seem to work best when those who manage the organizations that interact in them are not accountable to a central authority. Let us assume, then, that for a society to choose a market system is also for it to narrow the choice of constitutions for nongovernmental organizations to those that give different nongovernmental groups the right to choose managers. Which of these alternatives has the weightiest moral support?

A noteworthy feature of a market system is that organizations are responsible for their own economic viability, an important part of which is insuring enough investment to maintain existing productive resources and to augment them with additional resources. One question a society must address in deciding between alternative constitutions for nongovernmental organizations is whether making managers accountable to employees, as the values of fairness and welfare maximization prescribe, is compatible with achieving a socially optimal level of investment. If not, the values that support organizational democracy and the values that could be more effectively promoted if investment were socially optimal will point toward different constitutions.

It might be argued that in posing the question in this way, I have overlooked what is most important about investment from the moral point of view. For decisions about how investment funds are to be allocated are properly social decisions, and we have already established that there is a presumption that social decisions, at least when they involve the exercise of C-authority, should be made democratically. But this may mean that investment funds should be disbursed by democratically accountable agencies of the government, rather than by private individuals.[5]

---

[5] This need not involve management in accordance with a central plan. The various public agencies responsible for these decisions could invest in market-oriented entities. For a market socialist view of this sort, see Schwieckart (1980).

The quick reply to this objection is that as long as the society decides democratically to create whatever forms of property it contains, investment is democratically controlled. Presumably society monitors what is done with the property its laws provide for, and it modifies property rights when the overall results are not to its liking. This can be done democratically. It is also worth noting, however, that in a market system with private ownership of productive resources, the whole society exercises some control over investment decisions by making consumption decisions, since investors want to invest in the production of what people will buy. Of course, there is room for debate about how much control society actually exercises in this way, and, in any case, control will be imperfect because of externalities. But here we are making a comparative judgment. Thus, the relevant question is whether the members of a society could exercise *more* control by acting solely through the electoral process—that is, by voting for candidates who propose to follow certain investment policies if elected—and this seems unlikely. Such policies could not be specified in much detail, and in the end heavy reliance would have to be placed on the judgment of officials who would have only imprecise information about what people want.[6]

Let us, then, suppose that nongovernmental organizations will be responsible for attracting at least some of their investment funds from nongovernmental sources,[7] and consider whether a society could plausibly decide that its goal of achieving a socially optimal level of investment would be more fully realized if managers were not accountable to employees. We can distinguish two arguments to this effect. The first alleges that democratically managed firms will not reinvest profits in the way that would be optimal from the social point of view, and the second holds that democratically managed firms will not attract adequate outside investment.

The argument that democratically managed firms will not invest in a socially optimal way is basically an argument that worker-owned cooperatives will not do this. By a worker-owned cooperative I mean an organization in which all of the incidents of ownership, including importantly the right to the income, are held by the workers. The claim this argument makes is that an organization in

---

[6] Roemer (1992) suggests that public control of investment could be accomplished by establishing a public agency charged with adjusting the interest rates on the basis of which firms in different industries could borrow from banks. This would reduce the bureaucratic encumbrances associated with direct public investment, but would still provide no way of exploiting, for the public good, the different attitudes toward risk found within each society. I say more about this below.

[7] This supposition is compatible with a role for governmental agencies in providing investment funds as part of an industrial policy.

which the employees have the right to the income, and seek to maximize the return on their assets, will decline to use their resources to expand production. Although expanding production may increase total profits, it will usually mean hiring more workers, with the result that average income—income per worker—will decline.[8] This will be of concern to society as a whole because firms contribute most effectively to the value of social prosperity if they act so as to maximize total profits.

One reply to this argument is that the case for managerial democracy does not require that employees have the right to the income but only that they have the right to manage: to choose who the managers will be. Thus, arrangements in which employees choose managers while outside investors retain the right to the income are possible, and in such arrangements the incentives employees face might not be adverse to optimal growth. In the end, however, the question is empirical, and it is by no means clear that the evidence supports the alleged suboptimal performance of worker-owned cooperatives.[9]

The more important objection to democratically managed firms points to the effect of democratic management on outside investment. The claim here is that outside investment enables a society to take advantage of the fact that its members have different attitudes toward risk. Outside investors might, however, be less willing to invest in, or lend money to, a firm whose managers were accountable to the employees than they would be to invest in, or lend money to, firms where investment carried with it the right to choose managers. Achieving a socially optimal level of outside investment might, then, require making managers accountable to investors rather than employees. In discussing this option, I assume that the distribution of wealth is in accordance with the requirements of justice. Thus, we are concerned with securing socially optimal investment of savings from justly earned wages or profits from previous investment of justly held funds.

That there is a legitimate worry here can be seen by considering the case of small firms. It is unlikely that someone who was contemplating using her life savings, and additional funds provided by friends and relatives, to start a business would be willing to do so if the law required that managerial decisions be made by a majority vote of all a firm's members. She would probably not want to risk her money unless she could control the business herself. But of course

---

[8] For this line of argument see Ward (1958). See also Buchanan (1985), pp. 113–14.
[9] See Dahl (1985), pp. 122–25.

societies benefit from people investing their savings in small businesses. Thus, a society probably should not dictate constitutions for small businesses that require them to be democratically managed by their employees.[10]

It might be thought that the case of large firms is different since they could raise adequate funds by borrowing or by issuing nonvoting stock. Even in this case, however, there may be reasons to provide for investor control. The problem is not that funds will not be forthcoming if managers are accountable to employees, but that because of the risk of expropriation, a premium will have to be paid, and paying it will be inefficient. Higher premiums might mean that any given enterprise will be able to obtain less outside investment than it could if premiums were lower.

Oliver Williamson makes this point using his transaction cost approach to organizational design. His general project is to display the institutional structure of contemporary firms not as a manifestation of class power but rather as serving a good economic purpose, namely, economizing on transaction costs. We saw in Chapter Eight how he thinks that hierarchical organization will sometimes be preferable from this point of view to arrangements in which combinations of actions are secured by contracts between independent producers. This latter point does not by itself have any implications for managerial democracy; the hierarchy could be democratically controlled. But Williamson also thinks that the structure that corporations currently have, with ultimate managerial responsibility being held by a board of directors accountable to investors, can be explained as making it possible for the firm to reduce the costs of securing adequate investment.

The core of Williamson's argument is contained in the following passage.

> Suppose that a group of workers wish to create opportunities for employment without themselves investing equity capital in the enterprise. Suppose further that the business in question has the need for a series of inputs, of which investments in nonredeployable durable assets are included. We can imagine the workers approaching a series of input suppliers and asking each to participate. . . . Considering the above described problems of crafting a well-focused safeguard for equity capital

[10] If the law provides for this, it could still mandate employee democracy in larger firms by stipulating that when a firm reaches a certain size, control will pass to its employees. This is discussed briefly by Dahl (1985), pp. 154–55. But this, too, might affect the willingness of people to invest in small businesses.

(which, by definition, is used to finance diffuse but specific assets), the equity suppliers initially offer to hold debt at [greater expense to the firm]. Upon realizing that this is a very inefficient result, the workers who are organizing the enterprise thereupon invent a new general purpose safeguard, name it the Board of Directors, and offer it to suppliers of equity. Upon recognizing that expropriation hazards are thereby reduced, the suppliers of equity capital lower their terms of participation to [a reduced price]. They also become the "owners" of the enterprise.[11]

Inventing the board of directors means creating an institutional device that has ultimate decision-making authority and is accountable, at least loosely, to the stockholders. Thus, Williamson is arguing that democratically managed firms would vote, for economic reasons, to transform themselves into dictatorially managed firms.[12] But we can imagine the larger society, looking at the matter from the standpoint of more effective promotion of the value of social prosperity, making it legally possible to create firms that have this structure from the start.

To make managers accountable to investors is to give investors the power to choose them, and if they must be reappointed at certain intervals, this power may carry with it the power to tell them what to do.[13] This would be directive power, and on the approach that I take in this book, the exercise of this power is legitimate only if managers have a good independent reason to do what they are told. In the present case, this reason is provided by the fact that the larger society, through a legitimate authority, has directed the establishment of a constitution that confers such power.

The question of whether nondemocratic structures are necessary to secure a socially optimal level of investment is ultimately a question for economists, and I do not attempt to answer it here.[14] It is

[11] Williamson (1985), pp. 323–24.

[12] Our earlier discussion raised doubts about whether members of an organization who value fairness and welfare maximization can have a good reason, exclusive of a directive from a higher authority, to replace a democratic constitution with a nondemocratic one. But Williamson appears to be looking at the matter solely from the standpoint of the economic self-interest of the employees, and viewing democracy as an instrument to achieve this. The employees initially form a democratically managed cooperative because they think their incomes will be higher as a result, and then discover that they were mistaken.

[13] See Bowles and Gintis (1992).

[14] One relevant contribution has been made by Herbert Gintis (1989). He argues that employee-managed firms will be less attractive to investors because such firms would be too cautious for the taste of many investors seeking high returns. See also Bowles and Gintis (1993).

enough for present purposes to note that there is some reason to suppose that democratic management of firms would be disadvantageous from the standpoint of securing a socially optimal level of investment in productive activities. Thus, there may be good economic reasons why a society concerned with increasing social prosperity would not want to mandate legally that all firms, or all firms above a certain size, be employee-managed. A concern for liberty, however, dictates allowing those who would prefer employee-managed firms to form them even if they are economically suboptimal. The best arrangement, then, might be to make legal provision both for nongovernmental organizations whose managers are accountable to their employees and for nongovernmental organizations whose managers are accountable to investors.[15]

Expertise

The second consideration that may count against managerial democracy is the role of expertise in managing nongovernmental organizations. To the extent that some individuals are more expert than others in matters relevant to the decisions made within an organization, it may be appropriate to place them in offices that carry de facto authority. Because there is no presumption that E-authority should be democratically exercised, but rather the reverse, utilizing expertise in this way would seem to have antidemocratic implications. The issues that we must confront in exploring this possibility are complicated, however. It will be useful to begin by discussing an artificially limited case, that in which the only decisions that managers must make are decisions regarding the best means by which to promote preestablished ends.

Expertise in the best means to a given end is technical expertise, and those possessing it can acquire the status of E-authorities for others by displaying a history of correct judgment. The fact that someone is a technical E-authority can also justify compliance with her *directives* if the subordinates who receive these directives accept the ends the authority is trying to promote and find that they are better attained in this way. Many of the decisions made in organizations, for example in matters of marketing, finance, and engineering of all sorts, would appear to admit of differences in expertise that could justify compliance with directives. Moreover, since technical expertise is typically established by an external criterion, its posses-

[15] For a view of a society that would provide both traditional capitalist structures and worker-cooperatives see Krause and McPherson (1986).

sion can in principle be detected by anyone. If the occupant of an organizational office truly has greater technical expertise than her subordinates, then, they should all be able to accept her as a legitimate E-authority.

Now let us complicate the picture a bit. Technical expertise can manifest itself as directives issued to isolated individuals or as directives issued to groups. In the latter case, the relevant expertise will involve the ability to decide how the actions of various members of a group should be coordinated to achieve the desired end. As we saw in our discussion of C-authority in Chapter Four, coordinating expertise can also play a role when the members of a group are trying to advance independent ends, but could do so most effectively by coordinating their actions. For there can be expertise in the recognition of coordination equilibria. Neither of these possibilities involves the abandonment of the basic inductive strategy for establishing expertise, but each introduces a social dimension to the validating experiments. It is by jointly following a plan to coordinate their activities that the members of a group more successfully comply with reasons that they accept.

There is another form of technical expertise the possession of which might justify putting someone in a position of authority: leadership ability. Expertise in coordinating the actions of a group is an aspect of leadership. But leadership usually involves more than being able to make correct judgments about how best to achieve certain ends; it also involves being able to get people to do what they must to promote these ends. This latter ability can be regarded as a further form of technical expertise since it displays knowledge about how to produce certain results. It is not an ability that a manager needs when the members of a group are effectively motivated to achieve the ends she is trying to promote and accept that she is an expert on what actions would be most effective in realizing them. But one can acknowledge that one has sufficient reason to promote a given end while still not being effectively motivated to promote it—one may be discouraged, for example. The occupant of a certain office may also possess the technical expertise required to achieve certain ends, but not yet have established the record of success that would give her subordinates good inductive reason to regard her as possessing it. This is especially likely if the ends in question can only be promoted by the coordinated action of groups of people; an individual must secure compliance with her directives before she can display such expertise.

In these and other cases, the ability to motivate people to take action is an important attribute in the holder of an office. This ability may involve a knack for crafting inspirational communications or for manipulating the available psychological and sociological incentives to achieve the desired type and intensity of effort. It should also be noted that good leaders are often people who have the attribute that, for whatever reason, their approval is taken as a reward.

I have been presenting leadership ability as a form of expertise that can usefully supplement technical expertise in how best to achieve certain ends, but it can play a role in other forms of authority as well. In many agency relationships, the agent is motivated by an extrinsic reward (that is, pay) that the principal promises to provide in return for compliance.[16] Since the reward is extrinsic, however, it does not directly support the desired performance, and thus a principal may be able to achieve her ends more effectively if she—or those to whom she delegates P-authority—possess leadership ability.

Similar points can be made about C-authority. Leadership ability can facilitate the achievement of mutually beneficial cooperation among people with different aims. In this case, too, weakness of will or discouragement may leave people without an effective motive to cooperate in ways that would benefit them. Even when the members of a group are motivated to cooperate, however, the motivating potential of leadership can have value as solving the assurance problem. As we have seen, in both coordination and prisoner's dilemma situations, no one has a reason to cooperate unless he believes that enough others will as well. This means that the ability to incite others to action—especially if its efficacy is common knowledge within the group—can play the same role in facilitating mutually beneficial cooperation as coercive sanctions. No rational member of the group needs this reason to act if he is confident that enough others will do their parts, but he will find it easier to have this confidence if the person issuing the directives is commonly known to have the ability to inspire or motivate people.

The role of expertise in the management of nongovernmental organizations is uncontroversial. Even advocates of worker cooperatives, such as Robert Dahl, argue that expert managers will need to be employed.[17] The decision to employ them is a decision to live with less democracy than would otherwise be possible; for as we have seen, democracy undermines expertise. If managers are arranged in a hierarchy based on greater technical (including coor-

---

[16] As we have seen, the agent makes a promise too. But if this is only a promise to comply if he is going to accept pay, what actually motivates him is the reward.

[17] See Dahl (1985), pp. 128–30.

dinating) expertise or leadership ability, then, decision making will appropriately be nondemocratic at each level.

Now let us make our account of the role of expertise in the management of nongovernmental organizations more realistic. The first step is to note that the picture that has just been presented of the role of expertise in conferring legitimacy on managerial authority seems to be at odds with the general strategy that I have been pursuing in this chapter. This strategy has been to assume that managerial authority is C-authority and consider whether the presumption in favor of the democratic exercise of such authority can be outweighed by other considerations. On the account just presented of the significance of expertise for managerial authority, however, managers who have technical expertise were viewed as being licensed to issue directives by virtue of their status as E-authorities. This means that the situation is not one in which the presumption in favor of democracy created by the values of fairness and welfare maximization is outweighed by other moral values. Rather, it is a situation in which this presumption plays no role at all, since managers are not properly understood as C-authorities.

In fact, however, it would be a mistake to abandon the approach sketched at the beginning of this chapter. We can see why by bringing morality back into the picture. As was noted in Chapter Four, it is difficult for any one individual or set of individuals to win the status of moral expert for all the members of any large group. But as our discussion in Chapter Six revealed, moral considerations are relevant both to the choice of ends for an organization to promote—or the choice of basic policies that have the effect of setting ends—and to the choice of means to these ends. So in one fundamental respect, the moral respect, managers cannot plausibly claim expertise in the matters they decide. Consequently, it will always be appropriate to regard managers as, at bottom, C-authorities, authorities who facilitate mutually beneficial cooperation among individuals with conflicting (moral) aims.

Given that the moral dimension of management forces us to regard managerial authority as C-authority, how should we understand the role of expertise in management and the attendant implications for democracy? As we have seen, the presumption that managers who are C-authorities should be accountable to employees that is created by the values of fairness and welfare maximization might be rebutted if it could be shown that making managers accountable to some other group would enable nongovernmental organizations to promote certain morally important social values more effectively. But giving ultimate managerial authority to people who possess technical expertise of various sorts might make these organizations more effective social instruments for the promotion of any of a variety of morally important social values. Thus, a society could be well advised to choose a constitutional form for nongovernmental organizations, and in particular a constitutional right to appoint managers, that makes it likely that people possessing the required expertise will be placed in positions where C-authority is exercised. In doing this it would be opting for an arrangement in which the choice—that any C-authority must make—between the different directives on which mutually beneficial cooperation could be based depended not on the outcome of a fair procedure but on an expert's judgment about which of them was most conducive to some socially mandated end.

When the relevance of expertise to managerial authority is understood in this way, the reason that employees have to comply with managerial directives is not that they accept the E-authority of the person who issues these directives (although if they do, so much the better). The reason is that the manager has been chosen in accordance with constitutional procedures that were adopted or endorsed by a higher political authority whose legitimacy they accept. The higher authority provides for these procedures in the expectation that they will result in the appointment of managers possessing technical expertise, but whether employees have good reason to comply with managerial directives does not depend on this.

We must be careful not to go to fast here, however. Even if the values that could be more effectively promoted by giving technical experts control of nongovernmental organizations (that is, by making them dictatorial C-authorities) are more important from the social point of view than those supporting the democratic exercise of C-authority in nongovernmental organizations, it still does not follow automatically that managers should be accountable to, in the sense of chosen by, people other than their subordinates. Someone must be given the role of deciding who has the expertise required for a given managerial office, and the employees might be in the best position to do this. If so, higher authority could assign them the role (as trustees for the society as a whole) of determining which individuals had the technical expertise needed to occupy successfully the dictatorial offices created by their organization's constitution. The result would be a form of electoral dictatorship in nongovernmental organizations.

In discussing this possibility, it is important to distinguish between cases where expertise is established by an external criterion of success and cases where it is established by an internal criterion of success. If the criterion if success is external, it is plausible that employees would be as good as anyone at assessing the inductive evidence for expertise. But if the criterion of success is internal, expertise will be best detected by those who already have it to some degree. This will argue for making managers accountable not to employees but to other experts, that is, to other managers.

It might be thought that cases of this sort would be rare, since managerial success is usually determined by an external record of profitability or growth. Cases where an internal criterion would be appropriate seem restricted to, say, cultural institutions. Thus, the ultimate political authority might decide that aesthetic sensitivity was an important qualification for the post of director of an opera company, and in acknowledgment of the fact that this sensitivity can only be detected by others who have it, make legally possible constitutions for opera companies that place the choice of a director in the hands of a board of expert trustees rather than the employees. Like other employees, the employees of opera companies hold different conceptions of the moral good, and thus might find themselves contributing to a moral or political agenda that they do not share by complying with managerial directives. So, the authority exercised by an opera company's managers must be understood as C-authority. But under the arrangements now being considered, the director would not be accountable to the employees because the morally important social value of the development of culture was thought to outweigh the values that support democratic accountability.[18]

It is plausible, however, that there is also a large role for internal criteria in the selection of the managers of profit-seeking organizations and others where there is ultimately an external criterion of success. An individual candidates's previous record will rarely establish unequivocally that she possesses the technical expertise

---

[18] Here I am supposing, possibly contrary to fact, that the employees of opera companies, from parking-lot attendants on up, taken as a whole and acting democratically, would not possess the required expertise to the same degree as a board of trustees composed of experts in opera. I am making no claim that the boards of trustees of cultural institutions as they are presently constituted have a great deal of expertise in the aesthetic questions these institutions face.

It may be useful to mention another case in which expertise can be regarded as supplanting managerial democracy. The employees of colleges and universities, no less than other employees, may find that compliance with managerial directives means contributing to a moral or political agenda that they do not share. But in most such institutions, democratic decision making is restricted to the faculty, which constitutes a minority of the employees. The constitutions that provide for this can be regarded as reflecting a social decision that the value of the advancement of knowledge, which is better promoted when policy in such organizations is made by experts in education, takes precedence over the values of fairness and welfare maximization as applied to all the employees.

or leadership ability appropriate for a particular managerial position. Thus, the goal of the selection process will usually be to find
someone who seems to have the *potential* for success. Moreover, this
sort of potential might be most readily discerned by those who
already possess the corresponding expertise or leadership ability—
assuming they are free of prejudice. If so, it would be appropriate
for managers to be chosen by other managers, that is, other experts
of this sort. As we have seen, in contemporary corporations a self-
selected managerial elite has a large role in determining who will
exercise managerial authority. The considerations just adduced suggest that there may be some justification for this way of choosing
managers.

In concluding this section, it should be noted that these observations point to a general problem about the democratic management
of expertise. It is a staple of socialist thought that the productive resources of a society should be democratically managed. But
what are these resources? As long as they are understood to consist
solely of machines and land, there is no problem in principle about
their democratic management. But the talents of the people in a
society—its human capital—can be regarded as productive resources as well.

Liberal egalitarians such as John Rawls and Ronald Dworkin have
suggested that these resources should be regarded as common assets. What they appear mean by this, however, is only that the
whole society has a presumptive claim, through taxation, to the
income derived from putting these assets to productive use. The
management of these assets is left to those in whom they are depos-
ited, who can perhaps be regarded as trustees for the group. There
seems to be good reason for this, since it is not clear that the socialist
demand for the democratic management of productive resources
can be extended to human capital. To be sure, a society can control
the *use* of expertise by indicating to those possessing it what results
it wants achieved, perhaps by providing incentives for achieving
them. But the expertise itself can only be *managed* by individuals or
groups possessing greater expertise of the sort in question. The
essence of the resource lies in the judgment of the person who has it
about how it may best be employed, and if her judgments are sup-
planted by those of people who lack the talent in question, the
resource will be destroyed. Thus, there are limits to how much
control of any kind—and a fortiori, how much democratic control—
can be exerted over human capital by those who do not have greater
expertise in the matters to be decided. This argues for administrative

hierarchies in which the higher positions are given to those with greater expertise.[19]

These points could also be made by saying that a decision by a society to exploit differences in expertise inevitably carries with it certain meritocratic implications. The implications are not meritocratic in the sense that those who have the talents that society needs to a higher degree deserve a larger reward for their efforts. They are meritocratic in the sense that the decision about how socially valuable talents will be deployed must, in the end, be left to those who have them. This includes leadership talents. Direction of the talented by the nontalented can only take the form of indicating what results are to be achieved.[20]

One final point about expertise should be borne in mind. Experts are still fallible human beings. Their expertise consists in the fact that they are more likely to be right about certain matters than most other people, not that they are inevitably right. In designing institutional structures that enable it to capitalize on differences in expertise, then, a society will do well to diversify the risk associated with reliance on experts by decentralizing decision making. This is a further reason for a society to choose a market system.

Constitutional Choice

In the last two sections, I developed two arguments suggesting that certain morally important social values can be more effectively promoted if nongovernmental organizations are constituted so that managers are not accountable to employees. One of these arguments, which finds application mostly in the case of profit-seeking organizations, is that the value of social prosperity will be more fully realized if nonemployees invest in enterprises, and making managers accountable to investors may foster this. To be sure, employees could be investors, too, but in the normal case they will have the status of minority shareholders.[21] The second argument is that

[19] The problem of the democratic management of expertise can be viewed as an agency problem—a problem of the control of an expert agent by a less expert (collective) principle. Similar agency problems arise in other areas as well. The strict norms of professional conduct found in such fields as medicine and law can be regarded as responses to them.

[20] These points are not intended to support rule by an elite class. In an efficient society, everyone would receive training that gave him or her expertise in something.

[21] This is not just because they will seldom be able to satisfy the investment needs of their organization themselves. Given that it is rational to diversify the unsystematic risk in an investment portfolio, employees who own stock will have a reason to want most of their holdings to be in other firms.

any of a variety of morally important social values might be better promoted by placing individuals with technical expertise in managerial positions where C-authority is exercised, and the most reliable way of selecting people who have the requisite qualities will often be to have them chosen by other experts. Unlike the first, this argument can be applied to nonprofit organizations as well as profit-seeking firms.

These two lines of argument are somewhat at odds with each other, but it can be held that current practice represents a compromise between them, since boards of directors are to a certain extent accountable to investors but also possess a great deal of autonomy.[22] But we may not be able to rest content with the status quo. We should bear in mind the context of the arguments we are now considering. To justify the status quo, it is not enough to show that some morally important social value could be more effectively promoted by dictatorially managed nongovernmental organizations. It must also be established that the incremental increase in this value that would accompany dictatorial arrangements is significant enough to outweigh completely the values of fairness and welfare maximization as they apply to the exercise of C-authority in the workplace. If it is not sufficient to do this, we must face the question of whether some other institutional forms would be preferable, all things considered.

The choice a society would be making in adopting certain institutional forms can be illuminated with the device of a hypothetical social contract. The contractors would be at something like Rawls's constitutional or legislative stage—choosing constitutions for nongovernmental organizations as opposed to fundamental moral principles—but they would be guided in this choice not by Rawls's two principles of justice but by an understanding of when C-authority is legitimately exercised and by the moral values that support either the democratic or the nondemocratic exercise of C-authority.[23]

First, let us canvas the alternatives. As we have seen, property rights have implications for the legal accountability of the managers

---

[22] Large institutional investors—pension funds and the like—may be able to exert more control over who sits on boards of directors or holds senior managerial positions than individual shareholders. But in such cases, managers remain accountable to other members of a managerial elite, since the input of these "investors" is just the input of the managers of the funds. The argument in the previous section that experts are best chosen by other experts does not require that the top management of each organization be self-selected, but only that the holders of managerial positions be chosen by other managers.

[23] For the constitutional and legislative stages of Rawls's hypothetical contract theory, see Rawls (1971), pp. 195–201.

of nongovernmental organizations. Those who hold the right to manage have the power to decide who will occupy managerial offices. The alternatives that we shall consider differ not only in who holds this right but also in how legal property rights in general are defined.

The first alternative is the typical capitalist arrangement. In the purest case, the institutional structure of capitalism is one in which an individual or small group has full ownership of the productive resources utilized by an organization, and thus all the power that this entails. In contemporary society, however, the usual form that this alternative takes in large organizations is that of the "publicly" held corporation in which a board of directors formally accountable to shareholders exercises most of the property rights in the associated productive resources, with only certain decisions reserved for the shareholders directly.

As we saw in Chapter Eight, this legal structure confers more power on those who exercise the property rights it creates than can be justified on the assumption that they are P-authorities, at least if employees are trying to promote their conceptions of the moral good in their work. For the legal structure of capitalism to be justifiable, then, managers must be understood as C-authorities. However, in its basic form, capitalism makes no provision for the democratic accountability of managers to employees that the values of fairness and welfare maximization support when a given locus of directives is a C-authority. The remaining alternatives can be understood as attempting to remedy this defect either by designating other individuals or groups as owners, or by modifying in certain ways the rights associated with full liberal ownership.

The first step away from the standard capitalist arrangement is to retain the legal structure of capitalism, but supplement it (that is, these legal conventions) with moral conventions that put limits on how legal property rights can be exercised. The society is understood to adopt, in addition to a legal form for nongovernmental organizations, a set of norms of professional conduct that embody a certain understanding of how nongovernmental organizations should be run, which the society then enforces with informal social pressure. These norms could move organizations in the direction of accountability to employees if they called for placing representatives of the employees on boards of directors, for example. They might also attempt to replicate the results that could be expected if managers were accountable to employees by stipulating that certain practices be followed by organizations, such as practices designed to ensure a safe workplace. The point of trying to satisfy the underlying moral considerations by relying on informal social norms rather than laws would be to avoid the cumbersome apparatus of legal enforcement. Should the norms break down, society could legislate how property rights were to be exercised.[24]

We would move further in the direction of the accountability of managers to employees if the presence of representatives of employees on boards of directors was not merely urged by conventional morality but legally mandated. One arrangement that provides for this is codetermination. In its simplest form, this involves legally stipulating that boards of directors be composed in equal parts of representatives of employees and investors. Thus, some of the top managers of organizations are accountable to the employees. As we have already seen in the section on investment, if a society wants full accountability of managers to employees, it can take advantage of the fact that ownership consists of several component rights and allocate the right to manage entirely to employees (or their representatives), leaving the right to the income—that is, the profits—in the hands of outside investors. One way to accomplish this might be to restrict outsiders to holding nonvoting stock.[25]

The remaining alternatives call for full ownership of productive resources by employees or by the society as a whole. These arrangements, however, would not make managers any more accountable to employees than giving employees the exclusive right to manage. Thus, the reason for emphasizing full employee ownership must be that it would effectively promote moral values other than those that support democratic accountability. For example, it might be thought that giving employees the right to the income as well as the right to manage would be an effective means of promoting the value of distributive justice in a society—although this doubtful since there would be great differences in income and wealth received by the employees of different organizations.

Similar points can be made about arrangements that move even

[24] Donaldson's social contract for business can, I think, be interpreted in this way. Donaldson argues that the moral responsibilities that productive organizations have to society as a whole, and in particular to consumers and employees, can be regarded as established by a hypothetical contract. The idea is that society allows productive organizations to exist only on the assumption that they will serve certain social purposes, and the contract specifies what their part of the bargain is. This approach presupposes that the mere quest for profit in a competitive market environment by firms with the legal structure corporations now have will not suffice for the attainment of social purposes. See Donaldson (1982), chap. 3, and (1989), pp. 47–61.

[25] It is unclear how the other rights would be distributed. Assigning the right to the capital to investors would give them a threat advantage—the threat to liquidate—that they could use to influence the employee-managers, but it would not prevent the democratic management of firms by their employees.

further from the typical capitalist arrangement by replacing private ownership of productive resources with public ownership. Public ownership might be preferable to both employee-owned firms and the typical capitalist arrangement from the standpoint of distributive justice. Even if these public resources are ultimately controlled by officials democratically accountable to the society as a whole, however, instituting public ownership would not move a society any closer to ideal managerial democracy than giving the employees of organizations the exclusive right to manage the resources with which they work. Or at least this is so if democracy is understood as reflexive authority, the exercise of authority by those who are subject to it, in this case, the employees. Indeed, a society that adopted such arrangements would move farther away from the ideal of managerial democracy, since managerial decisions would be in the hands of individuals accountable in part to people who were not employees, such as the retired. The situation would be even worse from the standpoint of democratic accountability of managers to employees if the management of publicly owned productive resources was in the hands of a self-selected managerial elite, as in the form of socialism until recently found in the Soviet Union.

To these alternatives, I would like to add another suggested by our discussion in Chapters Seven and Eight. This is to use company unions to make possible the separate institutional expression of the competing considerations that count for and against the democratic accountability of managers to employees when managerial authority is C-authority.

On this alternative, the choice of managers is in the hands of a board of directors nominally accountable to investors but in fact possessing a good deal of autonomy. As we have seen, this arrangement can be regarded as a reasonable compromise between the values that are best promoted by making managers accountable to investors and the values that are best promoted by letting those who possess managerial expertise choose who the managers will be. The directives of these managers give expression to a particular conception of the moral good, and all in the organization usually have good reason to comply because implementing these directives is preferable to the noncooperative outcome.

By contrast, the values that support the democratic management of nongovernmental organizations in which C-authority is exercised are satisfied by the creation of company unions. These would provide a forum in which all who received managerial directives could decide democratically whether they wanted the organization to pursue the conception of the moral good that these directives reflected or to pursue it by the means management proposed. The unions must be company unions because democracy is reflexive authority, and thus we need a way to insure participation by all and only those whose actions are directed by a given managerial C-authority. In large organizations, democratic decision making in the union would have to be representative, with union leaders accountable to the members.

On this arrangement, the policies ultimately followed by the organization would be a result of the influencing of managers formally accountable to investors by union leaders formally accountable to employees. Since management would control the property associated with the firm, it would have a great deal of power, and unions would not be able to provide an effective check unless they had power, too. Various legal measures could provide such power. One would be to give unions the legal right to strike. As things now stand, however, the power that unions derive from the right to strike is diminished by the fact that those who control productive property are legally able to hire replacement workers. Thus, the power that the right to strike would confer on the company unions that we are considering would depend on how much solidarity possible replacements would display.

The power of company unions could be expanded by defining property rights in productive resources so that hiring replacements for the members of a striking company union was illegal, or by providing that doing so was permissible only after obtaining a ruling from a designated governmental agency. If the hiring of replacement workers was legally prohibited, managers ultimately accountable to boards of directors would have no alternative but to deal with company unions. Since a strike would be costly to both sides, there would be an incentive to reach agreement.[26] The larger society's decision regarding how much legal power to give to company unions by such devices would depend on its perception of the relative importance of the values that support and oppose democracy in nongovernmental organizations.

We have canvassed a variety of legal structures that could govern the accountability of managers who exercise C-authority. I shall not attempt to determine which arrangement is best all things considered. People with different conceptions of the moral good will disagree about this. But one conclusion seems clear: The typical capital-

---

[26] It might also be useful as a part of such an arrangement to place a representative of the union on the board of directors in a nonvoting capacity so that the union would have accurate information about the firm's situation. For a discussion of this alternative, see Williamson (1985), chap. 12.

ist arrangement and dictatorial forms of socialism are both highly implausible candidates for the title of best structure, all things considered. Given that managerial authority is C-authority, the values of fairness and welfare maximization create a presumption in favor of its democratic exercise. And neither dictatorial capitalism nor dictatorial socialism gives *any* weight to these values. Thus, constitutions for nongovernmental organizations that fail to provide the employees as a whole with some sort of role in formulating ultimate managerial policy are problematic. This is the second of the two main conclusions that I said I would try to establish in this chapter.[27]

Federalism

Our discussion up to this point has concerned itself with managerial authority in nongovernmental organizations, but the authority of managers over employees is found in governmental agencies as well. Before concluding, we should consider this case.

The basic approach to the problem of the legitimacy of managerial authority that I have developed for nongovernmental organizations is transferable to governmental agencies. Here, too, managers have a good deal of directive power deriving from their exercise of property rights, namely, rights ultimately held by the state, and the question arises of how we should understand the authority that underwrites this power.

For our purposes, governments can be regarded as performing two main tasks. First they pass laws directing their citizens to behave in certain ways, which we may understand as an exercise of C-authority. Second, they legislate the raising of tax revenues to promote certain ends for the society as a whole. This, too, is an exercise of C-authority. These two functions are not distinct since one of the ends promoted with tax revenues is the enforcement of laws, and the laws will include some directing the payment of the taxes that fund governmental projects.

[27] Instituting a mixed-property regime in which those who had a taste for participation could satisfy it (although possibly at the cost of reduced compensation) in workers' cooperatives would not render the typical capitalist arrangement unproblematic. My argument does not appeal to a personal preference for participation, which may not be widely shared, but rather turns on the presumption, created by the values of fairness and welfare maximization, that C-authority should be democratically exercised. If I am right that managerial authority in large organizations must be viewed as C-authority, there is a presumption that all such organizations should be democratically managed. The case is thus similar to that of government. We do not think that by allowing dissidents to emigrate a dictatorship can make itself immune to demands for democracy.

Governmental agencies promote certain ends by certain means. Let us consider the end-setting function first. The employees of governmental agencies could be understood as agents retained to promote the ends set by a principal. But this principal is the society as a whole acting through its government, and all employees of governmental agencies, as members of the larger society, form a part of this body. Thus, the reason they have to accept the ends that their organizations promote is the same reason that all citizens have to accept the ends set by government—that doing so constitutes mutually beneficial cooperation among people with conflicting conceptions of the moral good. The employees of governmental agencies just happen to have put themselves in a position to contribute to these ends in ways that other citizens do not, that is, in ways that go beyond obeying the law and paying taxes.

The account of means-choosing authority in governmental agencies is similar to that we have already provided for nongovernmental organizations. Even if all its employees accept the end a governmental agency promotes (as legitimately set by higher authority), means-choosing authority can still be regarded as C-authority that makes possible cooperation among individuals with conflicting aims. For they will have different views about which means would be best, and this will give them contrary intermediate aims. Moreover, as we have seen, viewing means-choosing authority as C-authority is preferable to viewing it as P-authority if employees seek to promote their conceptions of the moral good in their work.

In governmental organizations, as well, then, managerial authority is best regarded as C-authority. This has consequences with which we are now familiar. First, there is a presumption that this authority should be democratically exercised by employees. In democratic states, the democratic selection of ultimate policies is provided for. But our results imply that the employees of a governmental agency should decide democratically what means will be employed to carry out the tasks assigned to it by legitimate political authority. Although in the case of governmental agencies, this presumption cannot be overridden by considerations relating to investment, it can be overridden by considerations relating to the social benefits that can be obtained by placing the choice of directives in the hands of expert managers. Finally, unions—that is, the analogue of company unions—provide a good mechanism for meeting the demands of democracy while satisfying the moral considerations that argue for management by experts.

We should note the situation of high governmental officials. Whether C-authority is legitimately exercised in a given case depends on how well one could do, by one's own lights, in the nonco-operative situation, that is, the situation in which the authority to which one is subject was ineffective. But if high officials retained the ability to control those *below* them in this situation, they could often do much more to promote their conceptions of the moral good than ordinary citizens. On this hypothesis, then, they would be more likely than ordinary citizens to find it justifiable to ignore the directives of a C-authority, including a democratic C-authority, if they regarded accomplishing their moral ends as more important than fairness and welfare maximization. This is a reason for an ultimate C-authority to want the high officials immediately below it to actually share its values, and can explain why a change at the top usually involves changes in immediately subordinate high officials as well. Similar points can be made about nongovernmental organizations.[28]

Now that we have an account of how managerial authority is exercised in governmental agencies, we can see how similar non-governmental organizations are to governmental entities. Of course, this conclusion is trivial if regulation turns nongovernmental organizations into agents of the government, but it holds as well if they have some legal room to set their own ends. For in so doing, they organize cooperation among people with conflicting conceptions of the moral good just as legitimate governments do. The members of the various divisions and departments of a nongovernmental organization are like the members of governmental agencies. The sole difference that all of the citizens of these organizational "states" are employees of them.

This leads to a picture of the total system of authority in a society that contains independent nongovernmental organizations as a kind of federal system. A federal system of political authority is characterized by a nested hierarchy of governments, each of which is subordinate to those above it but also has a certain amount of autonomy in setting the ends for the political unit it governs. Further, the legitimacy of these subordinate governments as bodies that set ends derives from the fact that the policies they pursue foster mutually beneficial cooperation in the territories they control. But the account I have provided of nongovernmental organizations presents them as occupying a position in the overall system of authority similar to that of local or state governments. They are subordinate loci of C-authority.

---

[28] For a somewhat different view of why a governmental official might be justified in disregarding a directive from superior political authority see Applbaum (1992).

To be sure, there are differences. The authority exercised in non-governmental organizations is more prescriptive than proscriptive in character, and it is exercised not over all the activities that take place in a certain territory but over only some of them—or as we might say, over all the territories where certain activities take place. From the standpoint of authority, however, these do not appear to be important differences. It might be objected that the authority governments exercise is public authority while that exercised in nongovernmental organizations is not, but it is not clear what makes authority public. And on one plausible answer—namely, that a public authority is one that organizes mutually beneficial cooperation among people seeking to advance different conceptions of the moral good—the management of nongovernmental organizations is public.

If it is true that managerial authority is a form of public authority, the sharp distinction often made between systems that feature private ownership of the means of production and those that feature public ownership slips away. Of course, ownership has distributive implications, but any distribution of the social product can, in principle, be achieved in either sort of system with appropriate tax policies. The important consideration is the distribution of control, and to opt for private ownership of productive resources seems to be to confer all the power that access to those resources brings with it on individuals concerned only with the promotion of their personal ends. But once we address the question of the legitimacy of managerial authority, and derive the principle of the priority of authority to directive power, we find that private legal property rights, like the laws that underwrite the coercive power of the state, must be made to reflect morally valid C-authority. If they are, it does not seem to matter much whether legal property rights are held by governments or private individuals.

Similar points can be made about multinational corporations. These are usually multidivisional corporations one or more of the divisions of which are located in a different country from the country in which the main corporate office is located. On the present view, the fact that the ultimate authority guiding the management of a division of an organization lies outside the country in which that division is located does not change the fact that the division in question has the status, within the country where it operates, of a subordinate locus of decision making in a federal structure. The ultimate legislative authority of the society establishes the framework within which all organizations located within its borders must operate, and thus the decisions made at corporate headquarters regarding operations in other countries must accept the subordination of the divisions in question to the relevant political authorities. A corporation that decides to operate in a foreign country, then, commits itself to participate in a system of mutually beneficial cooperation among those residing in that country that is ultimately controlled by the local authorities.[29] Similar points apply to organizations that operate in territories controlled by different local authorities within the same country. Organizational decision making is subordinate to these governments as well.

Conceptual Change

Let us summarize our conclusions about managerial democracy. First, the case for democracy in nongovernmental organizations is weaker than the case for the democratic exercise of governmental authority because nongovernmental organizations are subordinate to governments that can make nondemocratic constitutions for them a legally available option. Second, constitutions that make no provision at all for managerial democracy, at least in the form of unions or codetermination, are deeply suspect. For if managerial authority is C-authority, there is a presumption in favor of managerial democracy. And although there may be other moral considerations that are capable of conflicting with the values that support democracy, it is implausible that these values can be completely outweighed.

Of course, these results presuppose those obtained earlier. I have argued that even in capitalist firms, managerial authority must be understood differently from the way the law understands it. It must be understood as C-authority (authority that serves those subject to it) rather than P-authority (authority which is served by those subject to it). Let us call a change of this sort—a change in our understanding of what makes authority of a certain kind legitimate—conceptual change. I should like to conclude by noting the parallels between the change that I have advocated in our thinking about management and a similar change associated with an important episode in the emergence of democratic government in Western societies.

The episode I have in mind is the constitutional struggle that took place in England during the seventeenth century, from James I to the

---

[29] For a discussion of multinational corporations, see Donaldson (1989). He explores the interesting question of what is required of a local division of a multinational corporation when law and conventional morality in the home country is more demanding than in the host country.

Glorious Revolution. At the beginning and end of this period, the institutions of government consisted of king and Parliament. Thus it might seem that all the turmoil of the intervening years was for naught. But something did change. At the beginning, the conventionally accepted reason for obedience was that associated with the doctrine of the divine right of kings. This is essentially an application of the model of agency to political authority. Everyone is understood to be an agent of God. Of course, God's status as principal is not established by a contract, as in most agency relations, but is simply part of the nature of things. The moral requirement to obey God is just something that confronts people. The king is then understood as God's lieutenant on earth, exercising God's powers as principal for him. The king, like everyone else, is an agent of God, but he has authority over all of the other agents because God has delegated his authority as principal to the king.[30]

What happened in England in the course of the seventeenth century was the replacement of this idea with the idea that the basis of political authority is the people. Political authorities came to be understood not as agents of God exercising his rights as principal but as something like agents of the people they ruled—if not in the sense that they governed under the direction of the people, at least in the sense that they governed on behalf of and in the interests of the people. That is, they came to be understood as governing in accordance with Joseph Raz's service conception; the reason for their subjects to obey them was that by doing so they better complied with the same reasons that would have guided their actions were no authority present. In the absence of generally acknowledged moral experts, this means that political authority came to be understood as C-authority. This change was accompanied by an expansion of the importance of Parliament, which could now claim to represent the sovereign people, but the king's authority was understood as having the same foundation. Thus, while the outward appearance of the institutions of king and Parliament was little different at the end of this period from what it had been at the beginning, the ideas that were regarded as providing a reason to accept them were completely transformed.[31]

[30] For a discussion of the moral background of this view of political authority see Schneewind (1984). According to Schneewind, the development of moral theory in the seventeenth and eighteenth century reflects a transition from a view of social cooperation which presupposed a divine supervisor who could be relied upon to insure that if everyone played his assigned part, the results would be morally satisfactory, to a view in which those engaged in social cooperation were understood as having to take responsibility themselves for whether it was successful.

[31] For an account, see Morgan (1988), part 1.

These changes coincide with the emergence of the social contract tradition in political philosophy, and it is instructive to consider how this tradition developed in the seventeenth century. The initial such theory in England, that of Hobbes, appears to been intended to justify possession by the sovereign of absolute authority similar to that which kings could claim under the theory of divine right. But later developments in contract theory, associated with Locke, present the government as an agent, or better trustee, of the people. The people's relation to the government is that of trust, just as in the case of a principal who authorizes an agent to act on his behalf.[32]

If the argument of this book is correct, with the growth of the moral dimension of management accompanying the rise of large organizational employers, there should be a corresponding change in our understanding of the basis of the authority of the managers of nongovernmental organizations. On the current understanding, the basis of their authority is their status as something like lieutenants of the corporate principal or the shareholders. And shareholders often have as little real control over what they do as God had over the kings and queens of England. But if managerial authority is best understood as C-authority, the basis of the authority of managers is that they serve the employees by enabling them to promote their conceptions of the moral good more effectively in their work.[33]

As in the case of the changes in England, this conceptual change need not carry with it a change in the basis on which corporate "monarchs"—the chief executive officers—are selected. The hereditary selection of the kings and queens of England survived the conceptual change that took place in the seventeenth century, and the selection of top mangers by other managers could survive the change that I am proposing in our understanding of what makes managerial authority legitimate. The important point is that the

[32] For an argument that Hobbes's attempt to establish the absolute authority of the sovereign on a contractarian foundation fails in its own terms, see Hampton (1986), esp. chap 7.

[33] It is interesting that in his early work "On the Jewish Question" Marx presents a similar picture of the supersession of bourgeois arrangements (1977, esp. pp. 55–56). According to Marx, in the feudal epoch, political and economic arrangements were both understood as particular relations between particular people. With the emergence of capitalism, life took on what Marx calls a universal character in the political domain, but not in the economic domain. Marx looks forward to the time when relations will be universal in the economic domain as well. Similar points can be made using the distinction between P-authority and C-authority. In the feudal epoch, all relations of authority were relations of personal obligation like that associated with P-authority. With the emergence of capitalism, political authority became C-authority while economic authority remained P-authority. I have argued that with the growth of the moral dimension of management, we have entered a time when managerial authority must be regarded as C-authority as well.

basis of legitimacy is taken to be service to the "people," that is, the employees. The justification of managerial authority is that it enables those subject to it to better comply with the reasons that apply to them.[34]

Of course, a look at English history shows a steady erosion of the power that kings had in 1688, and the ascendancy of Parliament. Perhaps if the reconceptualization of the moral foundations of managerial authority that I have suggested gains currency, there will eventually be, despite the disanalogies between the governmental and the managerial cases, a similar erosion of the power of managers chosen by nondemocratic means, and a transfer of all ultimate managerial authority to democratically elected representatives of the employees. But the first step is a change in our understanding of the relation of management to employees.

---

[34] Since I am not an expert on English history, I shall resist the temptation to explore the parallels between a political constitution that divides authority between a king and a parliament and an economic constitution that divides it between a managerial elite and a company union.

WORKS CITED

Alchian, Armen, and Harold Demsetz. 1972. "Production, Information Costs, and Economic Organization." *American Economic Review* 62:777–95.

Applbaum, Arthur I. 1992. "Democratic Legitimacy and Official Discretion." *Philosophy and Public Affairs* 21:240–74.

Arendt, Hannah. 1958. "What Was Authority?" In Carl Friedrich, ed., *Authority*, pp. 81–112. Cambridge: Harvard University Press.

Aristotle. 1985. *Nichomachean Ethics*. Terence Irwin, trans. Indianapolis: Hackett.

Arneson, Richard. 1987. "Meaningful Work and Market Socialism." *Ethics* 97:517–45.

———. Unpublished. "Is There a Right to Worker's Control?"

Arrow, Kenneth. 1963. *Social Choice and Individual Values*. New York: John Wiley and Sons.

———. 1974. *The Limits of Organization*. New York: Norton.

Austin, J. L. 1962. *How to Do Things with Words*. New York: Oxford University Press.

Axelrod, Robert. 1984. *The Evolution of Cooperation*. New York: Basic Books.

Baier, Kurt. 1958. *The Moral Point of View*. Ithaca: Cornell University Press.

Barry, Brian. 1979. "Is Democracy Special?" In Peter Laslett and James Fishkin, eds., *Philosophy, Politics, and Society*, fifth series, pp. 155–96. New Haven: Yale University Press.

Bates, Stanley. 1971. "The Responsibility of Random Collections." *Ethics* 81:343–49.

Becker, Lawrence. 1977. *Property Rights*. Boston: Routledge and Kegan Paul.

Benjamin, Martin. 1976. "Can Moral Responsibility Be Collective and Non-Distributive?" *Social Theory and Practice* 4:93–106.

Black, Duncan. 1958. *The Theory of Committees and Elections*. Cambridge: Cambridge University Press.

293

Bowles, Samuel, and Herbert Gintis. 1992. "Power and Wealth in a Competitive Capitalist Economy." *Philosophy and Public Affairs* 21:324–53.

———. 1993. "A Political and Economic Case for the Democratic Enterprise." In Copp, Hampton, and Roemer (1993), pp. 375–99.

Bratman, Michael. 1992. "Shared Cooperative Activity." *Philosophical Review* 101:327–41.

Brewster, Kingman. 1959. "The Corporation and Economic Federalism." In Mason (1959), pp. 72–84.

Brink, David. 1989. *Moral Realism and the Foundations of Ethics*. Cambridge: Cambridge University Press.

Buchanan, Allen. 1985. *Ethics, Efficiency, and the Market*. Totowa, N.J.: Rowman and Allanheld.

———. 1989. "The Communitarian Critique of Liberalism." *Ethics* 99:852–82.

Butler, Joseph. 1983. *Five Sermons Preached at the Rolls Chapel*. Stephen Darwall, ed. Indianapolis: Hackett.

Christiano, Thomas. 1990. "Freedom, Consensus, and Equality in Collective Decision Making." *Ethics* 101:151–81.

———. 1993. "Social Choice and Democracy." In Copp, Hampton, and Roemer (1993), pp. 173–95.

Cohen, Joshua. 1986. "An Epistemic Conception of Democracy." *Ethics* 97:26–38.

———. 1988. "The Economic Basis of Deliberative Democracy." *Social Philosophy and Policy* 6:25–50.

———. 1989. "Deliberation and Democratic Legitimacy." In Hamlin and Pettit (1989a), pp. 17–34.

Coleman, James. 1990. *Foundations of Social Theory*. Cambridge: Harvard University Press.

Coleman, Jules, and John Ferejohn. 1986. "Democracy and Social Choice." *Ethics* 97:6–25.

Cooper, David. 1968. "Collective Responsibility." *Philosopy* 43:258–68.

Copp, David. 1979. "Collective Actions and Secondary Actions," *American Philosophical Quarterly* 16:177–86.

———. 1984. "What Collectives Are: Agency, Individualism, and Legal Theory." *Dialogue* 23:249–69.

———. 1993. "Could Political Truth Be a Hazard for Democracy?" In Copp, Hampton, and Roemer (1993), pp. 101–17.

Copp, David, Jean Hampton, and John Roemer, eds. 1993. *The Idea of Democracy*. Cambridge: Cambridge University Press.

Cyert, Richard, and James March. 1963. *A Behavioral Theory of the Firm*. Englewood Cliffs, N.J.: Prentice-Hall.

Dahl, Robert. 1956. *A Preface to Democratic Theory*. Chicago: University of Chicago Press.

———. 1985. *A Preface to Economic Democracy*. Berkeley: University of California Press.

Dan-Cohen, Meir. 1986. *Rights, Persons, and Organizations*. Berkeley: University of California Press.

Davidson, Donald. 1969. "How Is Weakness of the Will Possible?" In Joel Feinberg, ed., *Moral Concepts*, pp. 93–113. Oxford: Oxford University Press.

De George, Richard. 1985. *The Nature and Limits of Authority*. Lawrence: University of Kansas Press.

Donaldson, Thomas. 1982. *Corporations and Morality*. Englewood Cliffs, N.J.: Prentice-Hall.

———. 1989. *The Ethics of International Business*. New York: Oxford University Press.

Donaldson, Thomas, and Patricia Werhane, eds. 1979. *Ethical Issues in Business*. Englewood Cliffs, N.J.: Prentice-Hall.

Dworkin, Gerald. 1988. *The Theory and Practice of Autonomy*. Cambridge: Cambridge University Press.

Dworkin, Ronald. 1977. *Taking Rights Seriously*. Cambridge: Harvard University Press.

———. 1978. "Liberalism." In Stuart Hampshire, ed., *Public and Private Morality*, pp. 113–43. Cambridge: Cambridge University Press.

———. 1985. *A Matter of Principle*. Cambridge: Harvard University Press.

Edwards, Richard C. 1979. *Contested Terrain: The Transformation of the Workplace in the Twentieth Century*. New York: Basic Books.

Eisenberg, Melvin. 1976. *The Structure of the Corporation: A Legal Analysis*. Boston: Little, Brown.

Estlund, David. 1990. "Democracy without Preference." *Philosophical Review* 99:397–423.

———. 1993. "Making Truth Safe for Democracy." In Copp, Hampton, and Roemer (1993), pp. 71–100.

———. Forthcoming. "Opinion Leaders, Independence, and Condorcet's Jury Theorem." *Theory and Decision*.

Feinberg, Joel. 1970. "Collective Responsibility." In his *Doing and Deserving*, pp. 222–51. Princeton: Princeton University Press.

Finnis J. M. 1990. "Authority." In Raz (1990a), pp. 174–202.

Foner, Eric. 1988. *Reconstruction*. New York: Harper and Row.

Frascona, Joseph L. 1964. *Agency*. Englewood Cliffs, N.J.: Prentice-Hall.

French, Peter. 1984. *Collective and Corporate Responsibility*. New York: Columbia University Press.

Friedman, Milton. 1979. "The Social Responsibility of Business Is to Increase Its Profits." In Donaldson and Werhane, eds. (1979), pp. 191–97.

Friedman, Richard. 1990. "On the Concept of Authority in Political Philosophy." In Raz (1990a), pp. 56–91.

Gauthier, David. 1986. *Morals by Agreement*. Oxford: Clarendon.

Gibbard, Allan. 1990. *Wise Choices, Apt Feelings*. Cambridge: Harvard University Press.

Gilbert, Margaret. 1989. *On Social Facts*. London: Routledge.

Gintis, Herbert. 1989. "Financial Markets and the Political Structure of the Enterprise." *Journal of Economic Behavior and Organization* 11:311–22.

Goldman, Alvin. 1972. "Toward a Theory of Social Power." *Philosophical Studies* 23:221–68.

———. 1991. "Epistemic Paternalism: Communication Control in Law and Society." *The Journal of Philosophy* 88:113–31.

Goodpaster, Kenneth. 1979. "Morality and Organizations." In Donaldson and Werhane, eds. (1979), pp. 137–44.

Gould, Carol. 1988. *Rethinking Democracy*. Cambridge: Cambridge University Press.

Green, Leslie. 1988. *The Authority of the State*. Oxford: Clarendon.

Greenawalt, Kent. 1990. "Promissory Obligation: The Theme of Social Contract." In Raz (1990a), pp. 268–99.

Grice, Russell. 1967. *The Grounds of Moral Judgment*. Cambridge: Cambridge University Press.

Gutmann, Amy. 1985. "Communitarian Critics of Liberalism." *Philosophy and Public Affairs* 14:308–22.

Gutmann, Amy, and Dennis Thompson. 1990. "Moral Conflict and Political Consensus." *Ethics* 101:64–88.

Hamlin, Alan, and Philip Pettit, eds. 1989a. *The Good Polity*. Oxford: Blackwell.

———. 1989b. "Introduction." In Hamlin and Pettit (1989a), pp. 1–13.

Hampton, Jean. 1986. *Hobbes and the Social Contract Tradition*. Cambridge: Cambridge University Press.

———. 1987. "Free-Rider Problems in the Production of Collective Goods." *Economics and Philosophy* 3:245–73.

Hardin, Russell. 1993. "Public Choice vs. Democracy." In Copp, Hampton, and Roemer (1993), pp. 157–72.

Hare, R. M. 1981. *Moral Thinking: Its Levels, Method, and Point*. Oxford: Clarendon.

Harman, Gilbert. 1965. "Inference to the Best Explanation." *Philosophical Review* 74:88–95.

Hart, H. L. A. 1961. *The Concept of Law*. Oxford: Oxford University Press.

———. 1982. "Commands and Authoritative Legal Reasons." In his *Essays on Bentham*, pp. 243–68. Oxford: Clarendon Press. Also in Raz (1990a), pp. 92–114.

Held, Virginia. 1970. "Can a Random Collection of Individuals Be Morally Responsible?" *Journal of Philosophy* 67:471–81.

Hirschman, Albert O. 1970. *Exit, Voice, and Loyalty*. Cambridge: Harvard University Press.

Hobbes, Thomas. 1968. *Leviathan*. Harmondsworth: Penguin.

Honoré, A. M. 1961. "Ownership." In Anthony Guest, ed., *Oxford Essays in Jurisprudence*, pp. 107–47. Oxford: Clarendon Press.

Hume, David. 1948. "Of the Original Contract." In Henry Aiken, ed., *Hume's Moral and Political Philosophy*. New York: Hafner.

Jackall, Robert. 1988. *Moral Mazes: The World of Corporate Managers*. New York: Oxford University Press.

Kant, Immanuel. 1991. *The Metaphysics of Morals*. Mary Gregor, trans. Cambridge: Cambridge University Press.

Kavka, Gregory. 1986. *Hobbesian Moral and Political Theory*. Princeton: Princeton University Press.

Keeley, Michael. 1988. *A Social Contract Theory of Organizations*. Notre Dame: University of Notre Dame Press.

Kim, Jaegwon. 1978. "Supervenience and Nomological Incommensurables." *American Philosophical Quarterly* 15:149–56.

Klosko, George. 1992. *The Principle of Fairness and Political Obligation*. Lanham, M.D.: Rowman and Littlefield.

Krause, Richard, and Michael McPherson. 1986. "A 'Mixed'-Property Regime: Equality and Liberty in a Market Economy." *Ethics* 97:119–38.

Kubrick, Stanley, Peter George, and Terry Southern. 1963. *Doctor Strangelove*. Screenplay.

Kymlicka, Will. 1990. *Contemporary Political Philosophy*. Oxford: Clarendon.

Ladd, John. 1970. "Morality and the Ideal of Rationality in Formal Organizations." *Monist* 54:488–516.

Locke, John. 1952. *Second Treatise of Government*. New York: Liberal Arts Press.

Lukes, Steven. 1973. *Individualism*. Oxford: Blackwell.

Lyons, David. 1973. *In the Interest of the Governed: A Study of Bentham's Philosophy of Utility and Law*. Oxford: Clarendon.

McClennen, Edward. 1992. "The Theory of Rationality for Ideal Games." *Philosophical Studies* 65:193–215.

MacCormick, Neil. 1972. "Voluntary Obligation and Normative

Powers. *Proceedings of the Aristotelian Society*, supp. vol. 46:59–78.

Machiavelli, Niccolo. 1977. *The Prince*. Robert M. Adams, trans. New York: Norton.

Mackie, J. L. 1975. "Causes and Conditions." In Ernest Sosa, ed., *Causation and Conditionals*, pp. 15–38. Oxford: Oxford University Press.

McMahon, Christopher. 1981. "Morality and the Invisible Hand." *Philosophy and Public Affairs* 10:247–77.

———. 1982. "Correspondence." (Reply to Charles Fried's criticisms of "Morality and the Invisible Hand.") *Philosophy and Public Affairs* 11:268–77.

———. 1987. "Autonomy and Authority." *Philosophy and Public Affairs* 16:303–28.

———. 1989. "Promising and Coordination." *American Philosophical Quarterly* 26:239–47.

———. 1991. "The Paradox of Deontology." *Philosophy and Public Affairs* 20:350–77.

Marx, Karl. 1977. "On the Jewish Question." In David McLellan, ed., *Karl Marx: Selected Writings*, pp. 39–62. Oxford: Oxford University Press.

Mason, Edward S. 1959. *The Corporation in Modern Society*. Cambridge: Harvard University Press.

May, Larry. 1987. *The Morality of Groups*. Notre Dame: University of Notre Dame Press.

———. 1990. "Collective Inaction and Shared Responsibility." *Nous* 24:269–77.

Mellema, Gregory. 1988. *Individuals, Groups, and Shared Moral Responsibility*. New York: Peter Lang.

Mill, John Stuart. 1958. *Considerations on Representative Government*. Indianapolis: Bobbs-Merrill.

Moore, G. E. 1959. "External and Internal Relations." In his *Philosophical Studies*, pp. 276–309. Paterson, N.J.: Littlefield Adam.

Morgan, Edmund. 1988. *Inventing the People: The Rise of Popular Sovereignty in England and America*. New York: Norton.

Munzer, Stephen. 1990. *A Theory of Property*. Cambridge: Cambridge University Press.

Nagel, Thomas. 1979. "The Fragmentation of Value." In his *Mortal Questions*, pp. 128–41. Cambridge: Cambridge University Press.

———. 1987. "Moral Conflict and Political Legitimacy." *Philosophy and Public Affairs* 16:215–40.

Olson, Mancur. 1971. *The Logic of Collective Action*. New York: Schocken.

Pateman, Carole. 1970. *Participation and Democratic Theory*. Cambridge: Cambridge University Press.

———. 1979. *The Problem of Political Obligation*. New York: John Wiley and Sons.

Parfit, Derek. 1984. *Reasons and Persons*. Oxford: Clarendon.

Parsons, Talcott. 1947. "Introduction." In Weber (1947), pp. 3–86.

Peters, R. S. 1958. "Authority." *Proceedings of the Aristotelian Society*, supp. vol. 32:207–24.

Pettit, Philip. 1986. "Free Riding and Foul Dealing." *Journal of Philosophy* 83:361–79.

Plato. 1945. *The Republic*. F. M. Cornford, trans. New York: Oxford University Press.

Pogge, Thomas. 1989. *Realizing Rawls*. Ithaca: Cornell University Press.

Quinton, Anthony. 1976. "Social Objects." *Proceedings of the Aristotelian Society* 76:1–27

Rawls, John. 1971. *A Theory of Justice*. Cambridge: Harvard University Press.

———. 1980. "Kantian Constructivism in Moral Theory." *The Journal of Philosophy* 78:515–72.

———. 1985. "Justice as Fairness, Political not Metaphysical." *Philosophy and Public Affairs* 14:223–51.

———. 1987. "The Idea of an Overlapping Consensus." *Oxford Journal of Legal Studies* 7:1–25.

———. 1988. "The Priority of the Right and Ideas of the Good." *Philosophy and Public Affairs* 17:251–76

Raz, Joseph. 1977. "Promises and Obligations." In P. M. S. Hacker and Joseph Raz, eds., *Law, Morality, and Society*, pp. 210–28. Oxford: Clarendon.

———. 1978. "Reasons for Action, Decisions, and Norms." In Joseph Raz, ed., *Practical Reasoning*, pp. 128–43. Oxford: Oxford University Press.

———. 1985. "Authority and Justification." *Philosophy and Public Affairs* 14:3–29.

———. 1986. *The Morality of Freedom*. Oxford: Clarendon.

———, ed. 1990a. *Authority*. New York: New York University Press.

———. 1990b. "Introduction." In Raz (1990a), pp. 1–19.

Riley, Jonathan. 1990. "Utilitarian Ethics and Democratic Government." *Ethics* 100:335–48.

Roemer, John. 1992. "The Morality and Efficiency of Market Socialism." *Ethics* 102:448–64.

Rousseau, Jean-Jacques. 1968. *The Social Contract*. Maurice Cranston, trans. Harmondsworth: Penguin.

Sandel, Michael. 1982. *Liberalism and the Limits of Justice*. Cambridge: Cambridge University Press.

Scanlon, Thomas. 1982. "Contractualism and Utilitarianism." In Amortya Sen and Bernard Williams, eds., *Utilitarianism and Beyond*. Cambridge: Cambridge University Press.

Schedler, George. 1983. "A Theory of Collective Responsibility and Some Applications." *Heythrop Journal* 23:395–412.

Scheffler, Samuel. 1992. *Human Morality*. New York: Oxford University Press.

Schneewind, J. B. 1984 "The Divine Corporation and the History of Ethics." In Richard Rorty, J. B. Schneewind, and Quentin Skinner, eds., *Philosophy in History*, pp. 173–91. Cambridge: Cambridge University Press.

Schumpeter, Joseph. 1950. *Capitalism, Socialism and Democracy*. New York: Harper and Row.

Schwieckart, David. 1980. *Capitalism or Worker Control?* New York: Praeger.

Sen, Amartya. 1985. "The Moral Standing of the Market." *Social Philosophy and Policy* 2:1–19.

Simmons, A. John. 1979. *Moral Principles and Political Obligations*. Princeton: Princeton University Press.

Simon, Herbert. 1976. *Administrative Behavior*. New York: Free Press.

Singer, Peter. 1973. *Democracy and Disobedience*. Oxford: Clarendon.

Smith, Adam. 1985. *An Inquiry into the Nature and Causes of the Wealth of Nations*. New York: Modern Library.

Soper, Phillip. 1989. "Legal Theory and the Claim of Authority." *Philosophy and Public Affairs* 18:209–37.

Sugden, Robert. 1993. "Justified to Whom?" In Copp, Hampton, and Roemer (1993), pp. 149–54.

Sverdlik, Stephen. 1987. "Collective Responsibility." *Philosophical Studies* 51:61–76.

Taurek, John. 1977. "Should the Numbers Count?" *Philosophy and Public Affairs* 6:293–316.

Ullman-Margalit, Edna. 1977. *The Emergence of Norms*. Oxford: Oxford University Press.

Waldron, Jeremy. 1993. "Special Ties and Natural Duties." *Philosophy and Public Affairs* 22:3–30.

Walzer, Michael. 1970. "Civil Disobedience and Corporate Authority." In his *Obligations*, pp. 24–45. Cambridge: Harvard University Press.

Ward, Benjamin. 1958. "The Firm in Illyria: Market Syndicalism." *American Economic Review* 48:566–89.

Wartenberg, Thomas. 1990. *The Forms of Power: From Domination to Transformation*. Philadelphia: Temple University Press.

Weber, Max. 1947. *The Theory of Social and Economic Organization*, Talcott Parsons, trans. New York: Oxford University Press.

Werhane, Patricia. 1985. *Persons, Rights and Corporations*. Englewood Cliffs, N.J.: Prentice-Hall.

Williamson, Oliver. 1975. *Markets and Hierarchies*. New York: Free Press.

———. 1985. *The Economic Institutions of Capitalism*. New York: Free Press.

Wolff, Robert Paul. 1970. *In Defense of Anarchism*. New York: Harper and Row.

Wollheim, Richard. 1962. "A Paradox in the Theory of Democracy." In Peter Laslett and W. G. Runciman, eds., *Philosophy, Politics, and Society*, second series, pp. 71–87. Oxford: Blackwell.

Zimmerman, David. 1981. "Coercive Wage Offers." *Philosophy and Public Affairs* 10:121–45.

Zimmerman, Michael. 1985. "Sharing Responsibility." *American Philosophical Quarterly* 22:115–22.

INDEX

accountability: conventional, 260; of managers to employees, 276, 283; of managers to managers, 9, 278, 280n; of office holders, 276; and right to choose, 8

agency problem, 279n

agency relations: agent-cooperation, 240; agent-democracy, 240; and bureaucracy, 237; defined, 47–48; and managerial authority, 18, 196; and P-authority, 49; and promises, 19

Alchian, A., and H. Demsetz, 243n

Applbaum, A., 287n

Arendt, H., 25n

Aristotle, 93, 209

Arneson, R., 3n

Arrow, K., 136, 163n

assurance problem, 104–5, 107, 118, 218–19

Austin, J.L., 188n

authority: absolute, 259; and accountability, 259; "an" vs. "in," 41n; and autonomy, 34, 36, 38; conjoint, 43; and consensus, 149; de facto, 26–27; de jure or legitimate, 27; defined, 25; disjoint, 43, 45–46; and domination, 45; and justice, 22; moral, 92; and moral disagreement, 22, 249; of morality, xi; noninstrumental justifications of, 235n; prescriptive vs. proscriptive, 171, 249n; public, 8, 288; and right to direct, 26–27; robustness vs. reach of, 85–86; service conception of, 126; structures, 48–49; and surrender of judgment, 32–33

authorization, 47, 49–50

autonomy: contrasted with liberty, 34; G. Dworkin's account of, 35

Axelrod, R., 106n

Baier, K., 106

Barry, B., 140n

battle of the sexes game, 113–14, 129, 215, 221, 248

Becker, L., 262n

Black, D., 136n

Bowles, S., and H. Gintis, 195n, 271n

Bratman, M., 80n

Brewster, K., 14n

Brink, D., 54n

Buchanan, A., 79n, 179n, 269n

bureaucracy, 49, 189, 237, 242

business ethics, 20

Butler, J., xi n

capitalism, 281

C-authority: and bureaucracy, 238–39; and capitalism, 281; defined, 44; and democracy, 129–30, 232, 240, 258; and E-authority, 120–21; and emigration, 253; in governmental agencies, 286; intermittent character of, 121, 236; and justice, 125; and moral goals, 122–23; in organizations, 238; as solving assurance problem, 107–8

chicken game, 114–15, 119–20, 211–12, 215, 221n, 234n, 245, 248

Christiano, T., 141n, 157n

civic humanism, 163

codetermination, 282

coercion: and autonomy, 36–37; and subordination, 36–37; and threat of dismissal, 198

coercive offers, 198

Cohen, J., 146n, 155n

Coleman, James, 43, 118n, 171, 189–90

collective rationality: and chicken games, 119–20, 215, 234n, 245; and the natural duty of justice, 124; and organizational cooperation, 245; principle of, 104; and the principle of fairness, 124; rationale for, 105–6; and thresholds, 217

collective responsibility, 208–9

collective wrongdoing: and causation, 212–14; and collective rationality, 214–20; of commission vs. of omission, 212, 214–15; distribution of, 208, 210; and individual rationality, 211–12; and overdetermination, 212; and unorganized groups, 224

common good, 83, 144

common sense morality, 70–71, 170

communitarianism, 78–82

303

The Princeton University Press series "Studies in Moral, Political, and Legal Philosophy" is under the general editorship of Marshall Cohen, Professor of Philosophy and Law and Dean of Humanities at the University of Southern California. The series includes the following titles, in chronological order of publication:

Understanding Rawls: A Reconstruction and Critique of A Theory of Justice by R. P. Wolff (1977). Out of print

Immorality by R. D. Milo (1984)

Politics & Remembrance: Republican Themes in Machiavelli, Burke, and Tocqueville by B. J. Smith (1985)

Understanding Marx: A Reconstruction and Critique of Capital by R. P. Wolff (1985)

Hobbesian Moral and Political Theory by G. S. Kavka (1986)

The General Will before Rousseau: The Transformation of the Divine into the Civic by P. Riley (1986)

Respect for Nature: A Theory of Environmental Ethics by P. W. Taylor (1986). Available in paperback

Paternalist Intervention: The Moral Bounds on Benevolence by D. VanDeVeer (1986)

The Longing for Total Revolution: Philosophic Sources of Social Discontent from Rousseau to Marx and Nietzche by B. Yack (1986)

Meeting Needs by D. Braybrooke (1987)

Reasons for Welfare: The Political Theory of the Welfare State by R. E. Goodin (1988)

Why Preserve Natural Variety? by B. G. Norton (1988). Available in paperback

Coercion by A. Wertheimer (1988). Available in paperback

Merleau-Ponty and the Foundation of an Existential Politics by K. H. Whiteside (1988)

On War and Morality by R. L. Holmes (1989). Available in paperback

The Rhetoric of Leviathan: Thomas Hobbes and the Politics of Cultural Transformation by D. Johnston (1989). Available in paperback

Desert by G. Sher (1989). Available in paperback

Critical Legal Studies: A Liberal Critique by A. Altman (1989)

Finding the Mean: Theory and Practice in Aristotelian Political Philosophy by S. G. Salkever (1990)

Marxism, Morality, and Social Justice by R. G. Peffer (1990)

Speaking of Equality: An Analysis of the Rhetorical Force of "Equality" in Moral and Legal Discourse by P. Weston (1990)

Friedrich Nietzsche and the Politics of the Soul: A Study of Heroic Individualism by L. P. Thiele (1990). Available in paperback

Valuing Life by J. Kleinig (1991)

The Lockean Theory of Rights by A. J. Simmons (1992). Available in paperback

Liberal Nationalism by Y. Tamir (1993). Available in paperback

On the Edge of Anarchy by A. J. Simmons (1993). Available in paperback

Authority and Democracy: A General Theory of Government and Management by C. McMahon (1994). Available in paperback